P9-EGJ-984

EXCURSIONS

Kennikat Press
National University Publications
Literary Criticism Series

General Editor
John E. Becker
Fairleigh Dickinson University

ROBERT BOYERS

EXCURSIONS:
SELECTED LITERARY ESSAYS

MIDDLEBURY COLLEGE LIBRARY

National University Publications
KENNIKAT PRESS   //   1977
Port Washington, N. Y.   //   London

PS
221
B58

4/1977
Am Lit.

Copyright © 1977 by Kennikat Press Corp. All rights reserved. No part of this publication may be reproduced, stored in a retrieval system, or transmitted, in any form or by any means, electronic, mechanical, photocopying, recording, or otherwise, without the prior written permission of the publisher.

Manufactured in the United States of America

Published by
Kennikat Press Corp.
Port Washington, N. Y./London

Library of Congress Cataloging in Publication Data

Boyers, Robert.
    Excursions: selected literary essays.

    (Literary criticism series) (National University publications)
        1. American literature–20th century–History and criticism--Addresses, essays, lectures. I. Title.
PS221.B58   810'.9'0054   76-22547
ISBN 0-8046-9148-7

FOR PEG
AND FOR LOWELL & ZACHARY MEYER BOYERS

CONTENTS

PREFACE

The present volume collects what I take to be the best writing I have done in the course of ten busy years. Though it omits several lengthy items I should like to see preserved, and which may well turn up some day in a second collection, I am satisfied that the book represents what a young man's first critical collection should represent. I have tried in these essays to ask serious and difficult questions about the art and thought of my time, and to be as persistent as I know how in pursuing this point and that. Though I suspect my literary sympathies are both wider and more provisional than some would like them to be, I have also been accused of a traditionalism which other readers find peculiarly unbecoming. I do not know how to answer such criticism in general terms, and so wish only to set down in this preface some first principles by which I have tried to be guided.

Most instructive on this score are the remarks of the late John Crowe Ransom, who urged the critic to ask of the work before him, "Is it up to his mental age or general level of experience? And is there any nonsense in it? The last question concerns the competence of the poet [or novelist or filmmaker] to carry out [his] intention consistently, whatever the limits of the intention. For the devoted critic must maintain that poetry [or fiction or film] on whatever level must make as consistent sense as [critical] prose, and he does not like being committed in it to nonsense; it cannot be the idea of [the work of art] to make us foolish, if that is not our habit, even though it must sometimes try to render something that is elusive and hard to render."

To Mr. Ransom's observations I would add the following considerations:

1. Does the criticism bring to life the work it presumes to discuss?
2. Does it resist the sorry inclination to reduce a plural work to the merely symptomatic status of an analyzable phenomenon?
3. Does the criticism think against itself, seek at least provisionally to go against the grain of its own largely unexamined and sometimes insupportable predilections?
4. Does it locate the particular critical enterprise against a background of general cultural ferment in which every discourse needs to take its place?
5. Does the criticism permit the critic, and in part his reader, to discover things he didn't aim at or insist he already knew when the specific project began to take shape?

The scrupulous reader will of course make up his own mind about the adequacy of my essays to the principles enumerated.

I owe a great deal to the many editors who have published my work and, in recent years, invited contributions to their distinguished journals. More especially I must thank Anne Farber, Leslie Farber, Henry Pachter, Ben Belitt, Jerome Mazzaro, Patrick Keane, and Robert Orrill, who have offered a fond mixture of personal and professional advice without which I should long ago have ceased to think of myself as a writer with a fine and sufficient audience. These, and others I neglect to mention, have done their best to keep up with my work and to offer, continually, the inestimable gift of their interest and support.

Also, I give thanks to Madelyn Gray who, through ten years, urged me to write, and did what she could to make it all possible. For her attentive and consoling sympathy there are no words of adequate acknowledgment.

I

LITERATURE and .....

ONE

THE FAMILY NOVEL

In speaking of the family novel we speak not merely of a work the burden of which is to deal with the various members of some family. Such a work is likely to focus attention on one family member more or less at the expense of others, whether because the one character is superior by virtue of intelligence, capacity for self-conscious reflection, or flair for self-dramatization, or because the novelist wishes to make certain points about loneliness, the difficulty of achieving independence, or some such thing, which requires that he deliberately limit his focus. What I should like to examine is a literary phenomenon one of whose main objects is the illumination of social process, more specifically, the way certain novelists have managed to show us how families grow, take shape, influence members, develop a momentum no one within that given family can control or even understand. That is to say, I am concerned with a novel for which the life of families is sufficiently interesting in itself not to be subsumed under some broader quest for the sources of alienation in society at large, for the key to the middle classes' loss of confidence, and so on.

There are a great many novels one might fairly describe as family novels. Surely the nineteenth century produced its share, more than its share, in fact, if one remembers the full range of novels attributed to a Trollope, for instance. In some ways the nineteenth century was the great age of the modern family, of course, and in its general movement towards genteel plausibility it demanded a family novel whose manner was sufficiently relaxed and even-handed as to suggest that all things may, in fact, follow an appointed, frequently kindly, course. There were substantial

From *Salmagundi,* Spring 1974.

individual differences among writers who wrote extensively of family life, but the novelists who spring to mind as most representative of that tradition, if we may so designate it, tend to conform rather closely to what one might expect. If, of course, *The Brothers Karamazov* is to be considered, we shall need to adjust our speculations, but Dostoyevski's book can hardly be said to typify the novel of family life. It is predominantly concerned with a variety of philosophical questions, rather than with domestic issues of a more or less mundane nature. In truth, it is not the novelist of the very first rank that we generally associate with the family novel, but a relatively minor figure — not Dickens, or George Eliot, but Trollope might have been a family novelist; in the United States, not Hawthorne or Twain or Henry James, but William Dean Howells. Now Howells and Trollope are hardly obscure figures in our literature, but they are clearly not in the first rank, clearly cannot be discussed in the same breath with a James or a Proust. In a sense it might be said that for our purposes, if we are essentially interested in families rather than in artistic or philosophic breakthrough and innovation, writers like Howells and Trollope are all we need. That is because their commitment is more to life and its representation than to those rigorous exertions on behalf of formal perfection that we identify with James or Proust. In Trollope, in Howells, we get the sheer flow and ebb of life, the suggestion that if here and there men clamor to destroy themselves and others, most men are mild and modestly satisfied, even decent, that conflicts are, if not perfectly solvable, at least bearable for all but the very weak and wilful few. Insight is a function of simple human need, so that we do not clamor to know what we do not need to know in the routine circumstances of our lives.

Now I do not mean to suggest that family novels of the sort I have begun so tentatively to describe are without intelligence or instructive potential of any kind. What we must come to terms with, though, is a work which insists, ever so quietly in most cases, on the relaxation of conventional ideological standards, which is, in Lionel Trilling's terms, "for goodness and gentleness, for 'life,' for the reservation of moral judgment, for the charm of the mysterious, precarious little flame that lies at the heart of the commonplace." I am not quite certain that the family novel in general may be said to speak on behalf of goodness and gentleness, but it does clearly celebrate the ambivalent blessings of the commonplace. The vision of the family novel is exercised not by the demon of extraordinary achievement and ferocious will to power and glory but by the staying power of the circumscribed and predictable. In this it goes against the grain of that literary modernism inaugurated at the turn of the century by Joyce and Proust and James, and represents a direct challenge to contemporary appetites hungry for novelty, excess, and consumption on a grand scale. For the writer of family novels, the family is unquestionably the source of much that is good, if also of much we should like to forget or cancel. While it is difficult to imagine a family novel, or any novel, that did not take as its central issue a threat to the integrity or comfort or success of its main characters, no authentic family novel in our sense would consider a threat to the family a familiar or indifferent or inevitable event. The underlying assumption in the family novel is that families must somehow find a way to preserve themselves, that the entirely liberated individual is not often better off than he would have been had he been able to make his peace in the family.

In the essay on Howells from which I have already quoted, Lionel Trilling reminds us that in our time "we are very little satisfied with the idea of family life — for us, it is part of the inadequate bourgeois reality. Not that we don't live good-naturedly enough with our families, but when we do, we know that we are 'family men,' by definition cut off from the true realities of the spirit." On the other hand, he goes on to say, "When we yield to our contemporary impulse to enlarge all experience, to involve it as soon as possible in history, myth, and the oneness of spirit. . . . we are in danger of making experience merely typical, formal, and *representative*, and thus of losing one term of the dialectic that goes on between spirit and the conditioned. . . . We lose, that is to say, the actuality of the conditioned, the literality of matter, the peculiar authenticity and authority of the merely denotative. To lose this is to lose not a material fact but a spiritual one, for it is a fact of spirit that it must exist in a world which requires it to engage in so dispiriting an occupation as hunting for a house." Now I don't know that house-hunting is really all that dispiriting an enterprise, but I think we can surely agree with Trilling that for most of our contemporaries, family life is not merely a viable life choice but a terribly limiting commitment, confirming their intuition that stability and nurturance are inevitably at odds with the life of the spirit. We have all read and thought about the Freudian family romance, and are familiar with the other originals of the attack on the bourgeois family, from Marx and Nietzsche to Kafka and Wilhelm Reich and R.D. Laing. In these various approaches it is difficult to say what precisely would constitute a common factor, beyond a hostility to the family as perpetuating a certain kind of repression that leads inevitably to misery and anxiety. Not all would do away with families, of course, and a number of these writers were driven to find ways of strengthening families against the murderous assaults of misanthropic radicals and disturbed family offspring. Freud, to be sure, knew that the problems to which he addressed himself had their origin in the family, and might well concede that a patient needed for a while to get away from a family situation that had grown oppressive and unmanageable for him, but he was surely unlikely ever to blame a family operating within the conventions of law and decorum for doing grave psychic injury to one of its members. For Freud, as for Trilling, "the actuality of the conditioned" was an unalterable fact. Men lived in families because they needed to be trained and nurtured, prepared for entrance into a society which was complicated and threatening in its availability to change and surprise. The dynamics of family life provided at once a testing ground and a refuge, in this view, for though anyone might find it very difficult adjusting to family life, with its frequently suffocating intimacies and gross challenges to one's self-respect, its very existence was bound up in, if not deliberately dedicated to, the life of affection. No matter how terrible the struggles might be, no matter how interminable the petty quarrels and intimidations, there were relative certainties in the restricted family universe that one could rely upon. In the face of accelerating social change, disjunctions in the familiar modalities within which ordinary men thought of time, succession, progress, the nineteenth century indulged a predictable though almost pathological nostalgia for the coziness of a family life that was often far from cozy.

Among fictional representations of the life of settled affection, there are a number of turning points, and it is well that we keep them in mind. Another commentator might well seize upon other key works, I know, for we are not dealing here with matters that are perfectly self-evident. There is no question, for example, that Henry James refined the variety of points of view that may be employed in a work of fiction beyond what any predecessor in the art of fiction had managed, or that Proust demonstrated ways to portray a character in the round that no one had previously attempted. But that Flaubert's portrait of Madame Bovary constitutes a crucial event in the life of spirit for men exercised by thoughts of family and worried over the threat to stable affection and parental responsibility, would be hard to prove. Suffice it to say, in introducing the issue, that Flaubert's novel, as a response to nineteenth century romanticism in its more vulgar and popular manifestations, is an important book. We do not need to recall the details of the novel to remember that it analyzes a woman who is violated by books, not bad books merely, but all books. A relatively ordinary person, with decent though not extraordinary endowments, is encouraged, by books and by a milieu in which fantasy readily fuels the wilfulness of narcissistic and shallow people, to think of herself as promised a deliverance from mundanity to which she is in no way entitled. Neither by virtue of intelligence nor invention nor breadth of feeling does Emma Bovary merit a liberated existence, for which she nonetheless yearns, and which she conspires to approximate in a series of empty and stupid affairs with men for whom she is tiresome and predictable. One of her lovers, in Mary McCarthy's account of the book, "feels something [for Madame Bovary] and convinces himself that it is nothing, while Leon [another lover] feels nothing and dares not know it." As for the woman, in McCarthy's terms, "*Anyone* could have prophesied what would become of Emma — her mother-in-law, for instance," for she is not gifted in the way one would need to be to carry off successfully these designedly adventurous liaisons. Flaubert's point is not that Emma should have stayed home bringing up her children and lighting her husband's pipe — even had he intended to say such a thing, the triteness of the sentiment would have disgusted him and turned him, in the process of writing it down, to say something else. Flaubert's vision, though, has to do with the pathetic extravagance and wastefulness of energy committed to a course which can issue in nothing even moderately satisfying to its subject. To be authentic, feelings like love and sincerity, fantasies of liberation and adventure, must somehow be grounded in the root experiences and expectations of characters. They cannot be manufactured or willed in accordance with the prescriptive delirium of sententious romantics. Madame Bovary gives up her family, for most purposes at least, because she has been violated by ideas current in her environment, ideas not in themselves evil or stupid, but trivialized and made potentially vicious in minds incapable of dealing with texture and nuance. That Flaubert's book is in no literal sense a family novel does not diminish for us its importance in pointing the way to developments in the view of the family which may be followed in countless novels written since 1850.

In Flaubert we get a critical, though still feeling, portrayal of individuals caught in the mesh of cultural developments working on a grand scale. McCarthy says that *Madame Bovary* "is the first novel to deal with what is now called mass culture," and she is perfectly right. Readers of the novel understand that a variety of historical crises, large and small, are direct components of the individual destinies of the main characters. The simple availability of popular novels to a wide range of people is a fact, for Flaubert, not to be underestimated even in considering so domestic an issue as a woman's treatment of her young child at bedtime. What happens increasingly, though, in subsequent nineteenth-century novels with pretensions to seriousness, is that family relations come more and more to be treated as a function of individual psychology. Families become stereotyped, role relations fixed and archetypal. We get *types* of father-son relationships, not particular fathers and sons with cultural destinies specific to the cultural features of their era. A split occurs between the individual-familial and broader sociological dimensions, and in this process history is degraded to the level of the merely trivial and archetypal. No detail of individual experience can be evoked without the novelist's seeing to it that the detail conforms to some given archetype which can label and account for it with little difficulty. The objects of social life, meanwhile, the literal paraphernalia of a social existence, are reduced to milieu, in the philosopher Lukács's terms, to the status of "picturesque atmosphere or immobile background against which supposedly purely private histories are unfolded." Surely this is not what Trilling intended to describe when, in speaking of Howells, he spoke of "the dialectic that goes on between spirit and the conditioned." For the conditioned is truly dialectical only in the sense that it participates at once in those broad historical necessities which lie beyond the surfaces of daily private life, and in the archetypal necessities described by Freud and others, according to which fathers and sons are fated to repeat patterns consistent with their roles. To overlook or diminish the persuasiveness of the one necessity in favor of the other is to impoverish the dialectic and reduce representation to caricature. A Thackeray can provide intricate psychological motivation for characters, but it is difficult to take from his work a clear sense of the dynamics of family relations — he writes of families, of course, shows us this family member and that moving in one direction and another, but he succumbs, in Lukács's terms, to stylization. Unable to see or imaginatively to invent a plausible relation between self and culture that would definitively account for the one in terms of its problematic intercourse with the other, he decides simply to mock pretensions of singularity and greatness, to show up great men and noble youths. In this view, no one is special, nothing really distinctive — heroes are made of the same stuff as other men and that is all we need to know of them. How such men are shaped by relatively objective circumstances we do not need to consider. Everywhere, at every social level, we have types of human development any one of which may be easily traced to particular tracks. If there is anything we may call process in such a view it is the developing and unmistakable control with which the novelist manipulates his characters. The writer functions in his fictional universe as a perfect god, responsive only to those laws which, without dialectical subtlety of any kind, see to it that characters never become more than an utterly cynical intelligence knew all along they would. Surprise is reduced to the level of stylistic extravagance or unaccountable eccentricity of behavior. In place of cultural depth perspective we have, at best, local color.

Where a Thackeray, partially recognizing the insufficiency of his own perspective, managed to gesture in the direction of history without really pretending to anything like historical authenticity, the great European naturalists imprison characters in rigid categories announced and explained in a variety of "scientific" theses, the burden of which is to account for human behavior in terms of clean causal relationships that everywhere violate the subtlety of actual human exchanges. In naturalistic novels by Zola and others, the open reduction of human lives to the status of things makes it difficult to speak of the family portraits they contain as more than predictive devices for charting in advance this progress or that. The adaptive element in any social interaction is here conceived in static terms — constriction and sameness characterize the stratagems employed by figures each of whom is victimized by a fate which proceeds with almost mechanical efficiency to lock him in and wear him down. The families one reads about in such novels are neither interesting nor plausible — for all the surface realism and close-grained texture one does not believe for a moment that it is the thing itself with which the writer is concerned. He seems instead worried about the power of prediction implicit in his own theories of human design and historical progress. Families, in this view, seem little more than seed-beds of narrowly adaptive behaviors fitted to generally inflexible historical circumstances. The drama is provided by the passion with which the novelist deploys various aspects of family interaction to prove here one, there another aspect of his thesis. The novelist as scientist is, of course, bound to present a melancholy spectacle, a spectacle described and analyzed in a variety of other contexts by Leslie Farber in *The Ways of the Will*. So eager are most such naturalistic writers to let the will do the work of imagination that they are little inclined even to consider the possible varieties of responses to a given human situation. A will given to systematic inspection of processes which in their nature do not lend themselves to objective quantification will find it increasingly necessary to forego all imaginative grasp of such processes. In the grip of so fanatical a will to prediction, fluid capacities become frozen gestures, and charm a function of ready acquiescence in impersonal designs.

All of which is not to argue that there is no value in works of literary naturalism, or that a Thackeray doesn't interest us because he fails to execute persuasively the intersection of psyche and culture. We are dealing here with the question of the family novel, and I have thus far intended only to sketch some of the difficulties encountered by writers who have addressed the family in their work. Flaubert represents the development of a view of the family according to which it becomes, in the popular imagination, identified with all that is constraining and inadequate in bourgeois life. Almost simultaneous with this development is a growing view of the family as a static entity, a condition whose rigid contours and assignments of role establish the necessity of a psychological approach based on the manipulation of archetypes. Such a novel, in the hands of a Thackeray, for example, nicely analyzes and accounts for the actions of characters conceived as types, as nothing more, really, than the immutable social roles they occupy, whether as ambitious sons, jealous fathers, or marriageable young women. Finally, in this altogether abridged perspective I have determined to work from, we have a variety of naturalistic works in which the family is treated as an aspect of a mechanistic universe controlled by impersonal laws that grind along without regard to the peculiar endowments of subject individuals. Despite the immense differences between a Flaubert and a Thackeray, or between Thackeray and Zola, it should be clear that in none of these writers can the family be looked at clearly in its own terms. Always in their hands it is a function of something else, not always larger or more important, but sufficiently compelling to ensure that the novelist will not care to give his undivided attention to the dynamics of family process. This does not constitute in itself an aesthetic failing, of course, and I should be the last to maintain that Flaubert ought to have devoted himself to a project other than what he wrote in *Madame Bovary*. What I should like us to agree upon is that approaches to the family, as a problem to which many novelists have addressed themselves, are many, and that some are better suited than others to understanding what is most essential in that institution.

A Howells, a Trollope, can better get at the actual feel, the pressure of family life by virtue of a capacity to focus a less divided attention on the vital details of such a life. Consider the following passage from Howells's novel *The Rise of Silas Lapham:*

It is a serious matter always to the women of his family when a young man gives them cause to suspect that he is interested in some other woman. A son-in-law or brother-in-law does not enter the family; he need not be caressed or made anything of; but the son's or brother's wife has a claim upon his mother and sisters which they cannot deny. Some convention of their sex obliges them to show her affection, to like or to seem to like her, to take her to their intimacy, however odious she may be to them. With the Coreys it was something more than an affair of sentiment. They were by no means poor, and they were not dependent money-wise upon Tom Corey; but the mother had come, without knowing it, to rely upon his sense, his advice in everything, and the sisters, seeing him hitherto so indifferent to girls, had insensibly grown to regard him as altogether their own till he should be released, not by his marriage, but by theirs, an event which had not approached with the lapse of time. Some kinds of girls — they believed that they could readily have chosen a kind — might have taken him without taking him from them; but this generosity could not be hoped for in such a girl as Miss Lapham.

Or consider this, from the same book:

". . . . The chief consolation that we American parents have in these matters is that we can do nothing. If we were Europeans, even English, we should take some cognisance of our children's love affairs, and in some measure teach their young affections how to shoot. But it is our custom to ignore them until they have shot, and then they ignore us. We are altogether too delicate to arrange the marriages of our children; and when they have arranged them we don't like to say anything, for fear we should only make bad worse. The right way is for us to school ourselves to indifference. That is what the young people have to do elsewhere, and that is the only logical result of our position here. It is absurd for us to have any feeling about what we don't interfere with."

"Oh, people do interfere with their children's marriages very often," said Mrs. Corey.

"Yes, but only in a half-hearted way, so as not to make it disagreeable for themselves if the marriages go on in spite of them, as they're pretty apt to do. Now, my idea is that I ought to cut Tom off with a shilling. That would be very simple, and it would be economical. But you would never consent, and Tom wouldn't mind it."

Hardly what we should call brilliant writing, and yet both of these passages have as their object a measured grasp of conventions by which families at a particular time and place managed their affairs. There is no sense of absolute conviction conveyed to the effect that universal laws have been illuminated and that questions of family process have been settled for all time. What we do have is the quiet authority of a careful and mild observation. Characters are not coerced by the novelistic imagination to do anything an amused and slightly disinterested reader might not expect them to. Where one fellow betrays a fanatical devotion, to his business enterprise or something else, there is generally a contrary force present to soften his passion and to suggest that any number of arrangements are possible under the sun, despite firm or single-minded resolutions held by one or another person. Moreover, though Howells does not have the accumulated density of scene and of heritage to work with, a fact James early observed in comparing the advantages of English and American novelists, he does give us more than the rudiments of a novel of manners. If he cannot quite give us the drama of forward-looking people bound in multiple ways by the inherited claims of tradition and simple habit, he can portray conflicts in which powerful appetites vie under the influence of vague doubts and misgivings that bear some relation to the past. In a sense, the custom of familial concern and affection is all the custom Howells's people have, and almost all the custom they need to have. The intricacies involved in family life are, in this view, sufficient to train us in the uses of tact, conscious reflection, charity, and stable affection. In fact, Howells may be said to love his characters precisely in the degree that they learn to get by in, rather than outside of, the family. This achievement constitutes for Howells a validation of the social ideal in which he believed, the notion that all of us must learn to be sociable creatures, to master the arts whereby men of modest abilities and limited goodness make way for one another. The family, for Howells, provides that certain ground to which all other aspects of middle-class experience must be referred, sooner or later. Like it or not, Howells knew what mattered most to most men and women, and though he did not ask the questions a contemporary reader would urge upon him, he would probably have been able to provide the answers.

The questions Howells fails to ask, of course, would consider the darker side of human intimacy, and inevitably raise doubts about the possible accuracy of any realistic account of close interpersonal relations. Such questions are so familiar to us, of course, that we need hardly think at all to be able to list them:

Who says that most families successfully instruct members in how to get along meaningfully in the world?

Why should intelligent people want simply to get along when to do so involves tolerating terrible abuses and severe restrictions on personal freedom?

Don't most families develop patterns of interaction that usually include scapegoating, ritual exclusion of some members from decision-making, and so on, patterns which encourage children to think of the world as essentially arbitrary and inscrutable?

Each of us can add to these many others, mostly standard for our time. To ask, then, is in a sense implicitly to recommend a criticism of Howells and other nineteenth-century writers centrally concerned with the virtues of family life and the decent promise of the middle classes. This seems to me acceptable, provided we do not equate criticism with dismissal or contempt, for there is in contemporary skeptical criticism a smugness which is in its own way narrow and a good deal more mechanical than it likes to think it is. There are any number of useful observations Howells is permitted to make by virtue of his generosity, which we should be hard put to recognize or concede in our insistence upon negative dialectic and that version of the Freudian proposition that nothing is what it seems to be. The spirit of contemporary disaffection from families and from other primary institutions is best captured in the work of Franz Kafka. In fact, it would be unthinkable to speak of family novels without at least mentioning such extraordinary works as *The Metamorphosis* and shorter fictions like "The Judgment." For in Kafka we have the purest expression of malaise and hysterical disability that we may hope to find, an expression, moreover, that has found an answering response in quarters one would have thought impenetrable to such "unreasonable" formulations. James once wrote of Howells that "he likes things to occur as in life, where the manner of a great many of them is not to occur at all," but even James could not have imagined what "not to occur at all" might mean for someone like Kafka. In *The Metamorphosis,* Gregor Samsa is forbidden to live with his family, which is to say, forbidden to live at all. Now the story of the man who wakes up one morning to find himself transformed into an insect is too familiar to rehearse, but it is perhaps not widely understood that Kafka's is more a lament than a satirical exposé of the middle-class family. In fact it is a species of neurotic disability, of hysterical withdrawal, that prevents Gregor Samsa from living in his family, not the fact that his family is an imperfect one. Kafka's protagonist is forbidden to live with his family by a law of nature — his own; by an inflexibility of temperament which is deforming and pathetic. His is not, contrary to what so many have said, a courageous refusal, but an unhealthy resistance to relation that can promise nothing by way of general improvement. Valuable insights about reciprocity in families are made available to us as readers, but it is clear that Gregor Samsa will not be able to use such insights. There is no doubt that Kafka has demonstrated with great authority how many neurotic and disabled people are forced into strategies of withdrawal and denial by others, usually members of their own families. Certainly the Samsa family bears a good deal of responsibility for what has happened to Gregor, but it is a mistake to formulate the case unequivocally. The most we can reasonably say in this case is that families can do terrible things to their members.

But let us consider more carefully what Kafka has to say to us about families, first by looking at a passage in his story "The Hunger Artist." It is one of the most painful moments in all of literature. The strange fellow who has, all his adult life, entertained audiences by feats of fasting, now lies in a heap of straw in a circus sideshow, no longer an awesome spectacle to anyone:

An overseer's eye fell on the cage one day and he asked the attendants why this perfectly good cage should be left standing there unused with dirty straw inside it; nobody knew, until one man, helped out by the notice board, remembered about the hunger artist. They poked into the straw with sticks and found him in it. "Are you still fasting?" asked the overseer, "when on earth do you mean to stop?" "Forgive me, everybody," whispered the hunger artist; only the overseer, who had his ear to the bars, understood him. "Of course," said the overseer, and tapped his forehead with a finger to let the attendants know what state the man was in, "we forgive you." "I always wanted you to admire my fasting," said the hunger artist. "We do admire it," said the overseer, affably. "But you shouldn't admire it," said the hunger artist. "Well then we don't admire it," said the overseer, "but why shouldn't we admire it?" "Because I have to fast, I can't help it," said the hunger artist. "What a fellow you are," said the overseer, "and why can't you help it?" "Because," said the hunger artist, lifting his head a little and speaking, with his lips pursed, as if for a kiss, right into the overseer's ear, so that no syllable might be lost, "because I couldn't find the food I liked. If I had found it, believe me, I should have made no fuss and stuffed myself like you or anyone else." These were his last words, but in his dimming eyes remained the firm though no longer proud persuasion that he was still continuing to fast.

The hunger artist, then, understands that his refusal to eat, to be a part of the everyday world, is a function of incapacity: "Because I have to fast, I can't help it," he says. Just so in the short novel *The Metamorphosis* Kafka's protagonist would gladly return to his accustomed position in the family if he could help it. Because he cannot return, because he must withdraw and make himself repulsive so as not to draw others into an intimacy he no longer feels able to return, the others must learn to do without him. This his family manages very well indeed, and though the others' optimism and successes are superficial and petty, there is no doubt that Kafka is more than a little jealous and peeved at their stubborn, some would say insensitive, resilience in the face of Gregor's disaster.

That is to say, in Kafka we have the definitive fictional version of the family romance, according to which something a little special, mysterious, and frightening inevitably goes on in relations between mothers and sons, fathers and daughters, and so on, and in which generational battles for dominance and attention inevitably make life for individual members a lot more tense than most will admit. In Kafka's families, of course, the struggle of naked wills is frequently on the surface of things, so that in a story like "The Judgment" a son can finally imagine that his father has sentenced him to death by drowning for harboring obscure patricidal wishes that make the son feel guilty without knowing exactly why he should. In Kafka's fiction, what is imagined is immediately actualized, and in "The Judgment" the son, following the sentence, leaps to his death. A horrible emblem, it is precisely this sort of grim transaction between parent and child that contemporary opponents of the family have taken up and elaborated in an all too literal way. Because Kafka seems literally bound by the figures of authority and guilt he conceives in no way suggests that his readers need be, and I have been alarmed by almost wilful identifications with Kafkan nightmares which so many literate people seem anxious to achieve. Only thus can flight from familial intimacies and responsibilities be justified, it seems. I do not mean to be unfair, but Kafka's families, bad as they are, are livable for most people, and strike the Kafkan protagonist as intolerable only because he persists in stripping away every trace of artifice and social concealment to reveal the bitter archetypal substructure. Kafka's inexorable vision of bitter struggle, guilt, and judgment is not a reflection of a will to demystify conventional social relations but of the will to mystify. Indeed, there is little mysterious about the routine conventions by which ordinary people learn to get along in families and in society at large. Such conventions seem terrible and false only to those who do not know how to distinguish manners from the indulging of deliberate falsehoods, fictions from lies. The fiction that is convention in society is a fiction founded on a deep truth, which is that most men and women require obliquity and indirection in their dealings with others. It is a fact of social life that human beings can never seem altogether what they are, but that for most purposes in social life it is necessary that they be taken as what they seem. Questions of sincerity and authenticity usually arise only when individuals are ill at ease in the social roles they occupy, either because someone else has told them they ought to be ill at ease, or because they are too self-conscious, too little concerned for their own capacity to function easily in the world, to submit to any convention without grave misgivings. The Kafkan protagonist is by nature a mystagogue, one who refuses ever to be satisfied with the surfaces of things, with the routines by which people act together in the world, rather than reflect bitterly on their isolation.

The Kafkan family, then, is a product of an imagination committed to mystifying what it sees. No word of a father figure but seems resonant with an authority and quality of intimidation most of us should be hard put to identify with fathers in our own experience. Nor were nineteenth-century fathers all *that* stern and intimidating in general, if we are to believe the accounts we read in novels of the period. We have in Kafka the inflation of an angle of perception into a full-blown vision, the marshaling of fragmentary insights into general statements. Families become, in this view, oppressive if frequently ineffectual machines which not only control but deny life. What makes Kafka's representation so striking and important is that he provides sufficient material for a criticism of his own dominant perspective. In *The Metamorphosis,* surely as close to a family novel as anything Kafka wrote, the Samsa family has obviously structured its life around an adult son who is expected to be everything to them — provider, contact with the world, and ritual scapegoat. As the novel begins, we see at once that the son, Gregor, has decided to withdraw, to deny his family the satisfaction of so using him. The decision to withdraw, however, is not made in the sense that most of us come to difficult decisions from time to time. For Gregor the decision is an aspect of fate, a fate which at once compels him to withdraw and to feel that he has no right whatsoever to do so. In this vision, to opt out of the nexal bind that is family life is to acquiesce in perpetual guilt and to sentence oneself to death, whether by drowning or by slow attrition of the will to live with guilt. From this perspective the family affords virtually no opportunity for imaginative collaboration and cooperative sympathy. Locked into the nexus, participants are routinely victimized by a system no family member can see or understand. Transactions proceed in undiminished obscurity, and the resentments generated by violations of systematic family procedure fester and burst without any hope of articulation and eventual redress. Even when family members act out, violently berate each other, they do so merely with respect to the forms that have been violated, the static role relations which have been disrupted.

In the course of *The Metamorphosis*, Gregor Samsa, who has ceased now to provide support for his family, to pay for his sister's violin lessons, and to accept blame for every little thing while assuming the full burden of the family, this now totally alienated Gregor Samsa is gradually forgotten, rather like the hunger artist, and soon dies. The members of his family pull themselves together and flourish. All of them find work, grow quite happy with their unfamiliar sufficiency, and look to the future with a foolish though quite charming optimism. Like families in general, or so Kafka would have us imagine, the Samsa family has successfully handled its unpleasant experience by agreeing not to think about it. One who had threatened to become too powerful in the nexus was made to feel his unworthiness and was maneuvered into quitting "the family trust." This was not a maneuver which any individual family member could have deliberately executed, but Kafka's point is that families are no less efficient for having to move unconsciously in such patterns.

There is more to *The Metamorphosis*, but we have one or two other texts to visit, and Kafka's work is instructive enough in the terms we have employed. It provides an excellent point of comparison for a novel like Joyce Carol Oates's recent *them*, for example. The most striking thing about Oates's book is the degree to which she manages to ground family and broader social relations in a densely imagined matrix of cultural and political realities without ever suggesting that any one level is merely instrumental to a consideration of another. Whatever Oates imagines has a weight and importance that no merely contextual consideration can in itself authorize. Thus, while family relations play a significant role in *them*, while the novel has much to tell us about family feeling, loyalty, and such, it cannot be, strictly speaking, a family novel, for Oates is concerned with a great deal more than the survival or redemptive power of families. In a sense the novel deals individually with three lives — with a mother, her son Jules and daughter Maureen. Strangely, though, we are never permitted to forget the Wendall *family,* the *unit* as nurturant and as nightmare. Even in the throes of jealous passion, the son is drawn to his family, thinks intermittently of his mother and her problems, wants to send money to his sister. Though he walks in a dream of erotic possession, he knows that he is a Wendall, that no single encounter or demon-lady can finally alter what he must inevitably be *because* he is a Wendall. At one point, Oates tells us, "Jules thought amiably, *'Jules Wendall is my fate'"* and this fate has much to do with his family, with bonds so powerful that they cannot be easily ignored. Also interesting is that Oates's characters, even where they have been most damaged by broken families and violent intimacies, seem headed always towards new families. It is not that they have not the imagination or strength to conceive anything else, but that they want, in the words of one character, to put their faith in things that are simple and clear. No matter that family relations are neither simple nor clear, or that even characters who articulate things in these terms know very well that families can be hells on earth. Compared with the perpetual flux in which unmoored lives generally revolve, family represents something solid and attractive.

Where a Howells tells us a great deal about families, Oates *shows* us what it feels like to be subject to their allure and tempted to violate their certainties. There is a quality of problematic warmth in Oates's families, and we sense how troubling it can be to various family members. In *them,* the main characters live in a family that is constantly menaced, both from within and without, but they continue to feel that families allow for such things, that it is possible to live with disruption and menace if only we remember who we are and where we have always belonged. This is no regressive mystique, but a reflection of Oates's conviction that most human beings can tolerate only so much confusion and violence in their lives. Readers of *them* will agree that there is no paucity of violence in the novel, and that most of it seems plausible enough. In the face of such violence, of so many threats to one's little satisfactions, the routines of family life represent for most people a welcome harbor, if not positively a retreat. In the following passage from *them,* an important though not central character is described in half-wakeful reverie:

. . . . Asleep, most himself, he was alarmed at the great range of his desires, and waking was always a relief to him. Waking, he understood who he was and what he was. He moved to embrace the woman sleeping beside him, his wife, taking comfort in her warmth.
At this time they had been married for nine years.
The depth of her sleep seemed to him a great trust, a treasure. She slept

silently in his arms. It stunned him to think that for nine years they had slept together, himself and this woman, that their lives had become inextricably bound, that he could not clearly remember a time when he had not known her. That time belonged to another, younger, more helpless self. He got no pleasure from thinking of it.

She was thirty-two. She had had three children, and the children slept along the corridor of this small apartment, two in one room, peaceful and miraculous to him in their sleep, a perpetual surprise, because he could recall a time in his life when they hadn't existed, when he himself had been no more than a child and unnaturally wary of the traps of permanence adults accepted so quietly. He had always been a wary person, beneath his kindliness and his gentle, patient smile. Before waking, drifting in a gray tangle of sleep that was like the tangle of a woman's hair, he felt his wariness rise in him to become a kind of evil. What is he waiting for? What is going to happen? Is he going to do something to his life, something irreparable?

Such a man, an intelligent, even thoughtful person, is one for whom marriage and family constitute a core of affection and trial, for whom the routine certainties are consoling in the degree that it is always possible to half-imagine or dream their dissolution. In such a construction, family represents not merely security but challenge, abandonment always ready to replace responsibility. Precisely because family ties bind individuals so very firmly, family members are given to imagine the breaking of the bonds, and Oates would not have it any other way. For her, the life of affection is arduous, and must be so if it is to bind anyone and sustain wayward fantasies.

Oates's imagination is not limited to the delineation of dream-states and trance-like ardors. Her sense of family intimacy is astonishingly sharp. At one point, the family man who wondered whether he would do anything irreparable to his life looks over at a student who is trying desperately to win his affection and take him from his wife, at Maureen Wendall, in fact. What he sees in her knowing gaze inevitably recalls to him his wife and their life together:

What did she think of him? Intelligence. Tenderness. His wife might glance over at him and see everything there was to see, having heard years ago everything there was to hear, helpless herself to change this fact, a fact of history. She saw through him — why not? She had constructed him, partly. She had helped imagine him for himself. She could not help seeing through his try at calm, elegant language (in imitation of a favorite professor) to his panic, his exhaustion, to the shabbiness of the tweed jacket he wore, the feeble exoticism of his necktie of red and green scimitars, or parrots' beaks, this crazy necktie he had had for too many years. Did his students notice his shabby clothes, or him?

The juxtaposition of wife and student in this passage is masterfully handled, and allows us to see how the idea of family, the sense of being truly seen, even seen through by one's familial intimates, may operate on a decently sensitive person. For Oates, families may brutalize, may suffocate their members, but it is rare that they do so in anything like a predictable and systematic way. So complex and challenging can life in families be that it is only in exceptional cases that imagination is entirely quieted — so long as there is imagination, the capacity to project change and to adjust perspectives on stable realities, so long will families provide substantial opportunities for growth and satisfaction. Contrary to what liberationists of various stripes have lately told us, Oates feels that imagination may be numbed and incapacitated precisely at the point of withdrawal from the binding familial nexus. A commitment to random or unconsidered change may well bespeak a refusal of those imaginative labors that enable us to handle what we know we ought to handle. When the young college professor in *them* moves finally to embrace Maureen Wendall, drifts into a situation in which he vaguely knows he will lose his wife and his family, it is done, in Oates's words, "without any particular reference to his wife, whom he can't quite remember."

them is a wonderful book, but I do not think it is a prime example of the family novel, any more than most of the other works we have looked at. It was not, I am sure, conceived in such terms, nor was Kafka's *Metamorphosis*. A book that was, clearly, conceived as a family novel, is *The Man Who Loved Children*, by Christina Stead. In an afterword to the novel written in 1965 when the book had been out of print for twenty years, the late Randall Jarrell wrote: "It has one quality that, ordinarily, only a great book has: it makes you a part of one family's immediate existence as no other book quite does. When you have read it, you have been, for a few hours, a Pollit; it will take you many years to get the sound of the Pollits out of your ears, the sight of the Pollits out of your eyes, the smell of the Pollits out of your nostrils." And that is the sort of thing we should have to say of any real family novel, that when we have read it, we feel we have been a member of a family not actually our own. In this case the fictional family seems a very special family, eccentric, boisterous and violent in a degree most of us would not associate with our own families. And yet, there is something wonderful and strangely representative in all of the crude antics of the Pollit bunch, not any one detail, or several, but the pattern of family life.

Consider the mother Henny, for example, for she is as important as any figure in a novel for which the *family* is what chiefly counts. In many ways a horrible, really terrifying woman, her bitching and moaning and hitting and frequently vicious behavior to her children would seem to ensure that she strike us as a grotesque pure and simple, the bizarre creation of an imagination given to excess and monstrous distortion. In fact, we are struck by how well Henny instructs us in the true impact of families on women who have neither the strength nor the imagination to make them work according to their real needs and the needs of the children for whom they are responsible. Henny's strength is all show, her hysteria an expression of permanent incapacity and largely self-inflicted dissatisfaction. She is a figure psychoanalysts have treated and described in meticulous detail, though rarely with the patience and genuine tolerance of Christina Stead. Such patience and tolerance are not reflections of mere charity, but of an imagination committed to looking at every figure in the round, according to his impact on every intimate and as the product of social forces he controls only in part. Henny Pollit is a mean-tempered, witch-like figure whose repertoire of stratagems includes many of the staple ploys a number of us have come to identify with women in general, legitimately or not. Her husband, the man who loved children, tells his eldest daughter about one of these devices:

'Men call it the tyranny of tears, it is an iron tyranny — no man could be so cruel, so devilish, as a woman with her weakness, recrimination, convenient ailments, nerves, and tears. We men are all weak as water before the primitive devices of Eve. I was patient at first, many years. You were too young then, Looloo: you did not see how kind I was, hoping for an improvement,' and on.

What we cannot miss in all of this is that the fellow who bemoans the tyranny of tears is himself given to brutal insensitivities when the fit is upon him, and that his own stratagems are no less calculating and treacherous than Henny's. In a sense he is a more lovable fellow, but when we think about him we feel that is only because he is so good at playing the poor oversized boy. If we like Sam Pollit, we like him as a hopeless fellow who will never grow up, as an eccentric barbarian whose narcissistic whining and bombastic verbosity are both somehow colorful and attractive. Confronted by Sam Pollit, it is almost essential that Henny learn to write herself large, to rave and complain and battle on a scale that would seem to defy human proportion. Like the therapist who discovers himself perpetually acting out with almost theatrical extravagance as an extension of his professional attempts to reach a withdrawn and silent psychotic patient, in the Pollit family behavior takes on a dramatic scale and coloration. People find themselves shouting and cavorting all the time, forgetting finally that it might be possible to get through with softer words and modest gestures. The family life takes on a texture and pressure that communicate themselves to every member. Constant threats of murder and suicide encourage family members to resort to such terms even when the specific provocations are relatively slight, though quite terrible for people accustomed to a milder environment. The resort to such extreme verbal gestures, and to terrible thoughts, represents in part an evasion of meaningful relation, an admission of failure to work through conflicts by examining this possibility and that. In the sense that such basic failures generally afflict families in our culture, we have much to address and correct in family life. While I do not think most families are as blocked in their modalities of communication as this might indicate, there is no denying that there are problems of this nature we have further to look into.

But what of Stead's representation of Henny as the tyrant of tears? Although some might well object that such a characterization is exaggerated and unfair, especially when it is said to describe women in general, it does after all make a difference that in the novel this view is Sam's. Accurate as much of it may be, we know very well, for instance, that men are not, as Sam claims, customarily weak as water, that they have harsh devices of their own, and that Sam's observations are tainted by his own wilful and neurotic impulses. But more important by far is Stead's ability to portray Henny always as *woman in a particular family*. She is peculiar in the extreme, her verbal tics alone entitle her to be considered an original, but for us she is a function of the Pollit family, of the house, the marriage, the children to which she belongs. In the first few pages of this very long novel, we read:

She had the calm of frequentation; she belonged to this house and it to her. Though she was a prisoner in it, she possessed it. She and it were her marriage. She was indwelling in every board and stone of it: every fold in the curtains had a meaning (perhaps they were so folded to hide a darn or stain); every room was a phial of revelation to be poured out some feverish night in the secret laboratories of her decisions, full of living cancers of insult, leprosies of disillusion, abscesses of grudge, gangrene of nevermore, quintan fevers of divorce, and all the proliferating miseries, the running sores and thick scabs, for which (and not for its heavenly joys) the flesh of marriage is so heavily veiled and conventually interned.

Or consider this passage, further on in the book, in which the daughter Louie recalls a small mission she had been given:

When quite small, she had been trusted to go to the forbidden medicine chest, to get out Henny's medicine — phenacetin, aspirin, or the tabu pyramidon — or her smelling salts; and even once had brought the bottle of spirits hidden behind all those bottles at the back, which all the children knew was there, and which none of them would ever have revealed to their father. None of them thought there was cheating in this: their father was the tables of the law, but their mother was natural law; Sam was household czar by divine right, but Henny was the czar's everlasting adversary, household anarchist by divine right.

Such extraordinary passages mark *The Man Who Loved Children* as a work of genius, as the apotheosis of the family novel, for it richly dramatizes the life of families as something of the greatest interest and importance. If it gives us a host of people who are neither gentle nor particularly admirable, there is nonetheless a combination of extraordinary decency and affection in the person who created them. In Trilling's terms, we cannot mistake the fact that the Stead novel is "for the reservation of moral judgment, for the charm of the mysterious, precarious little flame that lies at the heart of the commonplace." If no single character totally dominates this novel, if it is the family itself, its life process and survival that we care most about, then it is fair to say that *The Man Who Loved Children* celebrates life. In the terms of this vision, and here I think Stead must speak for family novelists in general, to celebrate life is to celebrate the family, at least in its ideal potential. For all the abuse and nastiness we cannot forget, the stench of human conflict we cannot get out of our nostrils, it is perhaps this passage from the novel that best accounts for its enduring hold upon us:

Sam said fretfully, 'You know, my friend, I would rather be at home, with my children, and hear the elms and sycamores and cedars rustle, and hear dear little Maretta, with her thin voice, asking if she will get her wish, and keeping my record of Georgetown birds, than even be near the throne of a God. And if I had to choose between such a Him, and them, I would choose them at once. And so would you, Naden. There never was a father would sacrifice his son to God, as the wicked old story has it: there never was.'

Of Sam Pollit, Elizabeth Hardwick once wrote: "He is modern, sentimental, cruel and as sturdy as a weed. There is no possibility of destroying him. After every disaster, he shoots back up, ready with his weedy, choking sentiments. In the end he is preparing to go on the radio with his 'Uncle Sam Hour' and it is inconceivable that the adventure should fail." That indeed is the unmistakable thrust of this novel: Looking at a family whose life is everywhere twisted by hypocrisy, shabbiness, and cruelty, Christina Stead concludes, "It is inconceivable that the adventure should fail." And we believe her.

TWO

NATURE AND SOCIAL REALITY IN BELLOW'S "SAMMLER"

One is apt to hear a great deal in our time about the return to nature and about the apocalyptic renovations likely to attend success in such an enterprise. It is as though, having failed quite miserably as a culture to manage our problems, having failed even properly to define them, we had decided that our only hope lay in pronouncing them less monstrous than they had originally appeared, and surely available to the rhetorical reductions we have collectively trained ourselves to execute. This is nothing new, of course. One has only to be modestly familiar with the vagaries of cultural fashion since the time of the French Revolution to recognize in contemporary cycles of reaction and renewal the rehearsal of a very old drama, and nothing has been so frequently proclaimed as original and promising in all these years as the tired notion of nature and the attributes of sheer being unmodified by cultural directives of any kind. There have been wide divergences among the various spokesmen for nature, to be sure, and one who has read carefully, say, Rousseau's *Confessions* or *Social Contract* cannot easily commit the error of linking him uncritically with German despoilers of the idea of culture in the Nazi period. What has generally characterized the best, the most enduringly useful of these spokesmen, though, is not really difficult to formulate. I speak of their resistance to the notion that reality conforms to rather simple laws, or that ambivalence towards one's society and prospects can be resolutely banished once an appropriate perspective is realized. That such resistance has been exemplary in the work of men like Goethe and Rousseau seems to me indisputable, but the romantic tradition they represent seems today

From *Critical Quarterly*, Winter 1974.

everywhere in ruins, its legimate heirs confused and hysterical in more instances than one would care to recite.

It has seemed to me for some time that we have in Saul Bellow a more hopeful variant of the romantic disposition than we had any right to expect. Surely, with a very formidable body of work behind him, he has shown us how difficult it is even for the most sensible of men to abandon the idea of nature to which American writers have been so uniformly compelled. He has, moreover, modified that idea and enlarged the context in which it is conventionally treated. Whether in so doing he has succeeded in making the idea more persuasive, or has stripped it of a singularity we always thought it had, we cannot decide confidently as yet. What is clear is that an element one could discern even in an early novel like *The Victim* has moved steadily to occupy a central position in Bellow's more recent fiction. What I propose to examine here is the idea of nature in Bellow and its relation to two others: the idea of social reality, and the idea of character conceived both in its moral and aesthetic dimensions. To do this, it seems a good idea to focus on Bellow's 1970 National Book Award winning novel, *Mr. Sammler's Planet,* for it is a compact volume with rather few characters and a carefully limited perspective on everything. It has, in addition, a sympathetically drawn protagonist whose intelligence is so fine as to filter a very great range of ideas and events. In *Mr. Sammler's Planet,* the idea of nature must necessarily be evoked as a complex and tantalizing thing, for the mind that entertains it is nimble and endlessly active. While it treats the idea of nature not as a learned treatise might, but as a learned work of fiction infrequently can, Bellow's novel allows us to consider the degree to which the idea can be compelling in a culture like ours.

Probably the most striking and insistent note sounded in *Mr. Sammler's Planet* is the protagonist's cry of alarm against what he calls ". . . the peculiar aim of sexual niggerhood for everyone." What he means by this is not as simple as one might expect, for Sammler, no less than Bellow, seems rather confused about just what constitutes "sexual niggerhood." Clearly the expression depends for its resonance on the stereotype of the black man as somehow more intimately "tuned in" to the rhythms of his own pulse than other men and as therefore more at ease with the demands of his own sexuality. From this stems the familiar notion of the black man's demand for instant gratification of every sensual whim, and the growing attractiveness of this attitude for many millions of white Americans recently liberated from outworn inhibitions. Crudely considered, the stereotype is not altogether misleading, though the human reality it ostensibly illuminates is largely concealed by so vague an image. Similarly, one would not want to take issue with the notion that demands for instant gratification have been sounded with increasing regularity even in those segments of the culture one would not ordinarily have looked to for such sentiments — I am thinking here especially of the intellectuals in American society, but the phenomenon is as current in European circles as it is in this country. Why Bellow's Sammler should be as exercised by the whole thing as he is we may justly question, however, for he is rather attracted by just those kinds of spontaneity and avowals of potency one is apt to identify with the stereotyped image of the black experience we have come largely to accept. It is not that Sammler is, or has been, an erotic type, if we may use so imprecise a term, or that his is a forcefully expressive personality of the sort we may mistake for erotic command. He is very much concerned, though, with what his intellectual enemies the existentialists call authenticity, and if he is less aggressive than they are about the wearing of masks and socially sanctioned ritualizations of concealment, he is never far from cynicism about the games most of us play, and we are not surprised to hear him say, "To be nearer to nature was necessary in order to keep in balance the achievements of modern method." In the long run, one has a good sense of what Sammler thinks on the subjects of war, peace, brotherhood, family, the responsibility of intellect, and the like, but one will be hard put indeed to locate a consistent pattern in these views. Not that we have any right to demand that Bellow provide one, of course, for what he does give us is a rich and believable character whose ambivalence moves us to the degree that it resists easy resolutions of every kind. Where the character Sammler succumbs to such resolutions, to patterns that would explain every particular view and experience, he strikes us as a little pathetic, hardly persuasive.

Mr. Sammler, for example, is not altogether moved in a negative way by the "niggerhood," sexual and otherwise, he has reason to descry. Readers of the novel will remember his compulsive returns to a west side New York bus to observe a handsome, elegantly attired black thief at work picking the pockets of passengers. Now it is nothing so fashionable as the fascination of the absurd that Sammler experiences on these daily excursions of his, but a positive admiration for carefully plotted depredations carried out with an assurance, style, and conviction that are almost calculated to embarrass an observer with the comparatively anxious and petty maneuvers to which he himself is habituated. Sammler reflects on the thief as follows:

The black man was a megalomaniac. But there was a certain — a certain princeliness. The clothing, the shades, the sumptuous colours, the barbarous-majestical manner. He was probably a mad spirit. But mad with an idea of noblesse.

Sammler suffers for this black man when he is finally cornered and humiliated, suffers for him not because he is a mere mortal who has fallen on bad times, but because the idea of noblesse he somehow incarnates has been wantonly soiled by those who have no real sense of what noblesse might mean for all of us. One is tempted, surely, to share Sammler's attitude, but it is a little hard to do so if one does not understand what it is he admires in the black man. Can one seriously admire a man for his sumptuous clothing and confident demeanor? What can the idea of noblesse amount to when it is embodied in a petty thief who shows absolutely no concern for his victims as people, and who brutally affronts an old man like Sammler as he does? (The thief, in a scene one is not likely to forget, traps Sammler in an apartment house and exposes his sex organ to him as an unmistakable sign of his mastery.) So much that Sammler says in the novel seems sensible and clear that one is almost willing to grant that he is right about the black man, that it is we who are blind to certain qualities largely absent in our experience of the modern world. It would be unfortunate to acquiesce in such temptations, though, for, as Bellow would himself say in his most lucid moments, we know better, and what we know Bellow has had a hand in teaching us. Surely the glorification of madness, whether princely or banal, is not a project one would associate with Bellow, nor with Sammler. Who would we expect to understand more clearly how the flight into psychopathology can be at best an abstract gesture, in that it contains no concrete criticism of the reality it would reject? That this is no easy criticism to produce we are aware, for we have lost all secure touch with what older writers might have called the concept of normality, and only such a concept can enable one to account for madness, to gauge its depth and consider reasonably its attraction. In all the talk of "sexual niggerhood" we overhear in *Mr. Sammler's Planet,* and despite the vivid evocation of a virile black man subversive of established western values, we are given very little sense of those particular social conditions that make possible the phenomena Sammler reacts to so unhappily. We never really understand why the black man, not merely in his person but as an emblem of values and life styles, should have been permitted to move into the center of western culture and to emasculate its older traditions.

What we can say, then, is that if the black man is not at the very center of Bellow's novel, the styles and values associated with him most definitely are, and to the extent that they weigh heavily on Mr. Sammler, they must concern us. These values and styles, only loosely imagined in the course of the novel, are about as close as we can come to what Bellow thinks of when he turns to the idea of nature. Obviously, it is not the nature of trees and blue skies and tiptoes through the tulips, nor the nature of pastoral swains and woodland nymphs, to which Sammler is drawn. Like other protagonists in Bellow's fiction, he is at least partially drawn to the idea and image of nature red in tooth and claw. Strange? Perverse? Not really, for Sammler is a survivor of a tradition forcibly isolated from pastoral pleasures of every kind. A Jew who has but barely escaped death in a Nazi concentration camp a quarter of a century earlier, Sammler is a gentle man, almost passive really, but in his heart he wishes he were a bit less civilized, less passive, that Jews in general had been less prone to play the role of victim to conquerors of every type. Nature for Sammler is purpose combined with the strength and energy to realize its wishes, grasp for its dreams no matter how unpleasant or occasionally indecorous. That this nature is necessarily envisioned as a little mysterious and frightening in Bellow's work is no surprise, for even substantial physical size and strength are insufficient to convince Bellow's protagonists that they are men capable of confronting the real world in all its harshness.

We think of Asa Leventhal, the central figure in Bellow's early novel *The Victim*. Though he is hardly an intellectual, and hardly the throwback to old-world dignity we meet in Sammler, he is nonetheless a prototype of Bellow's latest protagonist. Without rehearsing the details of his story, we may say he is victimized because he does not know how to look at nature, let alone deal with it maturely. One well-known critic complained of Bellow several years ago that his protagonists' sense of sin and excess was boyish, and when one thinks of figures like Leventhal and Augie March, one is hard put to disagree. When we meet Leventhal he is living alone, his wife having gone to visit a parent for a while. We see at once that he is ill-equipped to live by himself, and he is subject to morbid uncertainties, the prey of distressing memories out of a past that should have been settled and buried. He remembers an affair his wife was having with a married man while she was making plans to marry Leventhal, and he thinks of this as of an event so absolutely terrible and incomprehensible as to constitute a reality from which he must forever be excluded. Just so is he awed at the small spectacle of his neighbor's dog panting in pleasure as its belly is rubbed, wholly given over to delight in the moment. Attracted to an emblem of sheer abandon, Leventhal relates to the dog as a mysterious and wonderful creature, again existing at a level of feeling Leventhal cannot acknowledge as potentially his as well. When his friend tells him to get close to himself later in the novel, Leventhal seems to grasp what he means, that he must acknowledge his own propensity towards a variety of feelings and experiences he has sought resolutely to repress or to banish. What Leventhal must learn is that there need be no absolute victims, no total oppressors, only men who do injury to one another and who are capable of forgiving both what they have done and what has been done to them. But like Bellow's other protagonists, Leventhal never really learns this as well as he should, and he is therefore inordinately tempted to view as reality only what is sordid and ruthless. All the rest is suspect as mere sentiment or idea.

So the nature Sammler looks upon in the guise of a handsome black thief is a nature ruthless and sordid, and all the more attractive for being so. In a sense one may say this nature is conceived as a corrective to the humane sentiments and gentle manners in which Sammler feels somewhat enclosed, though at the same time he is very much at home with old-world manners and assumptions. What Sammler suspects is that the other nature, the nature one associates with the divine flow of things passively regarded, is not really the sort of thing one can rely upon in the modern world, much as one would like to, and much as Sammler relies upon it from time to time. The nature to which Whitman and other American writers have delighted in yielding themselves is here rejected as inadequate, for it is unrealistic in its trust and in its failure to discriminate between a sense of the universe and a sense of social fact. That Sammler never successfully formulates or understands the distinction on an intellectual level only attests to the great difficulty western humanistic intellectuals have had in thinking in such terms. Sammler tells us he has abandoned most of the books he has read in and thought about in his life, so that he might dwell almost exclusively with Meister Eckhart, whose mystical works contain injunctions against entertaining notions of multiplicity and difference, of limitation and quality. Would Meister Eckhart have been gripped with admiration for Sammler's black thief? It is, of course, a preposterous suggestion, but it points up rather clearly the intellectual failure of Sammler's formulations, and of Bellow's fictional project conceived as a philosophical enterprise. No doubt it is possible by way of explanation to assert that it is Bellow's intention to dramatize Sammler's failure of insight, but we have no way of discerning just where Bellow's perspective deviates from Sammler's. It is hardly legitimate to claim that a character's revealed failures in insight constitute a necessary triumph for the novelist who has permitted us to see them. Unless the novelistic intelligence is unmistakably distinguished from a single character's perspective, as it is so often in Flaubert and in James, we can have at best a richly ambiguous confusion. We may not have a philosophical triumph, which is precisely what the wise-man accents that permeate *Mr. Sammler's Planet* would lead us to expect.

But we have not determined as yet precisely what is this nature to which Sammler is drawn and whose incarnation is the black thief. Is this nature no more than reality bluntly conceived? I should have to say that it is not, for reality would seem to me at least a complex of events and objects and living things which cannot be evaded or denied. Mr. Sammler's black man is something else altogether, for he *can* be evaded, can be denied. In his actuality he is as strange, as unrevealed to Sammler as though he had never seen him. Nature for Sammler is a fictive realm which can endow human beings with wondrous attributes otherwise undreamed of by cautious old-world Jews committed to esoteric speculations of an altogether otherworldly sort. Which is to say that for Sammler, nature is an idea, and as an idea it is available to manipulations whose basis in subjective need in no way compromises the persuasiveness of the idea. It is a nature practically protean in the number of shapes it can be made to assume. In Sammler's hands it serves at once to assuage a sense of alienation, of otherness, and to enforce it as a badge of distinction. On the one hand he will insist upon the viability of mystical experience, unorthodox though it may be, upon the necessary dissolution of that multiplicity we perceive in the physical world, upon the sensation of oneness with all that exists. This is the perspective of Meister Eckhart, so forcibly impressed upon us in *Mr. Sammler's Planet*. On the other hand we have a nature which is nothing if not multiplicitous, a nature which is movement, passion, struggle, disorder, the singular personality impressive precisely in the degree of its defiant singularity.

To ask which nature Sammler prefers is to compound the confusion. I think it is possible to conclude that he thinks he is on the side of Meister Eckhart and the mystics, but that he actually occupies several positions at once. Would he agree with Wittgenstein in the *Tractatus* when he asserts that "the solution of the problem of life is seen in the vanishing of the problem"? Surely this is to deny nature, if nature has anything whatever to do with what we ordinarily call reality, and if reality can be said to grip us by the throat from time to time. Problems conceived as difficulties in linguistic operations are surely susceptible to manipulations such as would please a Wittgenstein, but it is doubtful that Bellow would be satisfied with that sort of solution, or with that sort of problem. The problems he posits for his characters are not problems of mere explanation, not a matter of simply getting things straight or establishing manageable linguistic dimensions in which the problem can be more beneficially reconstituted. When Bellow's Augie March tells us, "That's the struggle of humanity, to recruit others to your version of what's real," he does so with some sort of conviction that this is ultimately an impoverishing struggle, that to become more attached to the version than to the reality it should serve or represent is a great misfortune. What is so baffling in our experience of Bellow's work, though, is that virtually all of his resolutions, certainly in the works of the last fifteen years or so, amount to simply getting things straight or rearranging the terms of a problem so that it at least appears more manageable, or less important. What does the mystic do if not banish problems conceived at a secular level? To seek to move beyond desire, for example, is to avoid having to determine appropriate objects which can satisfy that desire. Whether the character is Henderson the rain king, Moses Herzog, or Artur Sammler, we have in Bellow's more recent fictions the exaltation of a will to banish conflicts whose resolutions imply decision and discrimination. A decision is made at the conclusion of *Henderson The Rain King,* but it does not emerge from the novel itself, nor from anything the main character has learned in the course of his adventures. The decision is willed rather than achieved, and it is asserted largely at the expense of fundamental realities the novel has resolutely impressed upon us. I do not know any serious commentator who has found that novel's conclusion satisfactory. There is nothing like a concluding decision reached in *Herzog,* nor is there one in *Sammler.* Both decide, basically, that there is little point in the endless discriminations and explanations to which their lives have been largely committed. It is fitting that the final words of *Sammler* should be, "For that is the truth of it — that we all know, God, that we know, that we know, we know, we know."

What we know, according to Sammler, has a lot to do with the mystic bond men like Meister Eckhart have told us so much about. Secure in our affirmation of this bond, so Sammler's thinking goes, we shall be secure in knowing the terms of responsible behavior towards our fellows, we shall be decent men and women, grateful children and generous parents. Is it human nature to be thus secure, to seek simply to fulfill the terms of our contract with God which in our heart of hearts we know and understand? This is more difficult to answer, surely, for one can hardly claim that mystical affirmations are natural, that the discounting of physical phenomena is a thing readily accomplished even by the most mundane intelligence and flabby will. Nature mystics, from Wordsworth to Rimbaud and Tennyson, have of course described states of blissful absorption into boundless being achieved almost spontaneously, without the sort of disciplined attentiveness and wilful self-denial we associate with St. John of the Cross, or with T. S. Eliot, for that matter. What seems clear, though, is that the trust and spontaneity of a Wordsworth, lovely and moving though their expression can be in his poems, are simply not of the sort a sensible man can long maintain. That, in Wordsworth's words, "Nature never did betray the heart that loved her" is a gorgeous sentiment, but the grotesque developments in the life of Wordsworth's own sister Dorothy ought surely to have altered his faith in such a sentiment. Sammler's gentler nature, the nature he identifies with the mystic affirmations of Eckhart (rather than with the nature represented by the black thief), is not really very different from Wordsworth's, is similarly easy, accepted almost deliberately as against the facts. In an extended discussion between an Indian scholar named Govinda Lal and Sammler, we note especially the following exchange:

Lal: "I believe you intimate that there is an implicit morality in the will-to-live and that these mediocrities in office will do their duty by the species. I am not sure. There is no duty in biology. There is no sovereign obligation to one's breed. When biological destiny is fulfilled in reproduction the desire is often to die . . ."

Sammler: "When you know what pain is, you agree that not to have been born is better. But being born one respects the powers of creation, one obeys the will of god — with whatever inner reservations truth imposes. As for duty — you are wrong. The pain of duty makes the creature upright, and this uprightness is no negligible thing. No, I stand by what I first said."

Surely Lal's remarks seem the more cogent and sensible in this exchange, but we must remember that Sammler is a hard man to pin down. Only thirty pages earlier in the novel, speaking wistfully of Tolstoy's humanism, he reminds himself and his companion of a scene in *War and Peace* in which the French General Davout spared the life of Pierre Bezhukov: ". . . they looked into each other's eyes. A human look was exchanged, and Pierre was spared. Tolstoy says you don't kill another human being with whom you have exchanged such a look." Prodded by his companion to explain his sentiments upon recalling such an incident, he remarks: "I sympathize deeply. I sympathize sadly. When men of genius think about humankind, they are almost forced to believe in this form of psychic unity. I wish it were so." And further, ". . . though it's not an arbitrary idea, I wouldn't count on it." Which is to show only that Sammler is of many minds on many issues, that his attraction to Meister Eckhart and the black thief is no more contradictory really than his attraction to abstract ideas of widely varying merit and implication. That nature should be for Sammler at once an exhilarating idea, no matter how disparate his varying conceptions of it, and also a rather sickening notion laced with a kind of emotional excess he finds intolerable, should not surprise us once we have come to terms with Bellow's work. One may find it all a little dismaying, nevertheless, for it is not merely a narrow, a petty consistency that we fail to find in Bellow. What we have, again, and there is no getting around the fact, is confusion presented as complex wisdom, is a series of rejections of specious idea constructs which is itself thoroughly founded on intellectual quirkiness and easy indulgence.

We have claimed for Sammler a considerable intelligence and power of discrimination, yet we accuse him of intellectual quirkiness and vulgar expediency. The contradiction is not in the terms we apply, however, but in those confusions that we have cited. These confusions point to more than a split in the central character, a radical ambivalence the likes of which most of us surely know and share. I am concerned with a failure of imagination that refuses to work through the problems it posits at the level on which they are originally conceived. To fail of resolutions that are gratifying, or even modestly acceptable, is no great failure, for we live at a time when all resolutions are held suspect, especially among the liberal and literate people who will constitute Bellow's immediate readership. To introduce into serious discourse, though, considerations and perspectives that banish to irrelevance the central issues or insistently terminate them, is to opt for confusion, the fragmentary rather than the substantive response. And this is surely what we have in *Mr. Sammler's Planet.* For all that the central character is always on stage, for all his intelligence, his fine capacity to associate fluently among diverse materials and to stamp his personality on everything he touches, we necessarily relate to the novel as to a series of brilliant fragments, insights constituted in the spirit of the contemporary probe beloved of speculators in the stock-market of ideas. We may love or dislike Sammler himself, and surely that is a constituent of our response to the novel as a whole, but we will want as well a more coherent vision of possibility than the novel affords.

Some years ago, in an essay entitled "Art And Fortune," Lionel Trilling wrote of some of our best novelists that they ". . . have mixed what they personally desired with what they desired for the world and have mingled their mundane needs with their largest judgments. Then, great as their mental force has been, they have been touched with something like stupidity, resembling the holy stupidity which Pascal recommends: its effects appear in their ability to maintain ambivalence toward their society, which is not an acquired attitude of mind, or a weakness of mind, but rather the translation of a biological datum, an extension of the pleasure-pain with which, in a healthy state, we respond to tension and effort; the novelist expresses this in his co-existent hatred and love of the life he observes. His inconsistency of intellectual judgment is biological wisdom." The passage has always seemed to me rich and provocative, and surely it has a great deal to say about the idea of nature we have been considering. It speaks, after all, of "a biological datum," of "biological wisdom," in fact, and these are clearly notions dear to Sammler. For Sammler thinks he knows "what is what," speaks often of "fated biological necessities," and has something more or less definitive to say about everyone he encounters, as though confirmed in his judgments by some exalted authority seated deeply in his very blood. What the authority says corresponds roughly to the attitude of "holy stupidity" Trilling briefly describes, and might be put as follows: Be a judge, but don't believe over-much in the necessity or absolute validity of your judgments; believe that man is good, looking at the species archetypally, but understand that in fact we are miserable and cruel to one another and have it as our fun-damental project in life to overcome disgust; embrace only what is mys-tical, aesthetic, spiritualized, but be, at all costs, reasonable. No doubt about it, these are the messages Sammler turns over and over in his head, these are the imperatives to which he responds. Where the biology comes in is in our resignation to these contradictory imperatives as a kind of wisdom, in our feeling that nature enforces such contradictions as neces-sary, if not always satisfying to the critical intellect. None of this is a matter of cultivating experiences sufficient to convince us that what is, is. Experience has very little to do with it. In the view to which Sammler subscribes, we come to know what is necessary through an operation of mind which is not exercised by specific phenomena, by the accumulation and consideration of sensible experiences. Every mind must know by itself, somehow, what is necessary and true, those things that cannot be other than they are. A mind which cannot discover these things by itself will never understand them at all. We must anticipate lawfulness, form, regularity in nature, which is to say in the created universe, we must respect the rightfulness and necessity of some organizing principle, though we may not make regular contact with it. Duty will consist in our standing unperturbed, unintimidated in the midst of complexity, before the spec-tacle of inexhaustible contradiction.

This is all very well, it seems to me, but it does not yet refute the charges we have brought to bear in witness of Bellow's novel. "Incon-sistency of intellectual judgment" against a background of secure convic-tion in the orderliness of nature and the abiding authority of reasonable feelings is but an aspect of the problem, an aspect which gives us less trouble than others, I might add. What we really cannot understand in considering Sammler is what he desires for the world — to use Trilling's idiom, how he explains to himself the idea of society and its relation to nature. To "maintain an ambivalence" towards one's society is at least to have some sense of what it is, how it operates, what obligations partici-pation in its processes entails for the individual. This sense is difficult to improvise, for it is customarily rooted in a profound conception of neces-sity that takes into account both the peculiar, temporary needs of the self and the past it is impaled on. Sammler does not appear wholly to avoid the dilemma Bellow once described in an article, as follows:

American novelists are not ungenerous, far from it, but as their view of society is fairly shallow, their moral indignation is non-specific. What seems to be lacking is a firm sense of a common world, a coherent community, a genuine purpose in life.

I do not think Bellow's view of society is shallow — surely *Mr. Sammler's Planet* communicates the texture, the very feel of contemporary life as vividly as any novel we can name. What we must say, though, is that it is not sufficiently historical. We do not know what are the forces that have brought us to the moment the novel documents. In fact, there is no development of any kind in Bellow's novel, for while presenting to us a central figure who is nothing if not historical, Bellow is definitely more concerned with the revelation of the human condition. This condition we understand all too well in the first twenty-five pages of the book. As we read on, we come more and more to feel the absence of "a coherent community" as an aspect of the human condition, despite perpetual reminders as to the uniqueness of the present moment. The abstraction of "the human condition" finally is identified with reality itself, so that it becomes almost impossible to think of "a common world" or "coherent community" as concrete potentialities within the domain of contemporary experience. The novel, in other words, denies us the possibility of a social reality that is not a direct reflection of a corrupted nature, conceived here largely in static, immutable terms.

Set in such a context, the projects of selfhood assume a vaguely mystical air, and the attitudes that shape experience seem eccentric and insistently private. The strange thing about this, though, is that Sammler should stand out so clearly from all the others in the novel. While they do not collectively form anything like a "coherent community," surely they have a good deal more in common with one another than any of them have with Sammler, who often reminds himself of his distinction: "Mr. Sammler did feel somewhat separated from the rest of his species, if not in some fashion severed — severed not so much by age as by preoccupations too different and remote, disproportionate on the side of the spiritual, Platonic, Augustinian, 13th century." Is it simply that Sammler cultivates more assiduously than others certain aspects of personality which are relatively exotic in our time, or is it that he is really different as the result of some peculiar endowment more biological than cultural? The novel definitely stresses the cultural domain as the source of Sammler's distinction — continually he is referred to as a survivor of a very special kind, an old-world Jew with expectations and manners derived from an earlier world originally more orderly and decorous, later more unequivocally cruel and murderous, than the contemporary scene. Yet Sammler's mysticism does not seem at all a necessary outgrowth of his derivation from an old-world European tradition, the essential flavor of which was anything but occult and mysterious even in its darkest ravages. It seems to have emerged full-blown from nowhere, a wondrous flowering in old age. It is described in the novel not as an evasion of reality but as a commitment to a deeper, more abiding reality than mundanity impresses. That is to say, while Bellow wishes us to relate to Sammler as the product of a special cultural and social environment no longer available to us except by way of historical imagination, he evokes the character, in all his attitudinal dimensions, as a force of nature, something marvelous and unaccountable. No doubt, Sammler would not seem so marvelous and exotic were he presented to us with fewer explicit reminders of his difference, and did he not himself insist upon this so strenuously. In a universe of human beings struggling to keep afloat, to nurture some sense of individual, if not of communal purpose, a man whose habitual mode is "aesthetic consumption of the environment" is bound to seem extraordinary.

What remains problematical is the degree to which social reality in this novel reflects nature, or perhaps we should say, what is prior to culture. If Sammler's mysticism and his separateness cannot be strictly accounted for in terms of social realities either suggested or explicitly described, can we account any better for the other characters in the novel? Surely they do not seem to be forces of nature. In fact, each is the product of a situation Sammler himself would have us believe he grasps, a situation that is unmistakably cultural and social as far as he is concerned. What has happened, Sammler tells us, is that we have become so civilized, technology has had its way with us for so long, that it is no longer possible for most of us to think "nature" as we could in an earlier time. Even to say the word is to realize how little it resonates with the strangeness it once had. Where once nature called to mind primal energies and the necessary risks entailed in openness, it now has more to do with what Philip Rieff, in another context, calls "calculated spontaneity." Here is a description taken from the novel, a description of New York as the setting in which these various lives must make their way:

You opened a jewelled door into degradation, from hypercivilized Byzantine luxury straight into the state of nature, the barbarous world of colour erupting from beneath. It might well be barbarous on either side of the jewelled door. Sexually, for example, the thing evidently, as Mr. Sammler was beginning to grasp, consisted in obtaining the privileges, and the free ways of barbarism, under the protection of civilized order, property rights, refined technological organization, and so on.

What Bellow is giving us, in other words, and what Sammler sees, is a universe in which the very idea of nature has been altered, confused, deliberately turned around in such a way that it does not mean what it used to. And as the idea of nature has been wilfully perverted, so is it difficult any longer to think of social reality in the customary ways. Obviously, to think of the one idea is in some sense to compare it to the other, and this has become more and more difficult to do. The self has no secure home either in nature or in society, for neither constitutes a firm reality to which it can relate with confidence. Where once it was possible to speak of one's nature and authenticity in terms of understanding one's position in society — a fact brought home to us in Erich Auerbach's discussion of the seventeenth-century French idiom *se connaître* as signifying both recognition of oneself and of one's position in the social world — we have now reached a time in which it seems futile even to speak of the one in the context of the other. That this is not an entirely familiar situation we may be certain. Even Rousseau, whose exaltations of nature we hear so much about these days, had a very specific sense of the coherent community, and understood that there could be no natural man in the modern world, at least no natural man in the old sense. Whoever urged men to drop out, to cultivate their own impulses and pleasures in an exclusive sense, denied them access to reality, and that reality for Rousseau was clearly social. Though it was not desirable for men to require others to tell them what to want, it was necessary that modern men keep in mind the sense of themselves as contingent beings, as social and historical figures confronted with particular inexorable demands. In *Emile,* we read that "Good social institutions are those best fitted to make men unnatural, to take away man's absolute existence and give him a relative one, to absorb the self into the common whole, so that each individual no longer regards himself as one, but as part of a larger totality, and is aware only of the whole."

The passage does overstate Rousseau's fundamental position, as a matter of fact, but it is clear that social reality was to him no specter to be casually dismissed or wilfully transcended. It was there and one had to deal with it. Individual impulse could be nurtured only under conditions that might threaten to limit its gratification, and this the individual himself would have to acknowledge and approve. So disaffected is Mr. Sammler from his own social reality, so disgraceful is it, in fact, as it is presented in Bellow's novel, that the responsibilities Rousseau outlines seem more and more impossible to recommend or to fulfill. The dilemma is easy enough to explain. For Rousseau and for Bellow, particular social conditions have encouraged a whole variety of unfortunate behaviors which hinder the development of trust, affection, and confident selfhood. For Rousseau, however, these social conditions must be met head-on by a generation of people who have been properly trained to decide for themselves what are their real needs and what are the peculiar contours of their independent selfhood. This selfhood is understood in advance to be fragmentary and insufficient, since to be whole it must acknowledge contingency and control itself in the interests of communal purpose. For Bellow, insofar as his position is clear at all, there is an authentic selfhood that is individual and perpetually resistant to the claims of social conscience, indeed even of the social-reality principle. This resistance is an aspect of Sammler and constitutes perhaps the most favorable aspect of his character structure, in Bellow's view. That such resistance can take several forms, Bellow knows very well, it must be said, and there can be no doubt that he feels strong aversion to some of them. Of madness and the attraction to coolly spontaneous violence he has Sammler reflect as follows: "The middle class had formed no independent standards of honour. Thus it had no resistance to the glamour of killers . . . Madness is the attempted liberty of people who feel themselves overwhelmed by giant forces of organized control. Seeking the magic of extremes. Madness is a base form of the religious life." Despite these aversions, however, and no matter how deeply felt and persuasive we feel Bellow's expression of them to be, his notion of genuine and positive resistance is largely insupportable, whether in terms of social reality or of individual human nature. It involves a syndrome of gestures and assertions which the psychoanalyst Leslie H. Farber has described as a distention of will, a willing of what cannot be willed, given what the individual agent happens to be. Bellow wants his protagonist to be a reasonable man, a humble though learned *mensch,* even as he wants him to be something a little more exquisite, a mystic in touch with occult realms. For a man who in *Herzog* so eschews potato love, that awful inclination to get rid of one's peculiar burden of selfhood by merging with the mass and proclaiming the supremacy of the universal, he seems strangely at ease with a passage like the following in *Sammler:*

No force of nature, nothing paradoxical or demonic, he had no drive for smashing through the masks of appearances . . . that one should be satisfied with such truth as one could get by approximation. Trying to live with a civil heart. With disinterested charity. With a sense of the mystic potency of humankind. With an inclination to believe in archetypes of goodness.

In other words, while we must not feel ourselves absolutely "overwhelmed by giant forces of organized control," and while any sense of coherent community is surely out of the question for the foreseeable future, "the mystic potency of humankind" is a plausible idea to which we should cling for dear life, though surely it cannot provide those "independent standards of honour" for want of which the middle classes are literally destroying themselves. Altogether a difficult set of propositions to recommend. We know, of course, that it is not the business of any novel to recommend particular behaviors, and we would be gravely mistaken were we to translate Bellow's propositions into actual suggestions offered us in the spirit of persuasion. Yet there is no doubt that we must take these propositions seriously, and to do so we must look at them concretely, with a specific sense of what they portend. If the novel is, in some sense, as Lawrence argued, The Book Of Life, we have an obligation to read it as real men and women occupying a more or less real and still habitable universe, not as hypothetical readers bent on mere aesthetic consumption of the sort Sammler imagines himself committed to. Sammler tells us that "he had no drive for smashing through the masks of appearances," but we know that he is drawn to "archetypes of goodness" and to mystical affirmations. Perhaps he insists upon both because he is confident of neither. Yet he is presented to us as very confident indeed, despite the modesty he wears so well to ensure that he will not give offense. Again, the question we must ask is, why this fundamental confusion in a novel that takes as its central intelligence so astute a mind as Sammler's?

Rousseau proclaimed the indissoluble relation between the nature of civilized man and the socialization process to which he would inevitably succumb. Bellow understands all too well this relation, but prefers to deny rather than to confirm its necessity. Authentic selfhood, radical integrity, consist for Bellow in the capacity to think of the mundane behaviors conditioned by social reality as fundamentally inane and finally insignificant. The specific and the finite are to him in the long run hideous and intransigent, especially in the degree of their relativity, the fact that they do not have an absolute value to which all of us can readily attest. When he looks about him at the range of human possibility, at the varieties of actual human behaviors and values clashing as fanatical ideologies, he feels sick at heart, and yields to the desire to step, perpetually, back. He wants to think of nature as of something antecedent to civilization, something the social process cannot really touch, though it can obscure it a little. What is so terrible, though, is that Bellow cannot really imagine this nature. It comes to us always besmirched, corrupted, deliberately exotic as though conscious of its own implausibility. In *The Victim*, it is communicated in the guise of the panting dog owned by a Puerto Rican janitor, but it finally calls to the mind of Bellow's protagonist sexual adventurism and depredations of various kinds that Bellow finds not only exotic but disgusting. In *Henderson* the attempt to make contact with nature, one's own and the broader nature conceived generically, is involved in disciplined identification with the spirit of the lion, an identification Henderson himself never really achieves. In *Sammler* the most potent image of nature is the black thief riding the New York City bus line, dressed in impeccable western splendor but described as ". . . this African prince or great black beast." What these various images of nature have in common is the element of primary animal vitality, but none of them is generated in a context that espouses the return to nature in an authoritative way. The emotional context in each case is clouded by guilt and by a self-consciousness all the more poignant in Sammler for being so complexly developed.

That guilt and self-consciousness color Bellow's fictions should come as no surprise, for what neither he nor his protagonist-spokesmen can freely abide is the decision to pursue selfhood apart from the more general responsibilities social reality customarily enjoins upon us. In *The Victim,* Leventhal feels painfully out of touch with the sordid realities Allbee resolutely thrusts before him, and suffers over his incapacity to respond sympathetically, with an emotion less tainted by horror and revulsion. In *Henderson* we have the resurrection of the service ideal, of the notion that we have no right to live for ourselves alone, that we must consecrate our lives to something greater than the enhancement of sensual pleasures. If the novel does not quite encourage a specific communal ethic, the spirit of the novel certainly instructs us in the special beauties of a life hallowed by purposes ratified and enforced by a community. For Sammler, though guilt may not be precisely the word to describe his characteristic reflections, there is a distinct discomfort associated with his sense of distance from the life of his fellows. Though he can denounce others for their failures of filial devotion, he relates to his own daughter Shula with a lofty amusement and distress which never amounts to genuine intimacy. He accuses the young of having "no view to the nobility of being intellectuals and judges of the social order," but he recognizes somewhere in his depths the impoverishment of being a judge without at the same time allowing oneself to participate in the conventional foibles of social creatures.

What Sammler is strongly impressed by is culture, but lacking a firm grasp of social reality, he is unable meaningfully to impress it upon others. How can they relate to Sammler if not as to a magical figure to whom one periodically pays homage without doing him the honor of adopting him as a model? His notion of culture is so special a thing, so rarefied, and though he speaks of judging the social order, he has virtually no sense of how men and women may be expected to live under particular conditions, what demands it is legitimate to make of them. Of experience, mostly brutal and alienating, he has had a bellyful, but he has become too much the adept at converting it to moral lessons and exempla to make use of it in establishing intimacies with others. He is a touching figure, but the odor of death does cling to him, as he himself suspects. It is not just that he is old, that his life has largely run its course, but that he thinks of himself as old in a special sense, as inhabiting another order, of being in touch with arcane truths not permitted people who consider themselves contemporary. Convinced that nature is corrupted at its very source by imposing social organizations that have been taken in by individuals and elaborated as communal structures of consciousness, he has decided that it is better to transcend nature than to work to improve it. He does not want to deal with a reality that is continuously uncivil and unlovely, though the novel makes it clear he will go on dealing with it, evasively to be sure, but persistently nonetheless. He will accept that perversions of nature are the most exotic and exciting things around, that he is almost as susceptible to their fascination as are most of his contemporaries, but he will insist all the while that there are mystic archetypes, human bonds we know and ratify in the blood, unutterable realities beside which social reality and perversions of nature are as insubstantial shadows. Of course, the tension is a necessary one for the would-be mystic, who cannot completely transcend the things of this world. Were he to be successful in such an enterprise, he'd have nothing left to transcend, nothing to sustain his ardor. The mind would go entirely dead, challenged by nothing, all phenomena having been reduced to absolute inconsequence. Sammler's mysticism is selective, asserted when he feels just weak enough to require an "out," when the specific density of objects and the clamorings of other pathetic selves for solidity and permanence become more oppressive than he can bear. For the encroaching and devouring event, perpetually subverting our tenuous equilibrium, Sammler would substitute absence, only he projects this absence, this steady negation of the phenomenal, not obsessionally but modestly. In the face of the unanticipated and irregular, the accidental and individual, Sammler retreats to the universal and archetypal. His devotion is more to truth than to reality, a preference not without dire consequences for the novelistic project, at least. For though we find a comparable commitment in the work of nineteenth-century melodramatists like Balzac, the social structure set as a backdrop for individual development in their works so convincingly revealed character and established the necessity within which relationships could take root and unfold that there was no danger of projecting eccentric behavior as if it were a force of nature pure and simple.

Can it be that the failure of the modern world to furnish models of strength wedded to integrity and civility has forced upon Bellow the stratagems he employs? Is it fair to say that the moral impoverishment everywhere illustrated in the daily routines of the social order has literally driven writers like Bellow into fragmentary and confused elaborations of an idea of nature that cannot possibly deal with our shared experience in a satisfactory way? Surely our time is no worse than many others, a fact one hears oneself repeating with a regularity that is apt to become deadening, but there are differences in the ideas we have of ourselves and of our possibilities as social beings when we compare this period to others. Sammler himself suspects as much when he says that "Unanimously all tasted, and each in his own way, the flavour of the end of things-as-known." Western cultural history has long been taken with the idea of apocalypse, no doubt, but never before has apocalyptic thinking so dominated a secular age. When Sammler wonders, at another point, "To a lunatic, how would you define a lunatic?" he follows the thought with, "And was he himself a perfect example of sanity? He was certainly not. They were his people — he was their Sammler. They shared the same fundamentals." Sammler does not characteristically identify himself with others so explicitly — we have already stressed his sense of personal distinction, his notion of himself as a judge — but it is telling that at least at one lucid moment he should recognize the fundamental disorientation of the entire period, a disorientation so pervasive that it is not possible even for Sammler wholly to elude it. Under such conditions, how are we to be objective, how are we to discriminate between values, between human affections, how are we to make sense of the social reality we must reclaim for our better purposes? How are we to distinguish between nature as inherent, as something given and fundamental, and nature as spurious or corrupt, though no less immutable for all that?

Mr. Sammler is no misanthrope. He feels there is something in each of us that deserves to be preserved and extended, some essence that can be nurtured by our learning to imitate what is good, by adopting proper models. "Make it the object of imitation to reach and release the high qualities," he tells us, "but choose higher representations." What he encourages is not idolatry but imitation, and this is all to the good. What is problematical, of course, is the very existence of appropriate models. Higher representations are simply not available to most of us, who will demand something more immediate. Lacking these, we shall decide, most of us at any rate, that we had best learn to get along without models, and shall cease the pursuit of ethical heights. It is this that so discourages Sammler, and why we find him so often "considering the earth itself not as a stone cast but as something to cast oneself from — to be divested of." Unable actually to manage this, Sammler posits a nature that is, if not edifying, at least essential. Though reality is more than he can tolerate, though human beings are in general too silly and clinging to be borne, he will have for himself a deeper dimension of reality, a dimension he can invest with whatever qualities he finds lacking as he looks about him. Princeliness, unself-conscious brutality, subversion as primal need rather than defensive gesturing: these are the fancies he frequently entertains. To be sure, Sammler likes from time to time to lose himself in the music of the spheres, to listen for that finer harmony mystics say they are able to hear. But there is a perspective in which the mystic's nature and the nature of the black thief coalesce. Both are called into being by an aesthetic attitude, a demand that there be achieved an adaptation of phenomenal reality to human faculties and human wishes. That we are denied such an achievement in our mundane lives does not mean that we may not continue to nurture a hope of its coming to pass. We speak here not of simple delusion, but of faith in the impulse to transcend, not of the drive to reshape actuality but to imagine the possibility of another dimension. The moral component is lacking here, not because it is in any way inimical to Sammler, but because in the social world he inhabits it more and more assumes the barrenness of a gratuitous emotion. It has nothing to feed on, no models of consistent behavior to imitate. Where it appears at all it takes the form of empty rhetorical gesture without impact or meaningful extension. The nature to which Sammler turns, no matter how disparate the modes in which he conceives it, bespeaks the still potent combination of imagination and nostalgia. For Sammler, what he dreams and aspires to in his abstract, ruminative way may never have been, but may still be invested with an aura of preternatural pastness, as though it had been, and might still be. Sammler is not interested in reclaiming nature for the present generation, or for some cloudy future available to utopians and visionaries. To the degree that it exists at all, he wants it for himself alone. He is generally disturbed only when his customary aesthetic consumption of the environment is riddled with stimuli it cannot accommodate, images that refuse to be imaginatively transformed by the mystic's determined internal decrees.

We continue to care for Sammler, though, and it must be because his mysticism is inhibited by more than a vestige of conventional sanity. He remains always a figure to whom we can relate, whose distinction has not, for all his occasional pretensions to the contrary, wholly removed him from the turmoils with which we associate genuine reality. He leaves us with the impression of a man we might have a great deal to do with, who is as little content as most of us have been with the edifice of reason as it has come to us in our time. If his mystical impulses lead him to ignore what many of us know of necessity, his memory is still vivid, and he knows in his better moments how foolish it is to demand what "the sum of human facts," as he puts it, cannot yield. Where he disappoints us is in his continuing incapacity to get beyond the realm of sentimental affirmation to a more acute apprehension of social reality. We are not inclined to demand of him that he abandon his ideas of nature but that he somehow manage to place them in the perspective in which they belong.

To make this point more clearly, and it is surely a crucial point in these considerations, it is instructive to examine a key passage occurring near the end of Bellow's novel. Riding along in the automobile owned by his favorite nephew, Sammler notices a crowd gathered in the street to watch a fight of some sort. Getting out of the car and coming closer, he sees that the fight is between the black pickpocket and Feffer, a young man of Sammler's acquaintance to whom he has confided his experiences of the black man. As the fight proceeds, Sammler feels himself growing physically ill and profoundly aware of his weakness: "He was old. He lacked physical force. He knew what to do, but had no power to execute it." There, if you will, is the dilemma that Sammler can do nothing to resolve or to overcome. He knows what to do — not what can actually be done, but what ought to be done. We must be careful to see that it is not moral knowledge as such that Sammler would invoke here, but a knowledge of propriety that is a function of a resolutely aesthetic attitude. From a strictly moral point of view, and to the degree that moral laws are at least in some sense communally sanctioned, it is proper that the black thief be brought to justice, that he be prevented from further depredations. This is not a consideration that carries much weight with Sammler, though he had earlier informed the police, to no avail, of the black man's conduct. For Sammler, what matters is that two men are fighting with one another on the streets of New York, providing a spectacle that is singularly unedifying and unsavory.

After a while, Sammler's estranged son-in-law Eisen comes along, carrying a sack of metal pieces which he will use in his work as a sculptor. Sammler pleads with Eisen to break up the fight, insisting that it must be done at once. The younger man complies, stepping in to do what he can, but finds that the black man is a difficult fellow to put down. They struggle, and Eisen begins hitting his opponent with the weighted sack, to Sammler's horror and amazement. Stung by Sammler's angry reproaches, Eisen responds: "'You can't hit a man like this just once. When you hit him you must really hit him. Otherwise he'll kill you. You know. We both fought in the war. You were a Partisan. You had a gun. So don't you know . . . If in — in. No? If out — out. Yes? No? So answer.'" Against which we read, "It was the reasoning that sank Sammler's heart completely."

Now I do not see anything especially heartless or inhuman in Eisen's reasoning. What he says makes good sense, though obviously it reflects his intellectual limitations. Were the occasion less pressing and perilous, perhaps even he might have explained his behavior more elaborately, but without the sort of flourishes a Sammler might applaud. We may not like to think of contemporary life in New York as similar to a state of war, but it is clear that for many of its inhabitants that is what it has become. That such people, subjected as they are to acts of effrontery and violence almost every day, are not apt to be enthusiastic about turning the other cheek or "taking it easy" should come as no shock. Nor is Eisen mistaken when he says, "If in — in." For that is precisely what too many people of humane and liberal persuasion refuse to acknowledge. One does not need to line up with the pigs, to be thought of as a repressive brute, because one has done what is necessary to restore order and protect one's narrow life-space in the immediate terms available to individuals in the social realm. Sammler is almost right when, recognizing the dilemma we earlier cited, he says that "To be so powerless was death." To attempt to hold together a social order and restore to sanity an entire culture on the basis of modest gestures and whining sentiments is a form of deadly foolishness — and that is something we must not only see but renounce as well. This seems clear to me, at least.

That Sammler will continue to see, but never come to renounce the foolishness, is similarly clear. We persist in our affection for him because he is a decent and interesting man, no matter how confused, because he has suffered a great deal, and because he is actually old, not just belligerently old-fashioned. Powerless as he feels himself, and as his sentimental idealism ensures that he must be, it is no wonder that he should conceive nature as he does, or that he should proclaim the merits of undifferentiated being. Such a resolution is, after all, entirely credible and acceptable for a man who cannot act effectually to stem the tide of events, even those that affect him most closely and visibly. To demand an aesthetic response to human experience, a response that includes recognition of enduring, *natural* human obligations is to ask of most of us, alas, more than we can manage, or want to. Sammler is not an acceptable model for most of us, nor are his ideas of nature, social reality, and authenticity such that we ought to acquiesce in them indiscriminately. He is, however, a portrait of a very special and moving individual who raises a great many questions about our lives. Saul Bellow may not know any more certainly than Mr. Sammler the precise shape and direction of his own sentiments, nor the social implications that may follow from them. But there is no doubt that he knows the terror and confusion that beset those of us who try to take in and respond responsibly to the contemporary experience.

THREE

BERGMAN'S "PERSONA": AN ESSAY ON TRAGEDY

Upon the procrustean beds of Hegelian and Aristotelian theories of tragedy, we have seen in our time a proliferation of various other doctrines, each purporting at last to refine and make definitive the merely tentative notions of those two great theorists. What is so striking about many of these recent efforts is that they have taken it as their object to demonstrate that for our time, and presumably for future generations, tragedy is no longer a possible art form. It has been proposed that we can no longer claim particular habits of mind and qualities of sensibility which are fundamental to the tragic view of life, and which permit formal tragedy to be written. While the accents of proposals to this effect have not been uniformly mournful, they have been terribly final, as if to foreclose any suggestion that there may yet be life in the corpse. The great Swedish filmmaker Ingmar Bergman has lately shown us that it is possible to write great tragedy of almost classical austerity while employing materials that are distinctly modern.

Persona is a film, but it is certainly our purest modern example of tragic art. If it is currently unfashionable to speak of cinema as theatre, or of theatre as literature, it is also true that those who have tried rigidly to maintain such distinctions have failed to show that their restrictive focus genuinely enriches our awareness of the work of art, whether film or play. Obviously, the medium is not the same in cinema as in the theatre, and works which are intended for performance are in many ways different from works which are meant only to be read. But the overlap from one medium to another is considerable, and there is no doubt that anyone

From *Salmagundi*, Fall 1968.

who wants to consider the merit and the meaning of a film or a play will have to apply a variety of literary criteria to these works. In the case of tragedy, which is at least as much a literary and philosophical concept as it is descriptive of a purely theatrical reality, we see how damaging it may be to dogmatize at the expense of a more vital response to artistic experience. Even in terms of pure theatrics, and the dynamics of audience participation in the work of art, tragedy suggests that stringent formulations may restrain our awareness of crucial relationships between one medium and another. Though Susan Sontag is correct, for example, when she remarks that "our eye cannot wander about the screen, as it does about the stage," it is also true that in classical tragedy there will not be very much to attract the eye to wander. We can say, as a matter of simple fact, that the tragic dramatist like Racine or Sophocles continues to exert as much control over what the audience can see as the film director. In neither case will the artist permit a dispersion of his intended focus.

Much more important, it seems to me, is the question of why we continue to classify works of art as tragedies, or comedies, or lately as metatheatre, to use Lionel Abel's term. No doubt it has something to do with our appetite for certainty, for definition, and our uneasiness in the face of anything that defies our complete understanding. *Persona* is a major work of art as notable for its originality as for the fact that it reverberates with a consciousness as old as western man's first consciousness of himself as an alien being in an inhospitable universe. We want to engage *Persona* uniquely, as it is a singular contribution, but we soon find that it escapes us if we approach it without some formal apparatus of perception which is more than simply the sum of our insights. Kenneth Burke explains the entire procedure in "Literature As Equipment For Living," in which he writes: "You can't properly put Marie Corelli and Shakespeare apart until you have first put them together. First genus, then differentia. The strategy in common is the genus. The *range* or *scale* or spectrum of particularization is the differentia."

How then does one put Ingmar Bergman and Sophocles together, a conjunction, by the way, considerably more functional than a conjunction between Corelli and Shakespeare? Probably the best place to begin is in a consideration of Sophocles' *Electra*, a play that is crucial for an understanding of *Persona*. In the film, Bergman explores the relationship between two young women, one an actress, the other a psychiatric nurse assigned to the actress, presumably for the duration of her psychotic withdrawal. The actress, we are told, had been performing the title role in a production of *Electra*. Somewhere in the middle of one of her performances, the actress had stopped cold, apparently unable or unwilling to recite her lines. Eventually, the actress completes her performance, but soon after vows never again to speak. Language is seen as a falsification of genuine sentiments, an obstruction to honest discourse, which should simply reveal that it is impossible for one man to communicate an essential image of himself to any other man.

Bergman has dealt with such matters before, but never has his treatment been so profound and so interesting as it is in *Persona*. It is remarkable that those who have written on aspects of the film have not considered the central importance of the reference to *Electra*, a reference which cannot but impress the viewer as he observes the actress standing immobile, mute, and bewildered on stage, handsomely adorned in the robes of Electra, her face heavily painted for the role. What I should like to suggest is that this tableau vividly etches upon the filmgoer's mind a consciousness of a peculiar identity: the actress as Electra, not cast in the role of Electra, but actively assuming the role in her daily life. It is a difficult notion to evade, especially insofar as Bergman's film develops in such a way that the identity is at least somewhat reinforced. And the parallels one may allude to are far from coincidental. Taken together they clearly indicate a perspective in which Bergman desired the film to be viewed, a tragic perspective, if you will.

In *Electra*, the protagonist is berated for persistently bemoaning her father's death at the hands of her mother, Clytemnestra. "It is only your discomfort. Why do you seek it?" the chorus asks. They do not understand her, they wish her to forget, if not wholly to forgive. Like the slaves of mediocrity they are, they are unwilling to view suffering and lamentation as valuable in themselves, as gestures, wholly apart from any use they might serve in effecting a change of circumstance. Electra is determined to suffer, to mourn, long after the object of her despair has flown from the memory, or grown indistinct in its contours. "These ills of mine shall be called cureless./ And never shall I give over my sorrows./ ... Come, how when the dead are in question,/ can it be honorable to forget?" What one cannot fail to remark in lines like these, and Electra repeats such determinations frequently in the play, is the degree to which Electra is aware of her *role* as mourner and avenger. The repetition of her determination seems directed more to herself than to those around her. That is to say, her lines seem as much a conjuring of her own powers of resistance as an explanation to others of what she must do. She fears she may weaken, and tries to buoy her hopes by means of her own stubborn eloquence.

She is assisted in her determination by the presence of her sister Chrysothemis, an unhappy young woman, nervous, guilt-ridden, and incapable of doing anything at all. Chrysothemis has observed the same events as Electra, feels as sick at heart, but fears the consequences that may follow upon the heels of any retributive action on their part: "I am sick at what I see, so that/ if I had strength, I would let them know how I feel./ But under pain of punishment, I think,/ I must make my voyage with lowered sails." Electra vilifies her sister, indicting her cowardice and her addiction to expedient considerations at the expense of that tragic necessity she herself exalts in every denial she utters: "Have your rich table and your abundant life./ All the food I need is the quiet of my conscience./ I do not want to win your honor./ Nor would you if you were sound of mind." How strange and yet predictable it is that the outcast Electra, earlier described as being "like some dishonored foreigner," obsessed by thoughts of killing her own mother, should yet accuse her sister of unsound or infirm judgment. For one in the throes of what can only be termed divine madness, normalcy is at once obscene and pitiful, a manifestation of weakness that calls into question the value of living in the world. It is an essential aspect of Electra's strength that she has long since abandoned any desire to get along in conventional terms. Her wish has been to engage the dominant realities in ferocious combat, to abolish them once and forever, at least to the extent that these realities are embodied in her mother and Aegisthus. But as the probability of Orestes' arrival diminishes, and with it Electra's chances for wreaking the revenge she dreams about, she conceives a complete withdrawal from the world which would constitute a perfect complement to the psychic withdrawal she has already achieved. She wishes to be sent away to an underground cave, she says, "that I may get away from you all, as far as I can."

That the actress in Bergman's film is an Electra-figure is unmistakable. This is not to suggest that the two characters are the same, nor that their actions are perfectly identical. What we can agree upon is that structurally *Persona* has a great deal to do with *Electra*. The actress in *Persona* has deliberately alienated herself from the mass of her fellow human beings. She mourns, not the death of an actual father like Agamemnon, but of a symbolic father, the death of her culture as the embodiment of those guarantees which enable the individual to go on living as if he were the master of his fate, and might mean something significant to others. The actress mourns her awareness of the fact that she is alone and defenseless, and that there is an impregnable barrier which must forever keep her from truly knowing a friend, a child, a husband. It is not terribly unlike Electra's perception when she requests permission to withdraw to that underground cave, where she can be safe at least from the illusion that anything matters. Like Electra, the actress is beset by those who would have her adjust. "It is only your discomfort./ Why do you seek it?" Doctors, nurses, husband, child — all want her to be their healthy, happy, docile little actress once again. And like Electra, she insists on her illness, on her sorrow, her difference, her "wound," as it were. "How, when the dead are in question,/ can it be honorable to forget?"

What is more striking, I think, is the way the actress's relation to her nurse calls to mind Electra's relationship with Chrysothemis. The actress's every gesture is a standing rebuke to the nurse, who feels herself small and hypocritical next to her patient. While of course the actress never actually condemns the nurse, her choice of silence and austerity as the defining components of her life inevitably imposes itself upon the conscience of the nurse, who is introspective and rather morbidly hypersensitive to her own deficiencies, both spiritual and worldly. At one point in the film, the nurse rather hysterically accuses the actress of an excess of pride, exactly as Chrysothemis resents the strength and passionate determination of Electra. And just as Electra seems to suggest that those who are able to tolerate corruption and hypocrisy are deranged, so the nurse comes to feel that she is ill to the degree that she continues to adjust to the world and to live comfortably amidst its corruptions. In both *Electra* and *Persona,* the character who will not adjust, who alienates herself from the mass of humanity, becomes a symbol of essential sanity, though doomed: one of them to horrible suffering, the other to an utter detachment which makes it impossible for her even to enjoy the pleasures of family and art which not even civilization can wholly pollute.

There are differences, no doubt. One could never imagine the actress pronouncing with Electra: "Evil is all around us, evil/ is what I am compelled to practice." The actress is aware of radical evil in the world, not only through a close examination of literary works, but through simple observation of what passes for normal in the life of her time. As she briefly watches the television set in her hospital room, she hears gruesome statistics, body counts of the recently dead in America's war with Vietnam. And she sees fanatical Buddhists immolating themselves, burning to death while onlookers stand by helplessly. But hers is not the temperament of the activist. She quietly turns the set off, and tranquility is restored. Nor, for the actress, is there any real alternative to withdrawal into that psychic enclave Electra conceives so despairingly. There is no deliverer, no Orestes, that the actress can possibly imagine or conjure. When we meet her, she is beyond hope, beyond despair, and her satisfaction is such that she is unlikely ever again to emerge into conflict.

Now it is the nature of the tragic hero that he proceeds before our eyes and astonished senses to precisely that state wherein both hope and despair are transcended. And clearly, it is the struggle against circumstance and against his own personality that allows the tragic protagonist to achieve such transcendence as we recognize in the luminous culminations of *Lear* and *Oedipos Tyrannos*. Rarely in Bergman's actress is there the kind of suffering and that commitment to apparently futile struggle that distinguishes tragic character. It is conceivable that her suffering and her struggles may have assumed tragic dimensions, but as we are not permitted by Bergman to witness them, we cannot respond to them emotionally, or comment upon them. All that we know is that in our experience of her, the actress has passed beyond the pain of neurotic conflict. We may make an ideological judgment if we like, and say we wish she had not withdrawn from experience. But we cannot pity her, nor ought we legitimately to fear or stand in awe of what has happened to her. She is relatively at peace with herself, and satisfied with her situation. She resents intrusions upon the completeness of her withdrawal, but she manages for the most part to deal with these efficiently, and with little strain. Her withdrawal is no longer willed, but achieved, and total, and is therefore psychotic. No tragic emotion will issue from contemplation of her condition, for it is not a condition that we can authentically know.

It has been assumed by all who have written on *Persona* that Bergman's major concern is with the actress. I think not. If *Persona* is indeed a modern tragedy built on classical lines, the tragic character is the nurse, and in fact I do not see how it is possible that the student of the film should respond more warmly to the actress. The nurse is after all a magnificent creation, a character of real stature. If she can on occasion become irritating and childishly petulant, it is also true that Oedipus' treatment of Teiresias is irritating in the extreme, and that Lear is almost infantile in his demands at the opening of Shakespeare's play. To be sure, the actress grows more and more attractive as the film goes on, but it is a superficial attraction that she exerts. She is in control of herself, decorous, if hardly ingratiating, while the nurse, on the other hand, becomes increasingly more hysterical, desperate, and confused. She does not present a pretty picture, pouting, blowing her nose, plotting maliciously. But then tragedy is not a pretty spectacle, as we shall remember if we think of Oedipus emerging sightless from the darkness of the palace interior.

If we are ready to accept the nurse as potentially the tragic hero of Bergman's film, we shall find structural parallels with other Sophoclean plays which are perhaps even more useful than the comparison with *Electra*. We may think of the nurse, for a moment, as an Oedipus-figure. Like Oedipus, she has been given the task of cleansing the community, ridding it of an alien element which grows more dangerous the longer it is permitted to survive. In neither case is the alien element identified, though the nurse is introduced to the actress. What matters is that at first she cannot understand, certainly cannot sympathize with the actress's illness, and has really little insight into the motives for her withdrawal. Both Oedipus and the nurse are ordered to do what they do by a higher authority, in each case representing the accumulated force and sanctity of the respective culture. Oedipus cannot in fact question the authority of the oracles, and the doctor in *Persona* smugly pronounces the therapeutic imperatives of the civilization she protects against unconformed elements.

More to the point, certainly, both Oedipus and the nurse know that as and if they proceed with their respective tasks, they will find that they themselves are largely to blame for the conditions that are to be mitigated. Just as Oedipus knows that the oracular prophecy ultimately will cast an accusatory finger at him, through the agency of his own implacable integrity, so the nurse knows that the indictment of modern man and modern culture implicit in the actress's renunciation will be proven upon her own pulses as a result of her self-doubt and desperate insecurity. And one must not overlook the nurse's affinities with that other great Sophoclean hero, Antigone, who in standard Hegelian terms is forced to choose between the good of the state as that good is conceived and exercised by those in power, and the dictates of her own conscience. In these terms, the nurse is faced with the task of assisting the "deviant" character to conform to what is expected of her, so that all members of the society can live comfortably, without having to consider the motives of antisocial characters like the actress — without, that is, having to examine the grim possibility that the social relations obtaining in their culture may not be such as to satisfy the more alert and sensitive persons among them. From the point of view of the psychiatrist in *Persona*, everything is clear, therapy humane in its desire to socialize the patient, and nothing ambiguous about the patient's resistance to such therapy. Whoever thinks clearly must certainly want to join his fellows in the world at large, and leave eccentric behavior to those who are hopelessly muddled.

It is precisely these blithe therapeutic certainties that the nurse is unable to accept — I say unable because there can be no question that she wants to accept them. Her entire life has been directed towards the object of mollifying any doubts she may have had. From the very beginning of the film, though, we see that she does not quite trust her own capacities of resolution and firmness. She hesitatingly expresses this insecurity to the psychiatrist in charge, suggesting that the actress may be too strong of character for someone as weak as she. What we come to see, of course, is that this weakness is in fact but a partial manifestation of great strength of character. The nurse is that rare healer who would learn the life-view of the patient before attempting a cure, thereby presumptively judging the validity of a psychic orientation whose roots may be largely alien.

It would be foolish to assert that the nurse decides upon this procedure by means of reflection, but it is part of her nature to be sensitive to the nuances of personalities other than her own, a quality in part attributable to her persistent need to justify her own life style to herself. Similarly, Antigone does not formulate the alternatives before her in terms of conflict between family and state, or between duty and conscience. What matters to Antigone is that she be true to what she feels, that she discover what is authentic in terms of her needs as an individual, the imperatives of her own self-image. Antigone decides to bury her brother against the wishes of her king and uncle Creon, not because she is a pre-eminently religious woman, who fears the wrath of the gods. Ultimately she fears only her own inability positively to represent herself to herself. She once loved her brother, he was of her blood, and if she would not take pains to bury him as he would have wished to be buried, who would? In such basic terms is the nurse drawn to the actress, whose integrity she admires, though as she gradually discovers, it is the integrity of the grave, and is not without its own hazards.

Finally, of course, one does not really understand why people like the nurse, and Antigone, behave as they do. Bergman insists on the irrefutability of what occurs in his film, as Sophocles did in *Antigone,* but it is not possible to locate the precise source of necessity in either work, beyond vague references to character or personality. The nurse is drawn to the actress not because such acquiescence will make her feel better, not because the actress exercises insidious powers over her; or if she does exercise such powers, she does not do so deliberately, but instead seems disturbed that the nurse should behave so unprofessionally. No, I'm afraid there must be no answer to certain questions of motivation which occur in the contemplation of formal tragedy. Characters develop in particular ways, and behave accordingly, for the simple reason that they must. If there are alternatives, they are not alternatives for Oedipus, nor for Antigone, and the nurse. Those options which, if taken, enable men to proceed through life without facing critical considerations about the nature and value of their existence, do not present themselves as perma-nently viable propositions to certain people. What is possible for the mem-ber of the Greek chorus need not be possible for Oedipus. W. H. Auden was correct to speak of the tragedy of possibility in his essay on "The Christian Tragic Hero," only that possibility is as much distinctive of Greek as of Shakespearean and Racinian tragedy, and of *Persona.*

Certainly one cannot argue with Auden's statement on Oedipus: "The tragedy is that what had to happen happened, and if one asks what was wrong with Oedipus, that such a terrible fate should be assigned to him, one can only say that it is a punishment for a hubris which was necessarily his before he learned of the prophecy at all." What Auden does not, and cannot explain, however, is why this should be genuinely different from that tragedy of possibility he identifies in the drama of Melville's Ahab. To say that something has or had to happen is to assume circumstances which are given, and qualities of mind and spirit that are inflexible. By the time we are introduced to Oedipus, certain terrible deeds have been committed, and Thebes is being ravaged by plague. The deeds cannot be undone, nor were they committed in a spirit of malevolence or depravity. At his worst, Oedipus is no worse than most men, responding rather violently to provocation, and reflecting in his treatment of Teiresias the same impatience with equivocation that is so characteristic of a figure like Lear, and of "normal people" in positions of power. Does he deserve the punishment he suffers? Certainly not, yet he is an intelligent man, and calls curses down upon his own head. Oedipus' is a tragedy of possibility in the sense that he might have chosen to reflect rationally on his circumstances, and ultimately decided against blinding himself and accepting exile (in *Colonus* he claims he did come to such a conclusion, but was then exiled against his will.). His tragedy is that he chooses to suffer in excess of his guilt, because he is not the man to compromise the integrity of his conviction. His major fault, if you will, is that he has never before acknowledged the degree to which men are slaves of chance. At the root of his pride had been ignorance.

Bergman's nurse had been similarly ignorant, having thought to feign innocence by frankly submitting to the conventions of ordinary experience. At the root of *her* pride was her sense of realism, the sense of having refused to idealize at the expense of those compromises "sane" people habitually exalt as the test of good sense. Like Oedipus', the nurse's pride is gradually eroded, and it is this process of erosion which constitutes the basis of her tragic stature. The false pride erodes because she allows it to, because she consents to it with the full force of her personality, though intellectually she must exhaust her every available resource to resist it. Her constant rationalizations, which take the form of assaults upon the actress who draws her out of herself, away from the social self she has carefully erected, serve only as a reminder of how futile it is to oppose one's destiny, which is the inexorable thrust of one's personality.

This is not to suggest that the tragic character loses all sense of pride. In fact, what is asserted is precisely the uniqueness of the tragic character, whose distinction lies in his ability to accept suffering and futile struggle as the norms of his existence, though they are decidedly abnormal for most people, and shunned as such. The late William Troy in "Thoughts On Tragedy" missed the point, I think, when he wrote "that tragedy, in its fully developed form, provides us with a means of vision for the correction of individual astigmatism by humility." We need only look at Oedipus to judge this description less than complete. What humility has Oedipus developed? Certainly a humility about his own relation to the gods, and about his fate as a man, just as Lear on the heath sees that man is as nothing, and that all his attempts to control his destiny by imposing absolute order on his surroundings, by forcing all about him to conform to his peculiar psychic needs, are doomed to failure. But neither Oedipus nor Lear has become humble with relation to his fellow men. Their suffering has set them apart and somewhere within them they are aware of their difference, and revel in it. Bergman's nurse struggles to escape this perception of difference, as Oedipus writhes in anguish when forced by the citizens of Athens to remember the special intensity of his experience in *Colonus*. They struggle to escape, but they bow to necessity with a seriousness and pride that make them remarkable, and beautiful. What so firmly separates an Oedipus, a Lear, or the nurse, from those sensitive people who are moved by their plight, that is from the audience, is a quality that Wittgenstein might have understood. We observe the unfolding of a tragic vision in the theatre, and we assent to the validity of those perceptions which explain the tragic hero's willingness to suffer, though his suffering will not improve his condition in any way that is tangibly demonstrable. It is the quality of our assent that calls into question the authenticity of our emotions, and that finally ought to leave us distinguished in our own minds from the tragic character. We perceive, perhaps, the truth as it is perceived by Oedipus, or the nurse. We must, that is, acquiesce in that radical judgment of man's role in the universe made by the tragic protagonist if we are to feel for him, and not merely to pity him as a demented eccentric. What Wittgenstein understood, though, in the words of Erich Heller, is that such judgments require "the sanction of the moral and intellectual pain suffered on behalf of truth." In Heller's account, even a true judgment could outrage Wittgenstein, who ". . . denied them because they were untrue in the self that uttered them." No doubt there is something ill-natured in a fellow who will make such demands of mere mortals, but one must acknowledge that even Wittgenstein would not have found Oedipus, or the nurse, wanting in those qualities of suffering he so admired. And both Oedipus and the nurse would be sufficiently self-aware to defend themselves to him on his own terms, could he put them to the test. Freud knew all this, and indicated his awareness in the essay "Psychopathic Characters On The Stage," where he wrote: "The spectator is well aware that taking over the hero's role in his own person would involve such griefs, such sufferings, and such frightful terrors as would almost nullify the pleasures therein; and he knows too that he has but a single life to live, and might perhaps perish in a single one of the hero's many battles with the Fates. Hence his enjoy-ment presupposes an illusion; it presupposes an attenuation of his suffering through the certainty that in the first place it is another than himself who acts and suffers upon the stage, and that in the second place it is only a play, whence no threat to his personal security can ever arise." And, we may add, as we must be aware of the gap that separates us from the tragic hero, so he must be aware of that gap when he looks at the frequently averted faces of those around him, the helpless bystanders, the chorus.

It is curious that the notion of humility has for so long been an element in critical and theoretical considerations of formal tragedy. Is Lear humble in his final scene when he shouts, "A plague upon you, murderous traitors all!/ I might have saved her; now she is gone for ever!/ Cordelia, Cordelia! stay a little. Ha!/ . . ./ I killed the slave that was a-hanging thee." He is pitiful, but awesome in his pride and rage. And is there no pride discernible in Phaedra's final speech, when she confesses all to Theseus: ". . . The sword had long since cut/ my thread of life, but still I heard the cry/ of slandered innocence, and I determined/ to die a slower way, and first confess/ my penitence to you. There is a poison/ Medea brought to Athens, in my veins./ . . . / Death veils the light of Heaven from mine eyes/ and gives it back its purity, defiled." She is not fit for Heaven, a defiler of all that is good, and she reveals her baseness to her husband so that he may look upon her with disgust. And yet there is pride, pride that she has chosen so to reveal herself, so to acknowledge what she has been a part of, and to what end she is destined.

Even Othello reveals enormous pride in the midst of profound lam-entations and utterances of self-loathing. It is not humility that counsels a man to say, after discovering what an utter dupe he has been, and that he has killed his wife for no earthly reason: "I have done the state some service, and they know't./ . . ./ one that lov'd not wisely but too well; of one not easily jealous, but being wrought/ perplex'd in the extreme;/ . . ./ Where a malignant and turban'd Turk/ beat a Venetian and traduc'd the state,/ I took by th' throat the circumcised dog,/ and smote him, thus." If despair and humility produce the implied equation between Othello and the malignant Turk he killed, it is unmistakably pride which permits him to equate his suicide with the justice implicit in the murder of the Turk. In each case he does what he has to do, what seems to him right and just. One must grant him that he is consistent — the justice he executes upon himself is as swift and inexorable as that he had prac-ticed upon others, according to his lights.

Othello is in many ways a characteristic tragic hero. "Men should be what they seem," he says, "or those that be not, would they might seem none." In just so many words did Shakespeare make explicit what is a central consideration of all tragedy. The tragic hero is one who loses confidence in reality as he has always known it, and articulated it. He comes to see how arbitrary the world can be, to understand, in Simone Weil's phrase, "the ultimate meaninglessness of all moral values," the courage required to act according to one's lights. The writer of tragedy creates precisely that situation to which his protagonist will be unequal, and immerses him in it in such a way that he cannot but be destroyed by it. Always, of course, there is an opportunity for the hero to evade the imperatives of his situation, or to ignore them, but it is not a real opportunity for him, given what he is. In Brecht's terms, the spectator of a play is to see ". . . that this human being is thus and so because conditions are thus and so. And conditions are thus and so because human beings are thus and so." Not all human beings, but those who are in some sense directly reponsible for, and implicated in, the prevailing state of affairs. Only if Hamlet were someone else entirely might he have ignored the provoking injunctions of the ghost, just as Macbeth might not have become so steeped in blood had he responded critically to the witches' prophetic gaggle. What I am suggesting is that as the tragic hero abandons "realism," as he refuses to abide by the "rules" as he ought if he is to get along without great conflict, he begins to ask questions about the nature of reality itself, about the relationship between men's cognitive faculties and the world outside his own skin. What Othello comes to understand is that he cannot trust his own senses, the irony being, of course, that his own senses are perfectly adequate to represent to him the reality of Desdemona's affection, but inadequate to show him the duplicity of Iago, whose honesty he never actually suspects.

The nurse in Bergman's film has throughout her life accepted what passes for common sense and social progress among the mass of relatively enlightened people she has encountered. On occasion, she has asked herself questions about her own physical and emotional propensities — she has difficulty assimilating into her ideas of correct ethical conduct, for example, her willing participation in a brief orgy with a couple of adolescent boys, which she recounts in great detail to the actress. But this is an exceptional instance, and the nurse has apparently been stunned by the casual approach to such matters demonstrated by most sensible people. By the same token, she has for a while expected to marry a young man she does not love, and to raise a family she can conceive only with apprehension, but her expectations have not been retained without misgiving. She suspects that the foundation of her existence is rotten with hypocrisy, and that her presumption of capacity to cure others is somewhat fraudulent in the light of her own doubts. She is an introspective character, like Hamlet, ripe for the disillusionment that the tragic circumstances will effect. Certainly she is a lot better prepared for what she will undergo than Lear, who had never asked himself fundamental questions with any degree of seriousness or sincerity. Mistrustful of professions Lear had always been, but had never been able to find anything within himself that would have permitted their displacement in the scheme of things.

To doubt the evidence provided by one's senses is to leave oneself open to a kind of despair which is likely to be accompanied by psychic dislocations of indeterminate magnitude. In desperation, tragic characters strike at those about them, persistently demanding that everyone behave with a degree of clarity, even transparency, which allows of no doubt as to their motivations. How utterly intolerant is Hamlet of circumlocution, of assertions which do not boldly thrust themselves before everyone, though Hamlet himself is less than willing to make clear what he imagines, and intends. And how furious Oedipus grows when confronted by prophecies that taunt, that deliver some of the truth, or most of it, rather than the truth itself. The nurse, of course, grows increasingly bewildered as thoughts she had always thought to repress emerge steadily into the forefront of her consciousness. These thoughts are not readily explicable in terms of content, as they tend actually towards a metaphysical skepticism about the content of the thought process in general. This is all the content we are permitted to discern, and all, presumably, that the nurse contemplates, though her thoughts would inevitably embrace a variety of concrete, if fleeting, associations Bergman thought irrelevant for his cinematic purposes, and ours.

If we remember the prime source of the nurse's uncertainty, or at least the nature of the catalytic agent that sets her speculations in motion, we will have to consider the actress. At the time we first meet her, she has recently achieved a transition from doubt to certainty, as we have suggested earlier. She has for the most part ceased to speculate on fundamental metaphysical issues, and has instead settled for the nihilistic assumption that the collision of the subjective consciousness with the objective reality it tries to appropriate will lead inexorably to dissolution of the subject. Her withdrawal represents a refusal to submit to this necessity, as though turning one's back on the world could somehow constitute a means of preserving one's humanity, though it depends upon the rigorous exclusion of natural instincts and the cultivation of an ascetic discipline to keep sentiment perpetually at arm's length. Her discipline, of course, is less than strenuous, for like many other ascetic patterns, it lends itself rather easily to habit formation, and actually entails a minimum of suffering. The psychotic is more aware of the tranquility she can savor than of those positive human contacts she must forever deny herself.

Now it is one thing to be mad, and another thing entirely to admire, not the manifestations of madness, but those perceptions which in certain people contribute to psychosis. There is no question that Ophelia does not wish to be mad, does not when she is rational wish to be drowned. But she loves Hamlet, and is sympathetic to his feigned madness. She does not think about the peculiar psychological vulnerability which forces certain men to retreat into psychosis in response to the world. Her fundamental sympathy for the man Hamlet allows her to overlook the question of abnormal vulnerability and to look instead at that world which so torments men like Hamlet. Her sympathy, that is to say, is transferred from Hamlet and his behavior to the roots of that behavior in those who affect his life. One might presume to say, in effect, that she comes to look upon her father and other members of the court with the same jaundiced eye we have recognized in Hamlet. And her nature, being so much weaker than his, breaks all the sooner. Ophelia responds to Hamlet's feigned madness with a distraction that is all too real.

The attraction of normally adjusted individuals to insane people arises from a deliberately wrought sympathetic orientation to that reality which is assumed to be responsible for producing psychosis. Ophelia looks at the world through Hamlet's eyes. This is not terribly unusual. When people have nothing to live for they frequently lament that reality which enables them to conceive the retreat implicit in the psychotic orientation. Frequently, in fact, a kind of prestige is attached to that orientation which produces psychosis, and this attribution of prestige is not always unjustified. We are in a position now to say that in the throes of those stages of psychic dislocation just preceding the onset of serious mental illness, a heightened sensibility, struggling to preserve or to locate an authentic identity, may perceive aspects of its situation which are hidden to most of us who can conveniently repress such intimations. On the heath, Lear is drawn to the lunatic poor Tom, another example of feigned madness. Tom, of course, is none other than Gloucester's son Edgar. Lear looks at him, studies him, sees that he is almost naked, and warms to him as "the thing itself." Truth, reality, is seen to reside in that sensibility which is most vulnerable, in that personality whose defenses against consciousness are no longer viable. The truth is not a product of common sense, but of a defiantly uncommon sensibility. Othello's "Men should be what they seem" is a sentiment upon which most rational beings can agree, but it is difficult to retain confidence that most men will in fact prove to be as they appear.

In *Persona,* the nurse is drawn to the actress as "the thing itself." As far as the nurse can tell, the actress has grappled with a knowledge that she herself has merely glimpsed, imperfectly. Precisely what this knowledge amounts to is something we can only surmise, but its effects on the actress have certainly been devastating. For the nurse she is the thing itself because she has suffered and has not come through her trial intact. She bears witness in her every gesture to the nature of her condition, and to her conviction that this condition cannot be altered, but evaded or endured. It is to Bergman's credit that he does not attempt to make graphic, by simplifying, the elements of her awareness. The background of random violence punctuated by moments of futile moral resistance on the part of a rare few is lightly sketched on the actress's television screen in her hospital room. What is greatly more important, though, is the brief sequence of images with which the film begins. Stanley Kauffmann describes the sequence in the following terms: "Before the titles of the film, we see a series of disconnected shots: a film projector's arc light hissing alive into glare, the 'leader' of a reel of film, a snatch of silent-film slapstick, a sheep's eye being gouged, a nail being driven through a human hand. In a morgue full of corpses an adolescent boy sits up, reads, then stretches his hand toward a pane of glass behind which is an immense face — later we learn that it is his mother's face (the actress). This disjointed beginning, made of splinters of horror and showmanship, is like a quick jagged tour of the actress' mind: images that terrify and also, in an Olympian way, amuse her."

The description is fine as far as it goes, but I am afraid I cannot agree with this country's most distinguished film critic that what we get "is like a quick jagged tour of the actress' mind" — much as I like the phrase. What the film establishes, on the contrary, is that such sequences, which operate largely in terms of flashback technique in a work of fiction, occur with considerable regularity in the mind of the nurse. They are not unique to her as an individual, but it is she who conceives them in the course of this film. When Bergman presents the opening sequence, we cannot possibly be expected to know whose mind is beset by such images. In retrospect, we may conclude that these initial images represent an available fund of imagery which may be drawn upon by any one of us. They are among the staples of the modern, Christian, or perhaps largely post-Christian, imagination at its most serious and reflexive. If one wants to conjure an image of brutality, he need do little thinking to come up with the slaughtered sheep, and the hand with a nail driven through it. Both images in the film are strangely, and appropriately, divested of any religious connotation, for we see only the treatment of the sheep's eye, and the crucified hand seems almost completely detached from any body, and evokes no profound spiritual reverberation. The images, then, are cool, neutrally affecting, and have become so clichéd in their secondary associations that we do not respond to them much differently than we do to the "snatch of silent-film slapstick," which involves a villain and a patently "scary" skeleton.

What the actress must think of these images, or images of a similar nature that actually occur to her, can be assumed from the particular form of her psychotic withdrawal. She must think of them as literal representations of man's necessity, rather than as contingent images developed within a framework of particular historical contexts. At the root of her psychosis is a confusion between symbol and reality, a confusion which has been finalized to the extent that the actress can successfully resist attempts to treat her. It is in the nature of mental illness that the patient will inflate out of reasonable proportion fragments of ordinary experience or figures of imagination which are handled rather easily by most people. For the seriously disturbed, though definitely recoverable neurotic, this inflation may alternate with other reductive processes of the psyche which work to restore proportion. Strategies are desperately marshaled, frequently abandoned after only brief periods, and struggle is normative. In the case of a psychotic like the actress, the inflating process can be said at one point at least to have gotten out of hand, to have abolished that pluralism of responses to reality which permits the organism to differentiate among phenomena, to apply relative and proportional means to handle challenges to its integrity. For the actress, one may say, the ability to select objects of concern with a view towards maintaining some degree of tranquility, was severely impaired, and her response was to seize upon a strategy which could guarantee she would not be implicated in those things she abhorred and feared.

The nurse, on the other hand, responds to the various conventional images in terms of the concrete realities of her experience, and of the actress's experience, for which she has great sympathy. She fantasizes within a context, one may say, though for a while she seems in danger of being drawn into the actress's total commitment to an evasive strategy. Madness, after all, is something we fear only to the degree that we are conscious of its temptations at the same time that we are conscious of moralistic imperatives about courage, facing up to responsibilities, and the like. The nurse does not so much fear that she may become mad as she fears she may come to understand what the actress sees and be unable to mitigate her subsequent despair by resorting to madness. She fears, that is, her own strength, rather than her gravitation towards psychosis. In the course of her early attempts to deal with the actress, the nurse is caught in a dilemma which Freud characterized as indicative of psychopathological drama, drama in which the source of the protagonist's suffering "is no longer a conflict between two almost equally conscious motivations, but one between conscious and repressed ones."

The images at the beginning of the film, which reappear with only slight modification later on, constitute more than a background. They represent to the nurse a vital means of objectifying her fears about her own inclinations. The stock images of brutality and neglect, which appear on the screen and in the nurse's mind when she has behaved with special brutality to the actress, are terrifying images, but familiar, and therefore somehow controllable for all that. Brutality and indifference to human suffering are not absolute, but relative phenomena, with histories. In the course of time, man's ability to deal with certain facts of his temperament has been manifested in formalizing conventions, like art. Ritualization, the creation of symbolic artifacts to simulate reality, has made reality tolerable, even when viewed from the grimmest perspectives. Stock images of crucifixion and the slaughter of the innocents are part of this entire process of symbolization, and it is significant that when the nurse conceives such images, they are formally related to less general images having to do with the actress's life, with the life she has left behind. (I am thinking for example of the fantasy in which a boy, in this context the actress's son, awakens in a morgue full of corpses and strives to draw upon a glass screen an image of the mother he does not want to forget.) The nurse really only briefly shows evidence of genuine distraction. The fact that she can use the stock images not to magnify amorphous fears but to achieve a humane perspective on the realities of her own condition, and the actress's, is a sign of her essential sanity, riddled by neurotic uncertainties though she may be.

For the nurse, if the actress is "the thing itself," she is not an attractive sample of humanity to which anyone should aspire. She is, however, a means of drawing the nurse away from those certaities, from those cynical hypocrisies which have heretofore defined her life. The emotional conflict that is set in motion within the nurse involves her conscious desire to treat a patient who is ill by every normal standard operant in her society, and her unconscious (though increasingly conscious) desire to see herself and her reality truly. This second desire she can achieve, she sees, by projecting herself into the actress, by seeing things from the actress's point of view. Throughout the duration of this projection, of course, she will maintain at least a minimal foothold in her own decidedly shaky but yet determined psychic orientation. There is grave danger involved in such a procedure, and Bergman brilliantly depicts this danger in uniquely cinematic terms, as when the nurse pursues for quite some time the fleeing actress along the beach outside their secluded retreat. In this scene the nurse appears to have lost all sense of her own distinctness, all desire to retain her own psychological equilibrium, and seems desperately trying wholly to enter that psychic enclave of madness which she cannot achieve. The actress repels her advances, jealous of her own "advantage," it would seem.

There is no doubt the nurse retains the capacity to protect herself. In the course of Bergman's film, she learns what it is the actress sees, but never at the expense of her own identity. One sees this in a crucial image Bergman presents as part of the nurse's fantasy, or dream. I speak of the imaginary visit made by the actress's husband. The audience is momentarily confused by this strange interlude, uncertain for the moment whether or not this is actually taking place. The man is obviously distraught, longing for his wife, and this is reasonable enough, though few words are actually spoken. Before we have had time to consider the probability of the visit, we are assaulted by a rather violently perverse tableau, in which the husband addresses the nurse as his wife, and she submits entirely to his embrace, while the actress stands coldly by their side, her expression registering neither surprise nor concern. Their passion consummated, the image of the husband dissolves, and we meet him no more, as affairs return to normal at the country retreat. Though the content of the dream must startle us, once we are aware that it is only a dream, and that it represents an important element in the nurse's continuing struggle to retain her dignity, we can think of it with no discomfort at all. It has nothing whatever to do with sexual jealousy. It simply indicates the nurse's frustration at having been unable to affect the actress. Having come so close to her that she is able to think as she does, to view the world from her perspective, and feeling able to function in the world at the same time, as it were, she despairs that the actress cannot both know and act as some people can. She despairs, that is, because she knows it is possible to view one's husband essentially as a stranger who can never be truly known, and yet to give one's body and one's concern to him, cater to him, please him, and in so doing minister to those instinctual needs of one's own that cry out to be considered. The nurse makes love to the husband in her dream because in the dream she can act as if she were the actress. She does what she feels the actress ought to do, which is to face up to her responsibilities as mother and wife. Any ensuing guilt the nurse might feel would be neither sexual nor broadly moral, but a kind of intellectual or aesthetic uneasiness at having acquiesced in the sentimentalities of this world, foregoing that austerity which is all men can know of honesty in this world. The actress, on the contrary, convinced that attempts to communicate with one another are doomed to failure, feels no pity, no tenderness, no inclination to try again despite what she thinks she knows. There is nothing tragic about her condition, for she has reached a position of rest which is akin to the grave. Anouilh had no justification for speaking of tragedy as restful in his colorful adaptation of *Antigone* in which the chorus is made to assert the following: "Most of all, it's restful, is Tragedy, because you know that there is no more hope, dirty sneaking hope . . . And there is nothing more you can try; that's that."

Undoubtedly there is something ironical about Anouilh's use of the word "restful," but there can be no question that he minimizes or does not recognize the element of hope as a source of tremendous tension in tragedy, and as the agent of the tragic protagonist's most desperate actions. For why should Oedipus go on with his quest if he does not hope to cancel or to transcend the sins of his life by means of the absolute integrity of his pursuit of the truth? The tragic hero does not hope for substantive gain or victory of a conventional kind, but for an insubstantial balm, the conviction that he may be worthy of his passion, perverse though it has often been. Once brought as low as any man can find himself, he will not hope to see the justice of his fate. As George Steiner reminds us, the Old Testament Job is a spectacle we do not readily forget, but is not tragic, for Job is compensated by God for his sufferings, and ". . . where there is compensation, there is justice, not tragedy . . . Tragedy is irreparable."

In what sense then can the nurse in *Persona* be said to constitute a tragic heroine? She does, after all, return at the end of the film to normal life, presumably to marry and raise a family, and to forget if she can about the actress whose experience she has shared. In her life, that is to say, the nurse will compromise, will not live absolutely in accordance with her perception of nullity, meaninglessness, and drift as necessary components of human experience. She has chosen to be, and to live, despite her knowledge. There is no sense of optimism here, though we cannot but be relieved to see the nurse board the bus that will remove her from the oppressive presence of the actress. What we are left with, in Lionel Abel's terms, is "a grave silence — a speculative sadness." These are qualities of response which need not be tragic, but which in this case are distinctly so; for *Persona* does indeed make us ". . . believe that the events presented, responsible for our sadness, happened once and for all." We believe that what we have seen is somehow definitive for our time, because the nurse's dilemma is ours, her resolution our possibility, provided we are willing to be honest, and thereby to make ourselves tragic. This is the source of our pity and fear.

Specifically, the nurse's resolution amounts to a decision to live with the knowledge she has discovered within herself as a result of her abrasive intercourse with the stricken actress. To live with such knowledge is to remind oneself, always, of how little one matters in the scheme of things, to take pride in the futility of one's pursuits, and to laugh, perhaps grimly, at one's illusions, even as new ones come into being to replace those which no longer give comfort.

Now there is no doubt that all of this presumes a considerable degree of self-consciousness, and that a number of our gifted writers consider the notion of a self-conscious tragic hero a contradiction in terms. Lionel Abel, for one, has written a book called *Metatheatre* which weaves a brilliant argument around this point. It is an interesting idea, but it is not literally defensible. Abel claims that since the time *Hamlet* was first performed, we have been unable to respect a character lacking a fundamental awareness of himself as an actor in a kind of open-ended plot — "life is a stage" became a watchword for any serious dramatic enterprise. Any character who blithely commits himself to a course of action without conceding that he may be acting a role rather than the one he ought to be acting, having perhaps mistakenly conceived the nature of his "plot" or situation, will be a fool or barbarian in our eyes, according to Abel. In a sense this is true, but the arguments which proceed from this assumption are not. In the first place, contrary to what Abel and others have said, self-consciousness has been a feature of the protagonist since tragedy began. In the second place, as self-consciousness does not stand in opposition to the spirit of tragedy, it is possible to conceive tragic art in our time. Abel's concept of metatheatre is important but it is not especially useful in distinguishing, say, *Hamlet* from *Oedipus Tyrannos*, or *Lear* from *Antigone*.

Abel speaks of Shakespeare's appeal, in *Hamlet*, "to a very gross opinion, that thought and action contradict each other. This opinion has helped make Hamlet loved by audiences, who feel him to be a victim, not of his situation, but of his thought." Surely there is no doubt that thought and action frequently do contradict each other, and that the notion has become commonplace. But how does this make it "a very gross opinion"? I would argue that the element of intellectual doubt is crucial in forming interest in a tragic action, and there is after all no tragedy without action. Hamlet does not make up his mind to kill Claudius, nor his mother, but he does act. He pollutes the emotional life of the court by playing out his equivocation in such a way that everyone around him is implicated in his own peculiar internal struggle. And Hamlet's self-consciousness is not all that different from Oedipus', or Antigone's. We feel for Oedipus because he is not certain that his movement in a particular direction is wholly justifiable. Why should he be so violently aggressive toward Teiresias and Creon if he does not somehow suspect his own motives, his own purity of intentions? Even Antigone speaks with certainty only of what she knows she must do, not of what is indisputably correct by every standard. She recognizes that it is possible to view experience from a variety of perspectives, and that she can make her final commitments because she has gone through particular trials. As she says to Ismene: "Take heart. You live. My life died long ago./ And that has made me fit to help the dead."

Probably the Sophoclean play which has presented more critical obstacles to commentators than any other is *Electra*. Kitto writes of the implacable, unlovely qualities of Electra and Orestes which make it so difficult for an audience to sympathize with them, as we sympathize with other tragic characters. No doubt they are implacable, but even they suspect that they may have done something terrible, for they know that if indeed the gods have not ordered the deaths of Clytemnestra and Aegisthus, there can be no power to whom they will be able to appeal. And Orestes speaks as though he were distinctly less than certain. That he kills his mother and her lover does not suggest that he alone acts, in contrast to Hamlet who does not. Both act in different ways, and Hamlet's sour looks, malignant utterances and feigned madness are as final in what they effect as anything Orestes does.

It is certainly instructive to think of Hamlet when one considers Bergman's nurse, for it might be said of her as of Hamlet that she does not act, preferring to rejoin the stream of her normal life. What are her alternatives? Clearly, the actress represents one possibility, though the nurse cannot really choose psychotic withdrawal. She can choose silence, and physical withdrawal, and unhappiness for the rest of her life. Once convinced of the inherent absurdity of efforts to speak the truth, she might pridefully resign from that arena in which those efforts must perpetually go forth. So Nietzsche strove in his later years to evade the seduction of his intelligence by language, and saw it as the aim of philosophy truly to assist in this process of evasion. But the nurse is a practical sort of woman, extremely sensuous and earthy. It is difficult to imagine her withdrawing in such a way that she could no longer conceive herself a woman. In her dream fantasy of the actress's husband, she assuages his anxieties by doing what for her would be most fundamental, most natural — allowing him to make love to her.

Suicide is another alternative. Early in the film the doctor tells the actress that suicide is a rather gross resolution to a subtle problem, explaining to her in these terms why she has chosen to withdraw rather than to kill herself. The doctor may be right, in that there is something intrinsically dramatic, even melodramatic in the decision to commit suicide not because anything has happened to the victim specifically, but because life appears abstractly evil or inauthentic. The actress has renounced the drama as mere imitation, as a mere parody of "the thing itself," and she will manifest a particularly sensitive aversion to anything which might be construed as mere theatrics. Unfortunately, we may say, she comes no closer to the truth of her own feelings or personality by repressing what she feels and refusing to think about the world. She cannot love either husband or child, because she will not allow herself to, and she looks upon the nurse's emotional crisis with almost clinical detachment, though it is easy to see that she would like to befriend her. The nurse, of course, is true to her own feelings from the beginning of the film, and would be temperamentally incapable of committing suicide not because she lacked sufficient courage, or was optimistic, but because such an act would tend to define its subject, to impose a permanent role which a spontaneous character like the nurse could not but abhor.

The other alternative available to the nurse would be in her terms a kind of compromise without honor — a return to normal life without retaining that sense of nullity and absurdity which she had so difficultly won. Had she taken this way out, she would have become no better than most of us, an onlooker, passive, relatively docile and unimaginative. Indeed, she finds she must live with an awareness that neither time nor novelty of experience will do anything to mitigate. Like the tragic figure she is, she will settle for integrity, an integrity which is never truly achieved without immense suffering. In considering her condition, I was reminded of a fairly recent essay on Tacitus' *Agricola,* a chronicle depiction of a period when human history seemed to have run its course, when nothing noble or heroic seemed any longer viable, or even conceivable, even to the best of men. In observing this period, Tacitus is said to have ". . . condemned those who opposed the regime, for he saw no alternative to it and they only worsened matters; and those who supported it, for it was base . . . the sole honourable behavior was to avoid contention and die bravely."

The nurse's understanding is not simply conditioned by observation of her immediate surroundings. Tragedy, after all, does not speak merely to the inhabitants of a particular place, or period, or circumstance, but to all of us at all times. Yet what the nurse conceives for herself is very similar to that path of "honourable behavior" Tacitus could admire so long ago, in response to a particular period colored by specific events. And what we see in Tacitus, and in Bergman, and in all tragic creations, is the image of the hero as victim, not as the victim only of his situation, but as the victim of his condition as man. It is perhaps strange that it should be thus, that those whom we admire above all others must be those who suffer more than we, and accept their suffering as necessary and ennobling to a degree that we must find unnerving. And yet it should not strike us as strange, for how should it be otherwise? Those who have so assiduously labored to convince us that our capacities for tragic vision are diminished, or flown, have articulated distinctions where there are none important enough to constitute a major difference between, say, the Greek sense of life and our own. Raymond Williams in his absorbing book on *Modern Tragedy*, for instance, discusses the nature of tragic martyrdom, and attempts to show how far we are from the Greek concept of martyrdom: "Martyrdom now is defensive; it is a death under pressure . . . It is not a consummation, the climax of a general history. It is often a willing event, but to preserve, not to renew. The sense of loss is ordinarily keener than the sense of revival. . . After such an action, there is not a renewal of our general life, but often a positive renewal of our general guilt."

Williams puts the case very well, but in so doing he accomplishes something he did not quite set out to do. What he successfully describes, in spite of himself, is the nature of any tragic martyrdom, the nature of the tragic enterprise as it relates to Oedipus, Lear, Hamlet, and Bergman's nurse. He does not demonstrate to us that our own psychological and spiritual limitations are any different than those that afflicted the Greeks or Elizabethans. When, I should like to know, was martyrdom not defensive? Needless to say, it must always have been broadly creative and renewing as well, for otherwise we should not have wished to return to the theatre and experience tragedy again and again. It is in the nature of tragedy that it can renew even as it preserves, and that the sense of loss we feel in no way interferes with our conviction of gain. Tragedy is a most paradoxical art, as we shall remember if we keep before us the example of those we have agreed to recognize as tragic. Does not Oedipus agree to suffer martyrdom only because he cannot retain his integrity in any other way? Surely his martyrdom is defensive — having seen everything else blasted from under his feet, he must at least preserve the only vestige of value left to him. He is an honest man who will be an object lesson to all men, proof of our common weakness, and witness to that strength of integrity which is our greatest and most difficult possibility. What does Oedipus preserve but this sense of possibility, which others around him are not men enough to realize in their commitments and activities? The chorus warns Oedipus to cease his pursuit of "evidence." And in Oedipus' case, the preservation of a human potential is tantamount to a renewal, for the life of a community is renewed by a reaffirmation of those possibilities which are in general realized only by a few men, the best men. The spectacle of Oedipus did renew the general life of the Greek community, but it could not do so without inculcating some sense of guilt as well, for the aroused spectator must have asked himself whether he could have acted as Oedipus did, were his circumstances similarly terrible. No doubt, the modestly honest spectator would have answered that he could not conceive himself making such commitments. He would agree that any glorious potential with which we aspire to define ourselves is kept alive by the presence in every generation of an Oedipus, or Antigone.

Bergman's nurse is in this tradition. As we observe her returning to her life, we know that she will keep alive within her, and in those who know her, the sense of man's precarious destiny. "Nothing," she says to the actress. "Nothing," they repeat together, and this is the final word spoken in *Persona*. The nurse has given us no reason ever to doubt her in this film. She means what she says. The life she will make for herself, we must assume, will always attempt to justify itself against this final reality. It will be authentic, because it will be conscious; it will be tragic, because to be conscious, and to go on living, is to suffer as only our heroes can.

FOUR

LANGUAGE AND REALITY IN KOSINSKI'S "STEPS"

There are at the moment few writers in this country who enjoy the esteem in which the Polish-born novelist Jerzy Kosinski is held. His reputation rests upon two works of fiction published here within the last several years,* *The Painted Bird* (1965) and *Steps* (1968), the latter winner of the National Book Award, the former much acclaimed but apparently misunderstood. Each is distinguished by a concern for sheer rapacity and violence that surpasses in intensity even what our more extreme fictional representations have lately led us to expect, and each maintains a coolness of observation, a distance from the respective fields of action, that must exert a chill of unease upon readers. Both *The Painted Bird* and *Steps,* moreover, are written with an economy of moral and descriptive expression that renders them severe as few American novels have ever been, aglow with a harsh clarity of outline that would seem to conceal nothing, but which casts shadows that call into question everything they encompass, including the very project of literature itself.

Because Kosinski was, it seems to me, less clear about what he wanted to do with his first novel, what effects he intended to evoke, the book would appear to have a good deal less attraction for those of us who are interested in the potentialities of literary expression at the present time, than *Steps,* a much more careful book, I think, more controlled, more precise. The critic Irving Howe, who as an admirer of Kosinski compiled some anxious and pregnant questions about his work without really offering any answers, yet had this very useful thing to say: "About

---

From *Centennial Review,* Winter 1972.
* Kosinski's more recent fictions have been, somehow, less interesting, though his 1975 novel *Cockpit* bears further consideration.

Kosinski's powers for graphic evocation there can be no doubt, but finally one wonders whether there is not in this book [*The Painted Bird*] a numbing surplus of brutality. *The Painted Bird* comes to seem too close to that which it portrays, too much at the mercy of its nightmare." And later, "As a self-conscious artist, Kosinski seems to have been aware of these problems and decided to free himself from expressionist detail while searching for another form, more serene in its external dress and likelier to allow for symbolic compression and ellipsis."

While I cannot really agree that Kosinski would have sought a form because it allowed "for symbolic compression and ellipsis," as Howe contends, there is no doubt that these are secondary characteristics of *Steps,* and as such worth looking at in the course of any examination of that novel. What seems to me greatly more to the point, though, is a consideration of the feel of Kosinski's novel, its textural consistency, so that we may begin to examine the quality as well as the weight of its impact on our sensibilities. This is no easy matter, of course, for *Steps* resists the various mechanical approaches that have become customary in literary criticism. It is hardly what one would call a symbolic novel, nor is it a work of realistic expressionism. Philosophically it is neither broadly humanistic nor existential in its treatment of ideas, and it neatly eludes the categories both of Marxian and archetypal criticism. One comes to it after a first reading with measured admiration and hope, but it leaves one always a bit weary, though never bored. We feel like the assiduous deep-sea fisherman who has caught something more than substantial in his net, but who is unable to lift if from the sea, and fears that he will have to drag his load homeward through the troubled waters, until something unanticipated will come along mysteriously to lighten the burden. What is strange is that so much of the novel seems at first randomly conceived, haphazardly thrown together, and that it is only as we consider its impact that we detect a uniformity of movement despite the many digressive gestures performing on the novel's surfaces.

"Life makes no sense, but it is ours to make sense of," said Merleau Ponty with that dogged sense of the absurd project that only the French have properly evoked in our time. The sentiment accurately locates what it is Kosinski has set out to do in *Steps,* as well as the burden of participation he has lain, not without a sense of our frailty, upon our shoulders. For *Steps* suggests the actions of a life, or of several lives, without ever yielding to us sufficient information for us to know very much about either the actions or the people who perform them, without quite, in fact, permitting us to know the necessary degree of our implication in what we imaginatively witness. We are thoroughly aware as we read, of course, that it is not life our author is attempting to show us, but a sequence of formalized abstractions so tightly organized within themselves as to suggest a completeness, a sufficiency reminiscent almost of an algebraic formulation. The tension in our experience of the novel resides in our temptation to settle for a vertical interpretation of individual sequences, so that we acquiesce in what is an unreal sufficiency, a merely aesthetic formulation as such, and the simultaneous inclination to map connections where there may be none, to move horizontally across the entire field of the novel and thereby to violate its purity of fragmentation. Though life may make no sense, we understand, the novel may make a great deal of sense, and any tendency to move laterally across and through the barriers it erects to the imagination that would too glibly humanize and vitiate the true measure of its potency must be held in contempt at the very least. This is the danger we face in approaching *Steps,* and that Kosinski must have seen, the danger that we will demand of a vision that it be pliable to our needs as men anxious for consolation, anxious as well for guilt and a complicity in guilt that cancels barriers, distinctions, realms, that would if it could make of imagination a mere handmaiden of behavioral imperatives. What we need to do, in reading *Steps,* is to make enough sense, not too much, to accept that there is a level of ambiguity in Kosinski's approach to his material that we can justly consider mysterious — mysterious because it is aware of what it is about and yet unable to effect the resolutions a strictly moral response would require of it. What we want, in other words, is to suspend the coercive impulse in our approach to Kosinski's work.

Steps unfolds in a largely disconnected series of episodes or vignettes, some following immediately upon the heels of others, some separated from the others by fragments of conversation between a man and woman who speak always just before or just after a sexual bout. These fragments perform a certain motivic function within the structure as a whole, serving as a kind of stable referent against which the varied episodes may be placed with some sense of context, no matter what their apparent recalcitrance. Howe posits the existence of a relatively identifiable protagonist in the novel, presumably a character who has been through many of the experiences undergone by Kosinski himself. In Howe's words, "It becomes clear that most of the incidents are set in Europe during and after the war, that the narrator lives in a country ruled by 'The Party' under circumstances suggesting Communist Poland, and that he then comes to America, where he undergoes several bits of comic initiation, somewhat like the protagonist of Kafka's *Amerika.*" I'm afraid that Howe's general thesis is not really plausible, in the sense that it imposes a singularity of perspective that a close reading of the novel will not allow. In the first place, it is impossible to conclude that any young man, no matter how dexterous and flighty, would or could hold down as many jobs as Howe's narrator would have to have held down were he a single personality. The first person narrator speaks of himself as working with an archaeological expedition, as a sniper in a tree, as a student, a skiing instructor, professional photographer, cosmopolitan traveler, truck driver, revolutionary adventurer, and so on. Sexually, moreover, he alternates between violent energy, an unflagging erotic disposition, and a self-consciousness that renders him thoroughly ineffectual as a lover, and the alternation is clearly not a matter of simple mood-swing. Kosinski has placed side by side a series of vignettes that are intended to depict not a single personality, but propensities that are, presumably, our common heritage, woven together as the black flag of our condition. He does not for a moment glory in what he has discovered, and refuses to exoticize what is plainly extraordinary, given what we have learned to accommodate in considering human experience. He makes no explicit claim to universalize what he shows, but deals strictly in the realm of possibility, not with how it is for you, but with how it just might be for us, together. He points no accusatory finger, writes often in fact as though it were too late for accusation, too late even to consider how we got where we are, or where we are going. The tone of the narration is so cool indeed that it often betrays a kind of detached amusement such as one is more likely to indulge when examining the depredations of creatures less than human, a pack of jackals perhaps, or baboons.

There are at least two major questions that one will want to examine in considering these aspects of Kosinski's novel: first, what is it in Kosinski's relation to our condition that has determined his decision to write of what he does with the alarming absence of heat, of actively expressed concern, that we have noted; and second, why is it that we can relate to him and to his creation as positively as we do, despite our misgivings? It is unlikely, of course, that any of us can presume at this time to speak of Kosinski himself with any degree of authority, unless we have had the privilege of knowing him during his thirty-odd years of life. And finally, I suppose, it is not Kosinski himself who will matter very much at all. What matters is the mode of his imaginative participation in a certain kind of reality, an imagined reality, and the degree to which he has proven capable of imposing upon us his will to order that reality.

In any case, we might do well to look at precisely what it is Kosinski deals in, and the cultural matrix that informs the behavior of particular characters, no matter how motiveless or inexplicable many of their actions may appear. There are moments in reading *Steps* when the idea of society seems to us nothing more than an abstraction, an unrealized atmosphere in which characters move with absolutely minimal contingency. And this is, in Kosinski's terms, as it ought frequently to impress us, for there is implicit in his vision of human potentiality no necessary correspondence between cultural norms and what they nourish. Not that Kosinski can be content to present a purely subjective point of view, for given what we know of the unconscious and the inevitable breakdown in our time of all previous conceptions of autonomous subjectivity, he would be positing something completely untenable. The old-fashioned independent personality that we can still read about in the nineteenth-century novel has given way to something considerably more fragmented, if not more complex, and to project anything like an autonomous individuality in our present moment is to engage in a distinctly regressive sentimentality that the novel can hardly afford, or worse, to go in for the writing of clinical case history as a substitute for imagination. Kosinski, it must be said, avoids both of these as well as we might hope. If his characters do often seem to float free of their moorings within the culture, we are never permitted wholly to forget what they have come from, not as individuals, but as men who have it in them to do terrible things because they are men, and because neither "advanced" nor "backward" cultures have been able to do anything fundamentally to alter that simple fact of their capacity for barbarism. Kosinski's ability unobtrusively to remind us of what we, most of us, already know is a function of the novel's structure, in which though not every scene illuminates all the others, as some have claimed, there is a certain reverberant density that liberates particular tropes to work in a variety of situations. Thus, in the novel's very first episode, which covers all of five pages, we are told of an encounter between a swinging young fellow who drives a sportscar and a simple country girl, an orphan who washes clothes to sustain herself. The pivot upon which their entire relationship revolves is the young man's display of the wonders that can be worked with credit cards, and her response to the cards as to the "sacramental wafer" of old, which no longer serves the imperatives of her imagination.

It is crucial to see that in this first episode Kosinski is doing nothing so simple as drawing an indictment of advanced western culture, with its rapacious corruption of a noble backwoods ethos. If *The Painted Bird* did nothing else, it surely demonstrated the deeply rooted brutality of Eastern European peasant cultures, a brutality no less terrifying though clearly different from the gruesome nightmares visited upon those same cultures by regiments of Nazi soldiers during the late thirties and early forties. Questions of kind and degree are always open to rational scrutiny, and one no doubt feels impelled to ask such questions in considering Kosinski's novels. But *Steps* is more concerned with the dialectics of human interaction than with the moral content of an event. The more difficult moral issues are to be located in the area of this interaction, in fact, and nowhere more critically than at that point where the literary imagination tries to define the necessity of its own relationship to the subject of its discourse. When Kosinski chose as the primary figure of his first episode the credit card, he did not intend for it to cast a shadow so pervasive that it would color our impressions of all other interactions in his novel. Nor can it cast such a shadow if we read aright, for there are a wide range of other figures that are generated in the course of the novel, and it is altogether safe to assert that not every situation in the book can accommodate even the shadow of that first primary figure.

Why, then, does Kosinski introduce *Steps* as he does, with this particular figure? It is, in the first place, a sure sign that the novel is very much committed to a consideration of, even if it is not finally about, the modern world. Why this should be important, I suppose, is not fully clear, but there is reason to insist that the literary imagination involve itself, or seem to involve itself, always in the course of concrete particulars. As the poet Wallace Stevens once remarked, "The gods of China are always Chinese." Though it can hardly matter, we may say, what they are, our responsiveness to the image they present is distinctly enhanced by our capacity to invest them with attributes that in time grow sufficiently familiar as to constitute an assurance that gods do in fact exist. It is very much the same with Kosinski's figure of the credit cards placed at the opening of his book as a signal to ward off interpretations that would see subsequent proceedings as playful fantasies designed to cure the wart of a sentimental optimism, or as sorcerer's incantations aimed simply at electrifying a mass audience while leaving it all but unruffled at a level of response that would mean something.

But there are other reasons for Kosinski's use of the credit cards. For one thing, they are described as plastic, and plastic is a substance that calls to mind a whole range of things associated with the modern world, but also with certain traditional values that are systematically betrayed in the modern world. It is a vulgar cliche, of course, to claim that it is this recent culture of ours, this age of plastic, that has done away with these values, whatever they may have been, but we know that there is a sense in which we have irrevocably destroyed even the idea that certain values could continue to exist, albeit as no more than ideas in the minds of people peculiarly susceptible to such frivolous notions. There is no pressing reason here to be drawn into the welter of arguments concerning Marx's theories of alienated labor — enough of those theories have been substantiated for us in our mutual experience of what it means to be alive today for us to move on to something broader, to questions of an alienation considerably more pervasive even than Marx would have

•

imagined. For what do the credit cards indicate if not a further element of alienation in the market process by which more and more modern men come to identify themselves, to measure their potency, their reach beyond the narrow confines of the self? With the credit cards, Kosinski would have us see, not because he is perversely angered by the convenience of credit cards but because their function is paradigmatic in a culture that operates as ours has, we cease even to have contact with the money we earn as it can be used to obtain things. Our sense of what we earn, why we earn it, and what we can realistically do with it to enhance our lives is progressively diminished as the market process grows more and more abstract, as we move further and further from the simple reality of exchange as the root of meaningful interaction.

"All this from the measly figure of a credit card?" we may want to exclaim, and not inappropriately. Obviously there is only so much that a given figure can yield, by itself, and one would be hard put indeed to draw from the first episode in *Steps* even so much as we have drawn at this point, were it not for the presence in the novel of numerous reinforcements to the view we have developed. And obviously, too, there is something in a mature literary style that enables us to envision possibilities of connection and interpretation long before these possibilities can be realized. Style can be, after all, a moral act, and in Kosinski's work that is exactly what it is. Usually when we speak of a style as evincing some sort of moral posture, we are referring to various emotional attitudes either implied or openly asserted in the course of a work. Because we have in Kosinski no such thing, no combination of attitudes that we can identify as a position, we cannot but feel uncomfortable in the presence of his energy, for he is unflagging in exposing what we do to one another, and never holds out any hope that we might do otherwise. Nor, as we have previously indicated, does it seem of very much moment to him whether or not we go on as we have. And yet, we feel as we read through his book that there is something akin to an attitude, a position even, that the appalling reality of our condition has been evoked in such a way that we cannot but be appalled. So appalled are we in fact that we may realize with Kosinski that there is nothing more to say, that we have progressed beyond any necessity for lamentation, beyond the capacity to weep or protest. What Kosinski evokes for us in fact are the rigid mannerisms of response that have brought us to where we are — linguistic betrayals, the rapacious hunger to know everything that can be known, the obsessive individualism that has all but destroyed authentic communion among human beings, the reduction of all feeling to modes of consciousness, and the like, a veritable catalogue of social science cliches, here mounted as anything but cliches. For Kosinski evokes while refusing to type, to classify, even to discuss.

Why, then, once again, do we have the credit cards? There are reasons, of course, dictated primarily by the exigencies of the particular episode in which they appear. For the young girl who leaves her home with a stranger relates to him as the possessor of magical cards, not as a fellow-being, and it is this tendency to project the Other as object, as function, which lies at the heart of *Steps*. The cards, moreover, are very much part of a universe whose other abstract commodities they set into reliable perspective simply by the fact of their intimate juxtaposition within a limited context. One of these abstract commodities that is bought and sold, courted and easily dissipated, is glamour, that insipid concoction of insouciance, clean good looks and vague eroticism that is as good an approximation of ontological inauthenticity as anything we have encountered. How predictable, almost, it is that the first episode of *Steps* should conclude as follows: "By then the girl was slightly giddy from the wine we had drunk at lunch, and now, as if trying to impress me with her newly acquired worldliness she must have learned from film and glamor magazines, she stood before me, her hands on her hips, her tongue moistening her lips, and her unsteady gaze seeking out my own." The girl will relate to her young man, we see, not in her own person, but as a project culled from a remembered idyll in which she has never been able to participate. What she knows of herself, though her knowing is wholly inarticulate, is that there is no self beyond the procession of cliches that fill her like a life's blood, an artery of responses that flow through her like a fate.

Is it clear that one knows how to respond to the credit cards, to the girl's feeble impressionism? Of course it is, and of course it is the severity of Kosinski's prose, its assiduous surface neutrality, that ensures the appropriateness, the incisiveness of our response. For what we have in Kosinski is a writing so often colorless, so merely functional at times that we want to speak of it as that "Writing Degree Zero" so memorably portrayed in Roland Barthes's book of that title. Only Kosinski's prose is hardly stripped of a verifiable intentionality, as Camus's is in *The Stranger*, for example. Nor for that matter is Kosinski's prose in *Steps* of the sort Barthes associates with Gide: "The very type of an author without a style [style being for Barthes an expression of the author's peculiar 'biological or biographical' necessity, 'a form with no clear destination, the product of a thrust, not an intention'] is Gide." Gide becomes in this view essentially a craftsman, whose prose exhibits an almost classical austerity and poise, qualities which are not to be encouraged in the degree and form they must take under certain linguistic circumstances: "For what does the rational economy of classical language mean, if not that Nature is a plenum, that it can be possessed, that it does not shy away or cover itself in shadows, but is in its entirety subjected to the toils of language? Classical language is always reducible to a persuasive continuum, it postulates the possibility of dialogue, it establishes a universe in which men are not alone, where words never have the terrible weight of things, where speech is always a meeting with the others. Classical language is a bringer of euphoria because it is immediately social."

Kosinski, as he is among the most demanding of American writers, surely benefits from a reading framed in such unfamiliar terms. We consider, then, how we know what an appropriate response to Kosinski's material would be, since the signs he sets out are scarce at best, and we understand that his style evinces a classical sufficiency with a difference, that no matter how completely all surface connections are managed, there hovers over every episode a doubt, the shadow of an incompleteness. And it is this, this incompleteness, which draws an intensity of concern to particular expressions, halts the narrative flow to promise — what? Perhaps no more than that what we will be considering, in looking at the novel, lies somewhere outside of the specific content of any episode or fragment of dialogue though never finally apart from that content. What we begin to suspect is that the element of mystery that plays within the narrative gaps is of more than passing importance, that the gaps call attention to patterns of imaginative response that are resolutely inexpressible, whether because of the intolerable freight of moral anguish they carry with them or because of a conviction that patterns betray the particulars they presume to encompass. Whatever Kosinski's fears, the origins of his reticence and the mystery he secretes like tiny deposits of fear set to go off in the reader in the manner of time bombs, we know after a while what we must look for. Often we are surprised by how much we are able to find, for we rarely confront novels with that scrupulous attention to detail, and to silence as detail, that we find necessary in reading *Steps*.

What are the shadows, the gaps, the mysteries? They may be nothing more substantial than what produces a puzzlement in our reading of the first episode of *Steps*, beginning with the words "I was traveling farther south." Farther south of what, we would like to know, but are never told, and are pleased that we can never know, for the otherwise perfect clarity of the word "south" is here diffused, shattered into a whole wave of possible colors, and an almost tropical weight of sensuality thereby clings to the pages of this episode, like an expectation bound to ripen into a presence. A small device really, but Kosinski has so many others. What, for instance, of the mystery we sense in that brief episode in which a flock of butterflies is tortured by a group of boys? Here is the concluding section of the episode, which covers all of three paragraphs:

One day we placed some butterflies in a large glass jar and set it upside down, its wide neck overlapping the edge of an old ramshackle table. The gap was wide enough to let in air, but too narrow for the butterflies to escape. We carefully polished the glass. At first, unaware of their confinement, the butterflies tried to fly through the glass. Colliding, they fluttered about like freshly cut flowers which under a magician's hand had suddenly parted from their stems and begun to live a life of their own. But the invisible barrier held them back as though the air had grown rigid around them.

After we had nearly filled the jar with butterflies, we placed lighted matches under the rim. The blue smoke rose slowly about the pulsating blooms inside. At first it seemed that each new match added not death but life to the mass of living petals, for the insects flew faster and faster, colliding with each other, knocking the colored dust off their wings. Each time the smoke dimmed the glass, the butterflies repeated their frantic whirl. We made bets on which of them could battle the smoke the longest, on how many more matches each could survive. The bouquet under the glass grew paler and paler, and when the last of the petals had dropped onto the pile of corpses, we raised the jar to reveal a palette of lifeless wisps. The breeze blew away the smoke — it seemed as if some of the corpses trembled, ready to take wing again.

One notices immediately that the writing here is considerably more lush than anything a reader will have come upon previously in *Steps*, and one wonders why. We enjoy what Kosinski has done — the surfaces of language are most attractive, to be sure — but we cannot but be uneasy when we think of the senseless destruction of lovely things. After a bit we may be able to consider again whether in fact the destruction *was* senseless, whether it did not serve some purpose, some process of perception. But this, we decide, is hardly a question we can afford to answer, for it would have us weighing and comparing values that are distinctly incommensurate. And besides, Kosinski does not really call upon us to make such considerations, or does he? Is he perhaps suggesting here that the ugly, the brutal, can be redeemed, can be made lovely, by language, that art can save us from the horror of what we do by creating values that can be approved without constituting a threat to our casual inhumanities? Or is Kosinski instead revealing how pathetic, how largely desperate and perverse are such attempts, which though we may call down upon them the ignominy they deserve, will continue to move us and bewilder our efforts to appease the fascination they exert? Here the creative imagination comes to grips with dilemmas of its own inexorable making, and discovers that the processes of creation are as darkly inscrutable to itself as for those who merely witness. What we cannot fail to see in examining this encounter, however, is that the texture of the writing itself, as it deviates from the relatively neutral functionalism of the writing in other episodes, is itself very much at the center of Kosinski's discourse, very much what it is all about.

A literary expression that comes to deal more and more with the dynamics of its own creation, to meditate increasingly on the processes of its own awareness, will tend at the same time to seek a stable point from which to launch its examinations. Disabused of all recourse to autonomous subjectivity, to wholeness of being, and unable to achieve an authentic solidarity with the notion of humanity as such, a humanity from which it must recoil in fear and disgust, it finds what it is seeking in the first person "I," in a narrative convention that can hardly be familiar to most of us. This is not the "existential 'I'" of which Barthes speaks, an "I" which contains the promise of a personality that is potentially unique and dangerous. Kosinski's is the "pure I" discussed by the philosopher-critic E.M. Cioran in a recent study of the French poet Valéry: ". . . seeking among our sensations and judgments an *invariable*, he finds it not in our changing personality but in the pure *I*, 'universal pronoun,' 'which has no history' and which is, in short, but an exacerbation of awareness, a boundary-line existence, semi-fictitious, devoid of all determinate content and totally unrelated to the psychological subject. This sterile self, a sum of rejections, the quintessence of nothing, an aware void (not awareness of the void but a void which knows itself and rejects the accidents and vicissitudes of the contingent subject), this self, the ultimate stage of lucidity, of a lucidity distilled and purified of all complicity with objects and events, lies at the antipode of the Self — infinite productivity, cosmogonic force — as German romanticism had conceived it."

Cioran's is an especially brilliant and, in terms of Valéry, wonderfully authoritative construction, but while it goes a long way towards clarifying Kosinski's relation to his material, a number of qualifications must be made if we are to see the novelist's project confidently. It is true that we really know very little of Kosinski after completing his book, that he withholds himself from direct communication with his characters. It is true, moreover, that if we can claim to know him at all, we can identify him merely as the sum of the many rejections he makes. What we must acknowledge, though, is that if he is in *Steps* no more than "an exacerbation of awareness," "devoid of all *determinate* [my emphasis] content," he still cannot be described as "a sterile self," nor as "a lucidity distilled and purified of all complicity with objects and events." For Kosinski's willingness to manifest this complicity is largely responsible for our response to *Steps*, beyond a numbed acquiescence in or rejection of what we are shown. Now we have made it only too clear that Kosinski refuses in *Steps* to be drawn in explicitly, or to have us directly indicted. What he does instead is to fragment his vision of the way things are, or might be, and to enlist our participation in the ordering of constituent events that comprise that vision. We have remarked upon the dangers peculiar to such imaginative procedures, both for an author and his reader. Once we have been alerted to these dangers, and have grown suspicious of the facile generalizations and easy humanistic reductions to which such fragmented visions may lend themselves, we are prepared to pursue Kosinski through the maze-like intricacies of his novel. And what we shall come to look for, to appreciate, to fear, is precisely that complicity that the surfaces of language, the sheer blocked-out contours of the narrative would seem to deny, even to reject. For Kosinski's is a self that proves its own vulnerability even as it struggles to hold itself aloof, a self that focuses inward, upon the processes of its awareness, only to find that it has been invaded by legions of Others. The self we see is a fortress that has been pried open and occupied, possessed at the very core of its being. The chaste appointments of language, the neutrality, are but masks that point to themselves, that can hide, finally, nothing at all.

What grips us as we proceed through *Steps* is this most difficult awareness. It steals upon us as we read of the narrator's enthusiasm, in a late episode, to encourage a young woman's freedom by introducing her to drugs — this after he has manipulated and used her like a toy in the most cynical ways, described meticulously in the course of this fragment, which concludes:

Her addiction might regenerate all that had become flabby and moribund in her and at the same time break down what was stiff and rigid; she would acquire new desires and new habits and liberate herself from what she thought of me, from what she felt for me. Like a polyp she would expand and develop in unpredictable directions.

"Like a polyp," we read, and what we have witnessed assumes a moral clarity we were not sure it had. We look at the other words in this paragraph, a prose that winds through the novel like a fine scarf, leaving a trail we are not likely to overlook, if we crawl on our hands and knees after it. We look at the word "regenerate," and wonder what it can mean in this context that would allow us to think of it in the positive terms that it ought characteristically to evoke. And we understand that what is here described as "stiff and rigid" is all a woman can have of a distinctive personality, a being as such by which she can gauge her own needs and desires, and this the gentleman would casually "break down" as though he were experimenting with plants. And then of course, that lovely verbal "liberate" acquires such obvious irony in its perversely unsuitable environment that we need say no more about it.

The language of the novel, then, is infected by what it had sought to exclude. The novelist, by merely depicting, setting off, fictionalizing, had hoped on a certain level of his consciousness to tame the insight, chasten the vision, relieve it of its necessity. But he has been unable to do so, and this is the special value of his work, the source of its glory and its tension and its ability to haunt our dreams. "My original fall is the existence of the Other," Sartre wrote in *Being And Nothingness*, and also, "Whatever may be my further relations with others, these relations will be only variations on the original theme of my guilt." It is this guilt that dogs our footsteps as we patrol with Kosinski the pale wastes of our common experience that slide by us like driven snow. It is this guilt of having bestowed upon others, as they bestow upon us, a glance which together we must experience as an alienation, that we cannot dispel, for we make each other realize that for the self, the other is always an object, and we can never really grasp the self that we are for each other. Kosinski's is a moral style because it evinces a necessity it would evade, and that necessity is guilt, guilt for the fact that it is no longer possible to stand apart from the reality we would plumb, as we can no longer simply admonish and strike postures; guilt too that we have no language adequate to the meaning we would impart other than the language of our infamy, our alienation, our otherness. And even this idiom, so obscene when it would justify the solipsism of the partial selves who are all that we can know, even this idiom fails fully to capture the degree of our otherness, the stupid pathos of our futility. A girl in *Steps* couples with an animal, accompanied by the frenzied shouts of onlookers who urge the animal to penetrate her even more deeply: "The peasants, still refusing to believe that the girl could survive her violation, eagerly paid again and again. Finally the girl began to scream. But I was not sure if she was actually suffering or was only playing up to the audience." Thus it ends. Can any language adequately represent the dissociation of feeling from consciousness that this passage portends? Might moral strictures, introduced into such writing, enhance perception, or tame it? The latter, we must suppose, and therefore are they omitted. But the meanings multiply, and they are all a single meaning, fitfully emergent though unmistakable, as in the conclusion of another episode set in the snowy reaches of a mountain resort housing tubercular patients. A thoroughly simple transformation of vision is effected, and yet, early as it occurs in the novel, it is a decisively reorienting figure: "Suddenly figures appeared between the snowdrifts. They scrambled through the fields toward the sanatorium, now and then lost, as if straining against the stifling dust storm of a drought-stricken plain." Here the hypothetical element authoritatively converts naturalistic detail. It is a pattern by which Kosinski's work has always to be apprehended.

What intensifies the pace of *Steps* and reduces whatever tendencies toward exoticism it exhibits are the fragments of dialogue mentioned earlier, italicized snatches sometimes covering only a few lines, sometimes several pages. The lovers who speak to one another in these pages seem often interchangeable with characters who flit in and out of the other episodes, and at one point a mere ten pages or so from the end of the novel Kosinski makes an explicit link, allowing an italicized voice to recapitulate briefly what has been reported in standard type on the preceding page. Again, to be clear, Kosinski does not here establish a connection because it must be so, but because it might be. In any case, these tremendously biting pieces of dialogue confirm for us what Kosinski has shown through a variety of narrative devices in the rest of his book. What is truly remarkable is the sense we have, from the brief fragments, of thoroughly articulated personalities working through the artifices of language at their own irrevocable corruption and confusion, a confusion that is a betrayal of what they can properly mean for themselves. They are terribly glib, these people, whoever they are. They are well-trained in the nuances of sophisticated discourse, and they have heard a good deal about authenticity, and the problems of the self, and they are not likely to be taken in by the psychotic ideal of romantic love. They are not products of any particular culture, nor are they especially typical of any one group within a culture. Their words are, perhaps, our words, in that they trail along in their wake a variety of dessicated linguistic forms that inhibit true expression of self. Though they have banished from their vocabularies sentimental cliches, theirs can hardly be a medium of authentic communion. Feeling has need, in their exchanges, to dress itself in ideas. What Kosinski makes manifest for us in these dialogues is the revenge of intellect, of ideology, of the structured moral conscience upon our humanity, and it is a terrible vision that transcends any concern we may express over a purely modern dilemma. In the long history of the West, it may be true that we have reached something of an apotheosis in this progressive alienation of ourselves from what we might be, and there may be no further along this line that we can go. But, as the critic Frank Kermode has recently pointed out, it is characteristic of a certain kind of imagination that it always senses itself at the end of something, an era, an idea. For all we know, we may have yet a long way to go.

If in fact we can expect more of what we have had, this, Kosinski suggests, is what it will be like. A young woman confesses to her lover that she has been seeing another man:

Why are you telling me about it?

I would feel awkward hiding it from you. I don't want to be separated from you by an experience you know nothing about. You see, after you told me you wanted us to live together, I had to find out whether I could still be interested in someone else, and whether someone else would appreciate me as much as you do. I felt I had an obligation to know myself better — apart from the self you have brought me to know. . . .

So to find out whether you loved me, you had to sleep with another man?

I didn't sleep with him.

But if you wanted to find out how you are without me, how did you refuse such a critical test?

I didn't refuse; he didn't ask me.

Later, when pressured, she admits that the stranger made love to her.

But since you spent several nights there, it's not too much to assume that he made love to you or — if you prefer — that you gave yourself to him?

I don't deny it, but an act of intercourse is not a commitment unless it stems from a particular emotion and a certain frame of mind. It wasn't an act based on love; but I had to make sure, in order to discover myself, whether it would lead to love.

What is one to make of this? Frightening? Well, not really. What is strange is that a woman so dexterous in the use of words should be able so easily to lie to herself. But then it is not really strange at all — how fickle language is after all. We must look at the word "commitment" as the young woman utters it, and smile, not without a trace of self-consciousness, but with a certain pleasure of awareness.

A better passage, better because clearly illuminative of our own complicity in Kosinski's vision, is taken from another dialogue appearing late in the novel:

I want you, you alone. But beyond you and me together, I see myself in our love-making. It is this vision of myself as your lover I wish to retain and make more real.

But you do want me for what I am, apart from you, don't you?

I don't know you apart from myself. When I am alone, when you are not here, you are no longer real: then it's only imagining again.

Then all you need me for is to provide a stage on which you can project and view yourself, and see how your discarded experiences become alive again when they affect me. Am I right? You don't want me to love you; all you want is for me to abandon myself to the dreams and fantasies which you inspire in me. All you want is to prolong this impulse, this moment.

This is more difficult to refute, it would seem, and we may justly ask ourselves whether we can want to refute it. Dismiss it, yes, it comes perhaps too near the truth for comfort. That we want to think otherwise there is no doubt; that we shall continue to find in ourselves the courage — is it the audacity — to tell others we in fact do think otherwise, seems a similarly secure assumption. But what shall we call upon to validate our claims? If Kosinski's portrayal is not the whole truth, and we may together console ourselves that it is not, it is a part of the truth we can least afford to forget. Language here is not alienated from what it would express. The gaps, the silences we detect so often in *Steps* are here diminished. We reach at this juncture a kind of still point in which contending forces that vie within Kosinski's language achieve a temporary balance, a harshness that in this imaginative universe is all that we can know of sufficiency. Confronted by such clarity, we must draw an ambiguous breath, and gaze again as into the bottomless depths of an oracle. The pain of recognition here, whatever it may be, will draw us back in *Steps* to another point perhaps, as bitter, as clear, a point that may a little console, despite our complicities, our guilt. For it is to the realm of sheer wish that Kosinski once in his novel guides us, a realm we will not want to overlook, though we know at last we shall have to reject it with all the other consolations:

Had it been possible for me to fix the plane permanently in the sky, to defy the winds and clouds and all the forces pushing it upward and pulling it earthward, I would have willingly done so. I would have stayed in my seat with my eyes closed, all strength and passion gone, my mind as quiescent as a coat rack under a forgotten hat, and I would have remained there, timeless, unmeasured, unjudged, bothering no one, suspended forever between my past and my future.

FIVE

GOMBROWICZ'S "COSMOS": THE CLINICAL FICTION AS NOVEL

> "We are sinful not merely because we have eaten of the Tree of Knowledge, but also because we have not yet eaten of the Tree of Life. The state in which we find ourselves is sinful, quite independent of guilt."
>
> Franz Kafka
>
> "Before God we are always in the wrong."
>
> Søren Kierkegaard

The last of Witold Gombrowicz's four novels, *Cosmos* is a work in which reality has completely given way to meaning, a book not so much about anything as a stewing in its own juices. It is, one might say, a quest novel in which the object of the quest is not only known from the start, but known to be forbidden, this object being nothing less than the self's engagement with the world on a basis of reasonable equivalence. And it is, finally, a book in which the Tree of Life, so dimly evoked by Kafka, has ceased its fruit-bearing activity and stands mute, barren, inviting all interpretations, all uses, and none.

Sartre once complained about "a kind of onanistic complacency"

From *Review of Existential Psychology and Psychiatry*, Summer 1972.

*The works of Witold Gombrowicz are still little known in this country, though widely read in Europe. A special issue of the French publication *Cahier De L'Herne* has been devoted to Gombrowicz, with contributions by Gunter Grass, Michel Foucault and Jean-Paul Sartre. Most of his major works are available in translation in inexpensive paperback editions: the novels *Ferdydurke* and *Pornografia* as well as the plays, *Ivone, Princess of Burgundia* and *The Marriage*. Gombrowicz died in 1969 at the age of 65 after spending many years in exile from his native Poland, first in Argentina and later in France.

in the work of Genet, and there is reason to urge a complaint of this sort against *Cosmos,* certainly one of the most meticulously patterned novels ever written. It is as if Gombrowicz had seen fit to give us nothing but the dream that haunted his waking life, a dream so peculiarly familiar in all its particulars that it could not be presumed to deny access to anyone at all. What is lacking is the pressure of reality beating against the confines of dream, the throbbing of life protesting its reduction to meaning, the thing itself denying the sufficiency of its symbolic representation. *Cosmos* is rather too secure in its resources, smug in the limitations it accepts for its own unfolding even as its characters seem less creatively dissentient than their counterparts in Gombrowicz's earlier fictions. What we suspect is not so much a failure of imagination as a failure of nerve, for intimations of revolt are strewn about these pages like a chain of corpses, and yet they come to nothing, betray really neither energy nor cunning. The devices of characters, like the devices of this novel, are a little tired, if still somehow worth one's attention, if only in the sense that Gombrowicz's vision of the universe seems so perfectly to have dictated the form of this book.

Cosmos involves an episode in the lives of two young men who have retreated from the city to the countryside. The narrator Witold is a student at a Polish university and must ostensibly have quiet to study for examinations. His companion's name is Fuchs, and really there is little difference to tell between them. Witold seems to know precisely what Fuchs is up to, though a certain element of mystery plays about him as it touches everything in the novel, and Fuchs seems if anything a slightly more cautious, more "normal" version of Witold while suffering from the same unfortunate afflictions. Each is in temporary flight from an authority figure who has for the boys assumed monstrous dimension, in Witold's case a father, in Fuchs's an employer named Drozdowski. The two voluntary exiles spend their summer vacation at a guest house run by the Wotjys family, including Leo and his wife Kulka, their daughter Lena and her husband Louis, and the family servant Katasia whose mouth has been suggestively disfigured in an accident and provides a source for many of the narrator's obsessive ruminations. Other characters appear in the second part of the book during a strange excursion to a mountain hideaway, but the basic constellation of figures with whom we are concerned is introduced almost at once and remains in view more or less until the final page.

The structure of the novel may be described as circular, in that nothing we care very much about really happens — we know at once that our protagonist will be involved in nothing more momentous than chasing his own tail, an occupation not without a very real urgency for the participant, but decidedly a melancholy spectacle for observers. And if in the novel a crime, or several, have been committed, as the book surely suggests, it is something in the nature of an unspecifiable, universal crime in which the author is interested, and virtually all pathways he is able to chart lead ultimately in the same direction. What the perspective of *Cosmos* enforces, in fact, is that if crime is universal, if as Kierkegaard says, "Before God we are always in the wrong," then nothing is worse than anything else, and all we have is the certainty of our sinfulness. Now to begin with certainty is to have the possibility of going nowhere at all, and indeed this is the problem of *Cosmos*, for Gombrowicz was not the sort of fellow by the time he wrote this book to harbor anything like a doubt about the structure of things and his place in the universe. The genuine fear and spirited rebelliousness of his protagonist in the early novel *Ferdydurke* have here become the bitter pranks and mindless drift of one who can no longer even pretend to care for his own dignity. Nor can he believe that there is anything like an authentic fiction which, like myth, can serve man by reducing the plurality of his perceptions to a consoling vision wherein even the painful and the intransigently eccentric particular can find its place. All Gombrowicz apparently can countenance as authentic is the quest for fictions of whatever kind. Like Thomas Pynchon's character Stencil in the novel *V.*, he suspects that he needs "a mystery, any sense of pursuit to keep alive a borderline metabolism." What can be more circular than the experience of a man who looks for fictions in which he knows he cannot believe? How can such a life have an end? Everything is reduced to process. The English critic Tony Tanner has said of Wittgenstein's opening proposition in the *Tractatus, Die Welt Ist Alles Das Der Fall Ist:* "The assertion that the world is everything that is the case repudiates the very notion of plots and arguably leaves things and events standing in precisely describable inexplicability." At the same time we must acknowledge that "people would rather detect an 'ominous logic' in things than no omens at all," and many of our writers find themselves writing "both to demonstrate the need for fictions and to impugn or revoke their validity." One can find no better statement of Gombrowicz's project in *Cosmos*, a novel without a denouement and without an ending, whose beginning is nothing more than the first stirrings of self-consciousness in the stricken organism.

The universe of *Cosmos* is riddled with a variety of disgusting objects, but none is as disgusting as the protagonist Witold is to himself, and this is the primary source of everything in the novel, its fears, hallucinations, smells. For everything in *Cosmos* has about it the substance of dream; all is so obviously interfused that no single item of perception can exist without reference to every other. We know what to look for in reading *Cosmos* because we know at once its origins in a guilt that is nowhere relieved, a guilt that colors everything in the manner of an obsession, and without which a gaping void would otherwise occupy the space reserved for Witold, presumably a mask for Gombrowicz himself. From the very first we are informed of Witold's trouble with his parents, "my rudeness to the old man," and about "Fuchs's troubles with his chief at the office," and we suspect that we are on the brink of a Kafkan nightmare. This is rapidly confirmed by Fuchs's outburst of several pages later, when he proclaims: "Sometimes I feel like going down on bended knee and imploring him (the chief) to forgive me. But he hasn't got anything to forgive me for." Witold follows with: "The two of us undressed like men rejected and repulsed."

There is perhaps something rather too easy in formulating such a circumstance at the beginning of a novel and using it to inform a reading of all that is to follow. The figure of Kafka looms too large on the page, perhaps, and as readers we become more concerned with literary relationships of a secondary nature than with the immediate tonalities of Gombrowicz's fiction. Soon, though, it is the figure of Beckett that emerges, as it becomes clear that Gombrowicz has pitched the mansion of his imagination in the place of excrement, but we come after a brief while to care not at all about the various echoes of Kafka or Beckett that reverberate from page to page. For the imagination at work in *Cosmos* is in thrall to its fears and guilts in a way that can only be called distinctive. It ambience is not as severe as Kafka's, and it is less conditioned to the minimal gesture than Beckett's imagination, though the range and amplitude of event are obviously impoverished by comparison with most other fictions we enjoy. If it is true that Gombrowicz's protagonist begins where Gregor Samsa and George Bendemann begin, his novelistic development is hardly theirs.

Witold's is a case of sexual despair, and all of his loathings, and his loathesomeness, are sexually inspired. We have intimations of comparable difficulty in Kafka, but they are relatively subdued in a work like "The Judgment," limited to a minor detail that one notices but hardly finds it necessary to emphasize in a reading of the tale. It may not be entirely useful to identify Gombrowicz as a Freudian, but surely he interprets human reality largely in sexual terms, and one remembers an element of the grotesquely sexual in each of his earlier volumes that, in the light of the present novel, seems almost prophetic. It is as though everything in novels like *Ferdydurke* and *Pornografia*, and in a play like *The Marriage*, all the verbal razzle-dazzle and virtuosic gestural dueling, were simply a screen for the author's real concern, now bursting full-blown onto the page, with virtually no redemptive qualification or conventionally "aesthetic" concealment. A modicum of artifice there is, of course, in *Cosmos*, and a good deal of symbol and metaphor, but all are so firmly gripped in the obsessive strait-jacket of Gombrowicz's neurotic vision that they can refer only to what the vision inexorably predicts.

If we ask, of course, what precisely *is* a neurotic vision, we come upon all sorts of dilemmas, and there is a sense in which any patterned vision may be described as neurotic, if only in the sense that it wilfully imposes an individual desire for order upon a reality that resists such imposition in the very plurality of its being. These are the grounds of neurotic conflict, and to the degree that they describe a circumstance which is universal, they verify Freud's contention that we are all sick. Conventionally, though, it is the way we respond to the often mild discomfiture associated with this basic situation that determines whether or not we are neurotic. Gombrowicz's protagonist is undoubtedly so in a very serious way, and he is surely the sort of fellow one might expect to find in a mental institution, for his disturbances threaten to involve all those in whose company he finds himself. So familiar are we, in fact, with the behavioral patterns Gombrowicz describes for his character, and with his specific emotional responses to his experience, that we actually find it difficult to dispel the sense that we are reading a clinical document rather than a novel. Here the novel does indeed seem to fulfill the function Lawrence has attributed to it as the book of life, though its impact is hardly as bright and uplifting as Lawrence would have contended. Only at rare moments does the literary imagination here break out ot the trammels of its neurotic obsession and transcend the patently clinical detail, which is to say that the sense of play for its own sake is in *Cosmos* so limited as to impair the quality of openness and fluidity the novel ought ideally to evoke. The dialectical interplay between the artist and the materials of his vision seems here almost resolved in favor of the vision, so that what we like to think of as the artist's command of his materials seems no longer even a relevant consideration. The literary imagination has almost abnegated, it would seem, in the face of its vision, that which it was to have mastered and made somehow tolerable. The peculiarly neurotic fiction, as distinct from any fiction in which neurotic conflict plays a part, is an arena in which art succumbs to obsession and the raw materials of a vision refuse to be transformed effectually. *Cosmos* seems an example of writing by immersion, the sort of thing Gombrowicz proposes only for a first draft when he speaks of such artistic procedures in his *Journal.* It would seem that in the drafting of his final novel Gombrowicz hit upon a symbolic structure which so perfectly embodied his deepest fantasies, and in so literal a way, that he was struck by its lucidity and pertinence, and unable to mar its surfaces for fear of spoiling what was so authentically "correct."

There is no doubt that Gombrowicz had confronted this sort of difficulty before — it is surely not without precedent in literary history — and one does well to recall that his other novels contain patches of writing on the subject. In one of several digressive chapters in *Ferdydurke,* he reflects: "In the last resort, is it we who create form, or is it form that creates us? Incidentally, some years ago I knew a writer who at the outset of his literary career gave birth to a book of the purest heroism. With the first few words he put down on paper, quite by chance, he touched the chord of heroism; it might equally well have been that of skepticism or lyricism. But the first sentences that flowed from his pen were heroic, and because of this, and by virtue of the laws of construction, it was impossible for him not to go on concentrating and distilling the spirit of heroism until he got to the end . . . But what about the author's deepest conviction? Could a responsible creative artist confess that heroism had flowed spontaneously from his pen and independently of him, and that his deepest conviction was not his deepest conviction. . . . In vain, the unhappy hero of this heroism, feeling ashamed of himself, tried to escape from his part, which, having taken a firm hold on him, refused to let go. He had to adapt himself to the situation; and so thoroughly did he do so that towards the end of his career he had completely identified himself with his part. . . . Such are the deep and weighty philosophical reasons which have prompted me to construct the present work on the basis of several parts."

This is no mere formal consideration as it is developed in *Ferdydurke,* nor is its reflection in *Cosmos,* and indeed Gombrowicz has long recognized and lamented the degree to which human freedom is circumscribed by form, even as he has sought it in the context of his own life and art. It is like the need for fictions we spoke of earlier, and the simultaneous compulsion we experience to "impugn their validity." Now there is a sense in which it might be said that *Ferdydurke* is constructed "on the basis of separate parts," despite the consistently whole-cloth fabric of its conception. The field of the novel is teeming with invention, one piece of outrageous buffoonery vying with another for our attention. Individual characters, no matter how nicely they work together in enforcing a particular attitude which it is the burden of the novel to communicate, have a sense of wholeness about them, of emerging from a project that is at least partially their own. They move about, awkwardly it is true, self-conscious to a fault, and yet one responds to a certain, an indefinable independence in them. They are bound, no doubt, but bound by contingencies which they have had a hand in creating, and if they are all types of a sort, they are not reducible to any single type. There is something distinctive about each of them, small though their distinctions may be, and if Gombrowicz's views on human freedom are no more optimistic in *Ferdydurke* than in *Cosmos*, he did manage in the earlier book at least to retain a lively curiosity in the subject. Beckett once said: "I am interested in the shape of ideas even if I do not believe in them. . . . It is the shape that matters." Freedom is one most important idea in whose shape Gombrowicz no longer seems to have been interested by the time he wrote *Cosmos*, and the novel suffers as a result; for without the possibility of freedom, without the strength of will to nurture even the idea of it, the human project dwindles to an almost mechanical abstraction, and man becomes merely the object of a power he cannot begin to comprehend. R. D. Laing, writing on Sartre's *Critique Of Dialectical Reason*, explains the absence we experience in *Cosmos:* "In one *moment* (in the Hegelian sense) man is subject to the dialectic as an enemy power. In another moment he creates it. This second moment is the negation of the first, which is the negation of man. This is the crucial negation of negation. It is necessary, we are condemned, to live this contradiction dialectically. Man undergoes the dialectic, in so far as he makes it, and makes it, in so far as he undergoes it. He is not subject to it non-dialectically, like a divine law, or a metaphysical fatality." What we miss in *Cosmos* is the attempted negation of negation, which we cite here not as an ideological imperative without which Sartre's peculiar brand of humanism cannot be nurtured. We speak of this dialectical process rather as essential in any meaningful conception of an experience to which we can respond sympathetically, that is, as more than the alienated witness in the conventional psychiatric encounter between sick patient and presumably healthy therapist.

When in *Cosmos* Witold cries, "Will no one ever be able to reproduce the incoherence of the living moment at its moment of birth? Born as we are out of chaos, why can we never establish contact with it? No sooner do we look at it than order, pattern, shape is born under our eyes," we must relate to his despair more with pity than with any immediate sense of our complicity, for Witold's perception of things is rather too stable, too neurotically fixated, too conditioned by "metaphysical fatality" to remind us of our own, more vital experience of process, of perpetual formation and deformation such as the dialectic of *Ferdydurke* suggests. Indeed, every particular in *Cosmos* has reference to a single obsession, and the author would seem to have exerted himself less than strenuously to escape its grasp, at least from what we can tell in reading *Cosmos*. In the face of all his previous work, though, it seems safe to say that there is nothing vaguely inauthentic about Gombrowicz's fictional evocation of this obsession. Unlike the fellow in the anecdote from *Ferdydurke*, the obsession he dwells upon in *Cosmos*, his compulsive literary chord or tonality, would seem to have chosen him not by chance, but inevitably. It was only as a result of an alternative commitment, a commitment to art and laughter, that he was able in the past to defer this unhappy obsession, to hold it at arm's length, as it were. And as the alternative commitment grew less firm, less sustaining, Gombrowicz succumbed more and more to his obsession, to his neurosis. It is not, of course, entirely clear that such a schematic sketch of an artist's progress can make the dialectic of creation as clear as it would like to think it can, but it is at least suggestive of a discernible progress in Gombrowicz's career.

What, then, is the nature of this obsession and the various compulsions to which it gives rise? In Wilhelm Stekel's *Compulsion And Doubt,* a psychoanalytic work which throws great light on Gombrowicz's novel, we read that: "Physicians who have worked with compulsives know that the first compulsion to which the patients were subjected was masturbation and that consequently the entire life of compulsives is a struggle against masturbation." "Compulsions serve as substitutes for tabooed actions, which are not permitted to penetrate into consciousness. Obsessions serve the same purpose. The symbolization of daily life, the complicated activity which changes the patient's life into a difficult pattern of existence, the problems which he seemingly can not solve, are all derived from the fear of a vacuum in the patient's thinking process.

"All obsessive patients suffer from this *horror vacui,* the fear of emptiness. They imagine they are able to think what they are not permitted to think, or that they can carry out what they are not permitted to do. The symbol serves as a concealment of the original idea."

In *Cosmos,* the word "Berg" serves as a parodic equivalent of "masturbate" or simply "excite oneself," and in its frequent repetitions assumes the force of a palpable thing — it is in fact the most substantial force in the entire novel, hovering over everything else with an influence at once playful and demonic. It casts a long arm backwards to the opening pages of the novel, for example, and illuminates all the talk of "men rejected and repulsed" and the expressed impulse of these men to implore forgiveness though they cannot identify the crimes they have ostensibly committed. If we can take the character Witold as a mask for Gombrowicz, and Fuchs as a mere extension of his friend, then we can make a case for *Cosmos* as a masturbatory fantasy designed at once to stimulate the author's imagination and give an onanistic pleasure, and to serve as a wedge into the "respectable world" whereby the author can exorcise his self-disgust and achieve some sort of reintegration into the body of humanity The first specific compulsion we can posit is perhaps masturbation, as Stekel recommends, but we can extend that to cover a whole range of forbidden pleasures which children must learn to do without. In the most conventional psychoanalytic sense, the forbidding of such pleasures, from masturbation to thumb-sucking, and the attendant frustrations experienced by the child, are at the roots of the conflicts we know as neurosis. In Stekel's terms, "The ego, pressed by fear, has accepted the demands of culture, but it remembers and seeks revenge. Culture is not forgiven for inhibiting the free flow of pleasure."

Gombrowicz's Witold pursues behavioral patterns in *Cosmos* that are patently obsessive, and much of what he does seems motivated by just that desire for revenge Stekel describes. The objects of this revenge might prove to be anyone at all, and there is a malicious character in virtually everything Witold thinks about. He claims in the course of his narration to be unable to understand what he conceives, why he should harbor the despicable notions of people he reports to us. But it is evident early in the novel that Witold sees quite clearly the pattern in which he is involved, and while all compulsive actions appear to unfold as by a will of their own, it is similarly clear that the neurotic personality knows and controls what he is doing. As we read on in the novel, we are drawn of course to the appearance of the protagonist laboring to deal with something he can neither recognize nor master. The whole novelistic ambience of lurking sin and impenetrable mystery feeds upon the appearance of an unconscious implication in the cellars of evil, and to the degree that we are in any way able to worry over Witold, we must retain a sense of his inscrutable victimization. Early in the novel, though, we realize that Witold is the source of his own plots, impelled by the *horror vacui* Stekel notes, and that the mental gymnastics he performs are not nearly as dangerous to him in the context of his suffering as they are conserving, a protective device to ward off intimations of sinfulness that would otherwise be intolerable. What he does, of course, in a most meticulous and craftsmanlike way, is to project onto the universe qualities he cannot explicitly attribute to himself, though at a certain level of his being he knows that is where such attributions belong. "The symbol serves as a concealment of the original idea," writes Stekel, and that is indeed its function in the universe of *Cosmos,* a universe in which all things, all people, all activities assume a symbolic function with a single emotional and intellectual referent: the sinfulness and filth of being in a world man was to have made hospitable to the operation of higher values.

There are, to be sure, no higher values actually at work in *Cosmos,* and those that are momentarily introduced are raised to be mocked as inauthentic, to have their hollowness revealed. Leo Wotjys sees the absurdity of such values, to which he has consigned his life in a suitably ironic manner, and is the author of a preposterous harangue that exalts the exemplary life of immaculate drudgery, his own life of stability, civic responsibility, family feeling, and general faithfulness. To which Witold replies, "You are a masturbator," and sure enough, he is, acknowledging as much and more, and locating the fount of his enthusiasm and good humor in his early acceptance of himself as the prime source of his pleasure and well-being. He had decided "that there was no point in wasting time thinking about touching somebody else's hand when you had two hands of your own...because pleasure, it seems to me, is a question of setting your mind to it, and if you persist you can get pleasure from your own body, not a great deal of course, but it's better than nothing." And Leo sings a brief ditty that he repeats to himself, apparently, quite often: "If you can't get what you want/ you must want what you've got." Altogether a healthy attitude, one might say, though not what a larger heart could decently wish. Leo's is a case of successful accommodation to the reality of his own weakness, his fear of engagement, his fear of judgment. The grin on his face is a defensive smirk, and it reduces to inconsequence everything it embraces. As he concludes, "You buy, sell, marry, don't marry, and it's all nothing. You sit on a tree trunk, and it's nothing. Like bubbles in a glass of soda-water."

Witold is not nearly so fortunate, and his hunger for ever more intricate, more rapidly proliferating fictions and mysteries is symptomatic of his anxiety. As Stekel notes, "One can see that compulsion symptoms are the consequences of unsuccessful repression. The successful repression does not lead to neurotic symptoms." There is an extended passage in *Cosmos* in which Witold achieves the illusion of buoyant camaraderie with Leo, as they sit together in the great outdoors wielding words like rapiers aimed at the treacherous heart of a world they feel they never made. It is all rather light, and yet reverberant with an intensity born of Witold's desire to be at one with Leo, and subsequently to still the gnawing sensation of his own inadequacies and betrayals. ". . . It now seemed to me that we were both working together at something, working hard. Working hard at a long-term job," reflects Witold, and truly there is a sense in which this is an accurate description. Masturbatory fantasies are indeed difficult to maintain, do call upon great reserves of mental energy. D. H. Lawrence once remarked that "the only positive effect of masturbation is that it seems to release a certain mental energy, in some people. But it is mental energy which manifests itself always in the same way, in a vicious circle of analysis and impotent criticism, or else a vicious circle of false and easy sympathy, sentimentalities." Lawrence writes as an arch-opponent of onanism, it is useful to remember, and he saw the masturbator as a threat to the moral fabric of the world to which his sympathies were committed. Gombrowicz, on the other hand, writes from within the perspective of the masturbator, and while his Witold is hardly at ease in his life, Leo manages very nicely, as we have seen. So it is not masturbation, or even onanism as a subject with which Gombrowicz is concerned. There is no conventional subject matter of a kind we can identify in the sense that we can speak of man's inhumanity to man, or greed as the root of corruption, or what have you. Gombrowicz writes, it would seem, because he must, and he uses Witold as a mask so that he can objectify his misgivings about himself, strike out and find a source for his difficulties in the world. There is nothing peculiar about this, and in a sense it is the staple dynamic of the serious artist's relationship to his material. What makes Witold as unhappy and desperate as he is, and makes *Cosmos* more a clinical document than a novel can afford to be, however, is that while Gombrowicz knows what he is doing, knows that his maneuvers relieve him hardly at all of his anxieties, and even create new cares, he feels compelled to believe that they are necessary and important, and as a result can do nothing to banish them. What we have in *Cosmos* is an extreme version of a phenomenon that confronts us as we contemplate a number of key passages in Proust's *A La Recherche du Temps Perdu,* a dilemma to which Edmund Wilson addressed himself briefly many years ago in *Axel's Castle:* "Proust's novel, masterly as it is, does perhaps represent a falling over into decadence of psychological fiction: the subjective element is finally allowed to invade and to deteriorate even those aspects of the story which really ought to be kept strictly objective if one is to believe that it is actually happening." Which is to say that Gombrowicz does not objectify successfully in his novel, that the mask of Witold and his various fantasy projections do not serve to take us beyond Gombrowicz's originating obsessions. As Wilson said of Joyce's *Ulysses*, what we have is a "confusion between emotions, perceptions, and reasonings," and not only does Gombrowicz fail to dispel the mists in *Cosmos,* he fails finally to make them either engaging or instructive. All a reader can do is chalk everything up to derangement, posit the hypothetical psychic origins in terms we have suggested, and turn off any further inquiry, metaphysical or otherwise.

The maneuvers one comes to expect in *Cosmos* are not only in the nature of vengeful or spiteful impulses, sometimes acted upon, more often hoarded and furtively nurtured. They are largely intellectual maneuvers, such as befit a confirmed masturbator, but they go much beyond the specific fantasies that feed physical self-abuse. They involve a predictable sequence of imperatives which cannot be interrupted, for they are connected to each other by a kind of logical necessity that has little of conventional philosophic logic about it. Stekel reminds us that "the compulsion neurotic is the prototype of the doubter. If compulsion did not intervene, doubt would paralyze all decisions, life would be impossible." And we think of the passage in *Cosmos,* so reminiscent of John Barth's portrait of Jacob Horner in *The End Of The Road,* in which

Witold finds himself trapped, confronted by the need to make a decision in the sort of casual situation one is usually able to handle unconsciously. Walking through the woods one day he is about to pass between two insignificant stones, when his attention is momentarily distracted by a loosened patch of earth and an old black tree root, and he consequently makes a small digression from the original path of his walk: ". . . it was a minimal diversion amounting to nothing at all, but there was no real reason for it, and that, I think, disconcerted me. So I mechanically made another minor diversion to pass between the two stones as I had originally intended, but I experienced a certain difficulty about this, a very slight difficulty, it is true, deriving from the fact that in view of these two successive diversions my intention to pass between the stones had assumed the quality of a decision, a trivial decision, needless to say, but nevertheless a decision. There was no excuse for this, of course, for the total neutrality of the objects lying in the grass justified no decision . . . Silence, drowsiness, sleep, dreams. In these circumstances I decided to pass between the two stones. But the few moments that had passed made the decision more of a decision than ever, and how was one to decide since it made no difference either way?"

Ultimately Witold is enabled to move by thinking of the chain of objects which he has invested with symbolic importance, and for which he has speculatively established an intelligible relationship of which no amount of reasoned refutation can disabuse him. He moves because the immobility, the mute incommunicability of these various objects (a hanged sparrow, a bit of wood dangling from a bit of slender thread in the forest, a cat which Witold has himself strangled) frightens him with the specter of his own frozen condition achieving a permanence that would fix him as these other projections of his obsession are fixed. Having posited a chain of objects and of related events, the shapes of mouths, the position of clenched hands, all conspiring together towards a vision of universal rot and evil design, Witold fears suddenly that he may become part of the chain, one more trophy to be left standing with the others, alarming and inscrutable. What he hates is the doubt that would take his life, paralyzing even the most basic functions, and this is a doubt that stems from his general inability to trust the evidence of his senses. Toiling under the burden of innumerable minor imperatives which he understands but partially, if at all, he is stricken by an appalling awareness of the absurdity implicit in our victimization at the hands of oppressor-figures, the authorities with which we must deal all our lives. To these imperatives he submits, from fear of punishment, but he harbors resentments and makes plans to take his revenge. The submission, then, is only apparent, not real or convincing where Witold is concerned. Stekel observes that "the compulsion neurotic accepts no law apart from his own. He hates the Logos. His actions, which often seem completely alogical, are to be understood only as protests against the rule of the Logos. *He obeys the secret laws of his own psyche.* He maintains a Logos of his own, and only by analysis can we study it. The meaningless then becomes the meaningful; the stupidities are manifestations of profound wisdom; and madness is method."

Witold's maneuvers, then, constitute a response to imperatives which to observers outside his psychic system of equivalences and symbolic units may well appear meaningless, stupid, mad, but they are at least his imperatives to manufacture and structure as he likes. What is so desperate about the entire scheme, though, is that while Witold conspires in every way he can to banish doubt by setting himself apart from the ordinary run of things to which most of us are acquiescent, he has no possibility of accomplishing what he wants. Stekel tells us that "doubt remains. A neurotic doubt cannot be settled with finality. Urgently, unceasingly it reiterates its demands for the solution of the one burning question which is unanswerable [usually, I should say, some version of: Whose needs are more urgent, mine or everyone else's? May I in good conscience look to myself, even at the expense of certain cultural imperatives to which I cannot willingly bind myself? Is there always to exist a naked opposition between me and the world I would appropriate to my wishes?]. Thus one compulsion symptom after another develops." Thus, as Witold completes one psychic maneuver, ridding himself of a momentary panic experienced in the face of something which had seemed to bear down on him and press him to its bosom, he concludes, "I felt I was in a state of mortal sin," and proceeds to the next compulsive maneuver. As he looks about him, at his companion and at himself, he conceives a way of evading the urgent necessity of resolution in the moment, of dealing in some substantial way with what always seems to him intolerably difficult, which is the coming together in meaningful communion of two separate beings. But he sees the futility of his intended maneuver: "Neither of us was sufficiently here, we were like projections from somewhere else, from the house we had left behind, we were weak and sickly phantoms not really here at all, like non-seeing figures in dreams who are bound up with something else."

Though Witold refers in this passage to the Wotjys house from which the country excursion in *Cosmos* began, the phrasing even in translation is unmistakably significant of more than may at first be noticed. For Gombrowicz is intimating nothing less than the futility of his entire imaginative project, pointing to the insubstantiality of his fiction, its failure to convince, to engage that suspension of disbelief the novelistic fiction requires to work its magic effectually. Witold is aware of himself, and of Lena, who stands beside him, as "projections from somewhere else," and that is indeed how we relate to them. The burden of the novelist's narrative was to have evoked a variety of presences as though they actually existed in the here and now of the reader's imaginative life, to have rendered them as present for us. This does not occur. The burden of imaginative endeavor for Witold within the structure of the novel was to have evoked for himself, in a similar way, the reality of everything around him *as symbolic representation.* What he had proposed to do for himself was to establish the eternal credibility of patent fictions, fictions that would validate his own sense of things as invariably focused in a single direction. What he experiences instead is the masturbator's revulsion from the inadequacy of his own fantasy projections, so that, as Steven Marcus wrote in *The Other Victorians,* "Recognition dispels the dream of omnipotence and returns one to oneself, alone and palely loitering on the cold hill's side." Between the subjective consciousness and its anticipated appropriation of reality, and the reality in itself, falls the shadow, and doubt is perpetual. It is one thing to say, of course, as the critic Taylor Stoehr has written, that serious writers are not "fooled by their own fantasies, nor do their readers imagine that the things described are actually happening — any more than the author or reader of a recipe is fooled into thinking he is eating when his mouth waters at the thought of it." But it is quite another thing to suggest that readers of recipes and readers of novels are engaging in comparable activities, or that we are not genuinely moved out of our habitual concerns and awarenesses to the degree that we submit ourselves to the novel before us. We do not like to think we are fooled, to be sure, and since we willingly give ourselves to the artistic fiction only if it gives evidence of deserving such an abandonment of our self-possession, only if we stand really to gain from the attention we will lavish on it, we cannot sincerely complain that we are fooled. What we do complain about is the failure of the serious fiction to handle its materials in a way that can be useful to us, so that it gives pleasure as it transfigures the experience upon which it is founded. "If art is anything, it is everything," claims Robbe-Grillet, "in which case it must be self-sufficient, and there can be nothing beyond it." The house Witold cannot seem to leave behind is the house of Gombrowicz's own stricken imagination, flushing its tired and dirty waters over everything in Witold's universe, turning the dialectic of experience into a frozen landscape. It is not a situation with which Witold can do very much, for it is responsive to him in one way only, having its origin in his subjectivity alone, and owing to him its very existence. It cannot resist the voracious singularity of his need, and weakens him by permitting him to tie ever tighter the bonds he fastens to himself. And it cannot but be an appalling, a de-pleting spectacle for us, who in our desire to connect with the fictive vision, to sympathize, are confronted with a closed system so rigidly determined that it is all but impenetrable to an alien emotion of any kind. It refuses both criticism and complicity.

What is left to us as readers, then, is understanding, and this we can claim only in a very limited way, for as Witold will not hold himself open to those imaginative incursions we might choose to make, incursions possibly of a therapeutic nature, we tend to hold ourselves more and more aloof from him, to resent the screen of absolute resistance the neurotic fiction erects. We come around more and more securely to a view of Witold, and of his creator incidentally, as simply and irrevocably ill, and to the degree that his behavior and his thoughts may be accounted for in a clinical document like Stekel's, we feel increasingly less involved in his "case." We are not, after all, therapists, and Witold gives no evidence of an intention to bring his problems before us in a way that would elicit a participatory, truly sympathetic response. In Michel Foucault's *Madness And Civilization,* we read that "the constitution of madness as a mental illness, at the end of the eighteenth century, affords the evidence of a broken dialogue, posits the separation as already effected, and thrusts into oblivion all those stammered, imperfect words without fixed syntax in which the exchange between madness and reason was made. The lan-guage of psychiatry, which is a monologue of reason *about* madness, has been established only on the basis of such a silence." What we long for, in reading *Cosmos,* is just the stammered accent the loss of which Foucault bemoans, an accent rich in implication which would surrender its meanings less predictably. What we want is the novelistic mystery that preserves for us a sense of the sympathetically human, richly ambiguous and unique personality, such as we recognize in figures as disparate as Tolstoy's Anna Karenina and Camus's Meursault. A novel like *Cosmos* almost demands that we adopt the language of psychiatry, that "monologue of reason about madness" which is indeed inadequate to deal with Witold and his creator as we would like.

And what then do we see in the novel, what is it we understand too well? The sources of Witold's disorder we have touched upon in sufficient detail, I should think, to justify our giving increased attention to the symptomatology of Witold's compulsion neurosis. Stekel notes that "the thought processes of compulsion neurotics are similar to those of primitive man. The primitive thinks alogically, or, as Levy-Bruhl states in his *Primitive Mentality,* prelogically. Equally apparent is the analogy to mystical thinking. The compulsion neurotic, like the primitive, thinks mystically. He joins the primitive in animism. He does not recognize the

difference between the animate and the inanimate. Everything is animate!"
Now there is a sense in which, again, the features described by Stekel do
correspond rather closely to what we might call poetical thinking, or
perhaps simply the artistic sensibility. But we must recognize that the
writer is successful only when there is a reciprocal interplay between
subject and object, between the inner and the outer worlds. When Robbe-
Grillet speaks of the self-sufficiency of the work of art he assumes this
interplay as a prime requisite without which such sufficiency is inconceivable, or sterile at best. If the poet or novelist must indulge a vision that is
determinedly alogical, and if it is analogous to mystical thinking in certain
respects, there must be in its final expression a control, an order that is
accessible as an object of our admiration and concern. The mystic vision,
the fusion of contraries it may effect, the expressed identity of wish and
fact, must be framed by a kind of severe decorum whose influence we
cannot avoid. This is not what we discover in *Cosmos*. When Witold and
Fuchs find the corpse of a sparrow hanging from a tree in the woods as
they make their way to the Wotjys household, they are infected by it as
by a disease, and it follows them about wherever they go. Witold reports:
"I was slightly annoyed at the sparrow's coming back and haunting us like
this, flaunting itself in front of us as if it were swelling and inflating itself
and making itself out to be more important and interesting than it really
was." We recognize in this passage the presence of reality, but it is more
modest than we could wish, and though Witold later acknowledges "the
futility of those so-called signs which were not signs," it is clear all along
that for him the impulse to create reality as by fiat is overmastering. To
look at a ceiling in a casual moment and come up with the following train
of reflections is surely indication of special psychic propensities: "But a
little farther away, near the window, the tedious whiteness changed into
a darker, wrinkled zone which had been affected by damp, and inspection
revealed a complicated geography of continents, gulfs, islands . . . and
other oblique, fugitive lines. In places it looked unhealthy, like a skin
disease, here raging wild and unbridled, there adorned haphazardly with
curves and arabesques . . . Totally absorbed as I was by these things and
my own internal complications, I gazed at them, persistently and yet
without any particular concentration . . ."

We notice here the way Witold slurs "these things and my own
internal complications" as though he were speaking of a single phenomenon rather than juxtaposing alien entities. It is the sort of slurring that we
find throughout the text of *Cosmos*, and where the peculiarity is as
explicit as it is in the passage cited above, we almost feel that Gombrowicz has consciously installed it to remind us of the kind of fiction we are
witnessing. Witold tells us, for another instance, that any random thing

"somehow increased my resentment against my parents and reinforced my revolt against Warsaw and everything connected with it." Here, of course, the identification of the parental authority with the Polish city of Warsaw brings us once again to think of the author's unmistakable implication in his own fiction, of Gombrowicz's resentment of his native Poland, the rulers of which have been so ungenerous to him and his work, enforcing his exile from 1939 to the time of his death in 1969. At still another point in *Cosmos* we read: ". . . with no thoughts in my head, I just looked, feeling weak among all those insignificant trifles . . .; and at the same time I felt like someone trying to recreate his own strange and inexplicable past life." And finally: "What was I looking for? A basic theme, a *leitmotiv*, an axis, something of which I could take firm hold and use as a basis for reconstructing my personality here?" Witold's problem is not that he lacks logic, but that he cannot use it, and insofar as the function atrophies from disuse, he comes to rely more insistently upon compulsive alogic, and the accents with which this alogic is evoked are hardly inspirational, hardly what the seeker after visionary truth might expect.

The consequence of Witold's disastrous affair with the world, of his refusal to deal with it at least in part as it demands, is the emergence of that bizarre method or system Stekel describes, a method reliant upon the conversion of the meaningless to the meaningful, the random fact to the status of symptom. We know that every literary vision revolves about perceptual conventions of one kind or another, and the matter of rigorous selection is taken for granted in accounting for the particulars of any work of art. In many novels an author will make the process by which we come to see this principle of selection the basis of our interest in the work. *Cosmos,* though, reads too much like a puzzle, the pieces of which are so obviously numbered that elements both of mystery and play are rigorously excluded. Even the more subtle and dexterous varieties of what we might label the fabulistic genre in modern fictional narrative, from Iris Murdoch's *Flight From the Enchanter* to John Barth's *Giles Goat Boy,* suffer a bit from mechanical excess, and if *Cosmos* seems more urgent and sincere than anything Barth has given us, it is still less satisfying as a narrative, less various and reverberant in universal implication. Particulars are related and combined like the elements in a differential calculus, all defined by a constant Witold describes as the perpetual "return to my own horribleness, my own dirt, my crime, my imprisonment in myself, my self-condemnation." The sense of sin and the necessary punishment which in the psychological scheme of things must follow is translated for Witold into a fear of castration — the masturbator will be served with his just reward! As he sits at the dinner table watching others eat, he focuses on

Leo Wotjys: "He laughed. He was carefully buttering and salting a radish, after cutting off its tail." An apparent clue in Witold's search for what seems to him a pervasive degeneracy is a broken pole, found pointing significantly to the maid's room, a room pulsing with the promise of perverse secrets. Looking up at a configuration of lines drawn on a ceiling that seem to suggest an arrow, Witold remarks: ". . . but the main thing, the shaft of the arrow wasn't there." And what should Leo show Witold as a relic of his one extramarital affair, the site of which is the goal of their family excursion into the countryside: "He suddenly rose from the table and came back with a dried-up stick. 'It comes from there,' he announced." And finally, though we might extend the sequence of details to include a great many others, what proves to be the most startling and momentarily baffling event in the entire first section of the novel is the deafening sound of Leo's wife Kulka beating a tree-stump with the blunt edge of an axe. "'I was only hitting the tree stump,'" she says, and Witold adds that she "extracted these words from a vast, an infinite, store of patience, the patience of a martyr." One, that is, who has been married for many years to a masturbator, exemplary though his behavior would seem to have been, and who can take out her frustrations in a violent display that for Gombrowicz, at least, must be chillingly appropriate. Like the raging skin disease Witold sees in the ceiling's linear geography, with its intimation of the severe penalties children learn to expect as a consequence of masturbation.

It is strange that a novel with a first-person narrator, with a single point of view, should yet fail to allow the world its status as an independent object of consciousness, for this is generally a function of such a narrative approach. In *Cosmos,* however, everything is contaminated by the narrator's obsession to the extent that what we take away from the novel is an experience of restriction, where the novel familiarly enlarges the field of possibility even as its problematical structures concede ultimate defeat, that is, our failure to experience the world as meaningful in terms of our individual projects. In a study of the philosopher-critic George Lukács, Fredric Jameson describes the novelistic hero as a solitary subjectivity who "must always stand in opposition to his setting, to nature or society, inasmuch as it is precisely his relation to them, his integration into them, which is the issue at hand . . . The prototype of the novel's hero is therefore the madman or the criminal; the work is his biography, the story of his setting forth to 'prove his worth' in the emptiness of the world. But of course he can never really do so, for if genuine reconciliation were possible, then the novel as such would cease to exist, would once more give place to epic wholeness." Now Witold, we know, is both madman and, to a lesser extent, criminal, for in the course of the novel he strangles Lena's cat and hangs its body on a laundry hook. Moreover, his sense of his own pervasive guilt makes him increasingly conscious of himself as a criminal as the novel develops, so that after killing the cat and leading his comrades astray he reflects: "While telling these lies I felt pleasure mounting inside me, pleasure at leading them astray, at being no longer with them but against them . . . As if the cat had put me on the obverse side of the medal and I was now in a realm of hieroglyphics, where occult and mysterious things took place." The cat, representing Witold's active, if destructive and momentary, engagement with the world, takes him finally further and further from it. ". . . By acting we shall create reality," says Witold at another point in the novel, and indeed that is what he does in a certain manner of speaking. Witold's murder of the cat validates for him, makes authentic and thoroughly credible, what he had long felt about himself though with pitifully little evidence to go on. He makes a brief foray into the world the better to confirm his isolation in the prison of the self and its monomaniacal obsession. The structure of *Cosmos* is for Gombrowicz a simple fantasy of wish-fulfillment, and this is not something we can legitimately find objectionable. What we must lament, though, is its consistent inability to stimulate our desires, and thereby in any way to gratify them, or to help us define our values. It is one thing for a protagonist to "stand in opposition to his setting," as Jameson contends, but to evoke that setting as a mere repetition of static forms is to render such an opposition both futile and meaningless for all but the author, who can imagine nothing else.

What we understand, of course, falling back once again on the single responsive function *Cosmos* allows us, is that the emptiness of the world Witold habitually confronts is nothing more nor less than his own hollow identity. Of this *horror vacui* we have already had something to say, but we have not perhaps suggested with sufficient emphasis the range of mechanisms available to the character who would mitigate this experience. Stekel notes that compulsion neurotics "believe in their own omnipotence. To these people a wish is capable of killing, or at least inflicting harm. They also attribute this power to the wishes of others." And later he writes: "In believing in his own miraculous power, the compulsion neurotic identifies himself with God and devil. As a child he played magician and devil, he played with thoughts of his own omnipotence, and now, in later life, he can not free himself of this belief." In other words, if we are to see Witold in these terms, though he may once in *Cosmos* "create reality" by acting, he in fact does nothing but create reality in his perpetual self-preoccupation. All we get in *Cosmos* are pseudo-events and concocted settings imposed by a will that is everywhere implicated in its own fiction. When Witold describes for us a setting to which his thoughts frequently return, we know it is a mental landscape we are shown, the manifestation of a wish to pollute the most harmless and chance encounter with the specter of his own infamy: ". . . there were some bird-droppings on the wall. But the heat was different here, and so was the smell, it suggested urine, and I had a sense of remoteness . . . not far away there was a compost heap." Attributions of personality characteristics flow from Witold with sheer abandon and the conviction of absolute omnipotence Stekel described. Unwilling to go back to the setting he has evoked, though wanting to rehearse it all just the same, Witold thinks of Fuchs, and is quieted: "I felt certain that Fuchs would be going to have a look for me. His interior void was bound to take him there." Later he returns himself, and the ambience of excremental filth originally evoked assumes for us the quality of a displacement, symbolic of a transferral of negative feelings from the true source of anxiety to something less specifically painful. The second visit to this focal setting gives rise to: "You could feel the heat coming off the wall, as well as a smell of urine or apples, and just to one side there was a drainage ditch and some yellowed grasses," and we recognize the locus of Witold's fear in the idea of heterosexual contact. Indeed, no more grotesque account of feminine sexuality, the alien nature of the absolute other, may be imagined, replete as it is with allusion to forbidden fruit, the fall of man from his original, onanistic paradise, and the whole panoply of archetypal, neurotic associations.

The sensation of omnipotence that Witold experiences, then, does not enable him to alter the fundamental bearing of his life, but to validate the initial trajectory dictated by his obsession. To state or conceive an idea may be for Witold to invest it with truth, but we may be sure that a very narrow range of ideas is all the character can handle. His fictive adventure does not portend revelation in any biblical sense, for what in other circumstances might be called "concealed meanings" are not concealed at all. *Cosmos* is complete, and in looking at it there is an end to interpretation. Having suddenly determined to kill Lena, near the novel's end, Witold knows precisely the explanation he will need to represent the notion as reasonable to himself. "If I wanted to kill her it followed that she must be in love with me." And in a sense of course, from Witold's point of view, nothing could be clearer or more inevitable, for feeling strongly about Lena as he does, what can he do but protect her from the vileness by which he measures his every gesture? And with what better reason than the threat Lena's affection might represent to the security of his self-absorption can he acknowledge his desire to violate and destroy her? It is all very involved, and perfectly obvious, and despite the tone of somnambulistic excess that filters its fine grains over characters and events in *Cosmos,* we know we shall see through the screen without difficulty.

Apprised as we are of Witold's basic wishes, and given the relatively consistent features of compulsive neurotic behavior we find in these pages, how can we but understand? During the rural excursion trip, attended by members of the Wotjys household and by two additional newlywed couples, Witold's responses are quite what we might have projected, though mounted with some versatility by Gombrowicz. The most aggressively sensual young woman on the trip, Jadeczka, is bound to inspire in Witold the reflection, or something akin to it, that she "was rather like those bodily smells that are tolerable only to the person who produces them." In this manner is the threat she might represent put down. And her husband, of course, is drawn as one who "tried hard to be at the same level of ecstasy as she. But there was a slight air of martyrdom about him." In fact, this air of martyrdom circulates stealthily in the novel, like a warm current that beats back the breath and leaves one exhausted and dry. Only the martyrdom and its related sufferings have their counterpart in a violence, an inclination to revenge, that are equally pervasive. If Witold is made to wince under what he considers "a sort of marital pressure" that weighs upon everything in the course of the trip, he will see to it that a compensatory fantasy will hold sway, or several. Thus a country priest is picked up on the road and taken along on the excursion: ". . . he was ungainly, rustic, pitiful, and it looked to me as if he perhaps had something on his conscience. What was he doing with those fat fingers of his? Oh those fingers moving between his knees." The ambience of the literary put-on vies here with the note of genuine neurotic obsession, but *Cosmos* is not a put-on. The absurd rings true in a peculiar way, and we find it hard to laugh even where we think laughter might just be legitimate. At the end of *Cosmos* Witold finds Lena's husband Louis dangling from a tree limb, hanged by his own trouser belt, and proceeds to toy with the corpse, putting his finger in its mouth and so on. "This absurd corpse promptly turned into a rational corpse," Witold tells us, and this we accept only in the sense that the monotonous dynamic of *Cosmos* would not have been drawn to its ordained conclusion without this hanging. Louis, after all, had earlier been "caught" by our peeping narrator undressing before his already unclothed bride and retiring with her into the darkness and privacy of their marital chamber, all in the most routine and casual way. What more appropriate ending for him could an obsessional thinking devise? All we can do, confronted by the pattern, is to mutter some equivalent of, "So he has come full circle," and consign Witold everlastingly to the mechanisms that course through him like a fate. Unless, that is, he'd be willing to have us recommend a good therapist.

In his book on Genet, Sartre writes that "The Marquis de Sade dreamt of extinguishing the fires of Etna with his sperm. Genet's arrogant madness goes further: he jerks off the universe." Now Gombrowicz's neurosis does not have about it that quality of arrogance, and it is perhaps more natural to compare the author of *Cosmos* to a Kafka, to one who is played with by the hands of the world, than to a Genet. And yet, as we have seen, there is an element of that very transubstantiation we associate with Genet in Gombrowicz's novel. The manipulation of reality to conform to the imperatives of erotic fantasy is unmistakable, and if Witold's exertions in *Cosmos* are hardly such as to culminate in orgasmic release, at least not in any direct way, some psychic version of that release is surely potentiated by his maneuverings. Both Witold and Genet devour the world, or engulf it, and work at its reduction to the stature of an erect phallus, compact and manipulable. The difference between them resides in the area of human will, or freedom, an area we earlier indicated was especially unattractive for Gombrowicz's character. Sartre makes the point that evil, as a concomitant of a certain kind of madness that stems from an individual's desire to be revenged upon the world, must yet be gratuitous, must like the pursuit of good be its own reward. "If you steal, or even kill, in order to live, living is a good. You have reduced plunder and murder to the role of means." In reading *Cosmos,* we feel that Witold is simply driven by his obsessions, that he exercises virtually no element of choice at all, and his example is consequently dispiriting. Genet, on the other hand, while what he does may be disgusting, is never dispiriting, for he has chosen himself, freely decided to elaborate upon the role originally imposed upon him by the authorities of culture, the role of outcast and criminal. To say that "he jerks off the universe" is to attribute to him the passion for perversity, for overstepping the grounds of the conventional, that he deserves. The field of action in *Cosmos* is a paltry spectacle by comparison. Where Genet is willing to be used by the good citizens of his culture, to be hated by them as the potentially revolutionary aspect of themselves which they must reject, Gombrowicz's character retreats before our eyes into the privileged sanctuary of neurosis, into a defensive behavioral pattern that is forever invulnerable to hatred, fear, or judgment of any kind. Gombrowicz is neither concerned with meaning in any broad philosophical or human sense, nor with an assertion of the self's contingent potency in the face of a world order that frequently refuses to compromise to satisfy our needs. His concern is with his own equilibrium and, in the final analysis, with himself in a way that Genet, no less than any of us, would find merely pathetic.

SIX

ATTITUDES TOWARD SEX IN AMERICAN "HIGH CULTURE"

Thirty-five years ago, in his remarkable novel *Towards a Better Life*, Kenneth Burke admonished us to remember "that as the corrective of wrong thinking is right thinking, the corrective of all thinking is the body." Set as it is in the context of an elegant and extremely high-toned fiction, Burke's sentence could not have meant for his original readers what it says for us. More perhaps than he knew, Burke anticipated an inclination which has become almost a formalized convention of the serious literature at present being written and discussed in this country. The body has become for our writers that oracle wherein lie value and truth, and balm for the pains of consciousness. Our literature is created under the same star which has guided the fantasies of pornographers since the origins of that frequently black, yet somehow sacred profession. If our more serious writers are more than pious pornographers, there is at the same time no doubt that they represent experience largely "as seen through the eye of a penis." Steven Marcus's sniggering, even condescending, indictment of pornography on this ground, as on others (in his book *The Other Victorians*), serves as well to describe manifestations rampant in contemporary high culture, though it is possible that we disagree on what is "high" and on what is "culture."

So that there shall be no mistaking what we are observing here, it may be necessary to mention that for our purposes the word "culture" is to be taken in its narrowest sense, signifying the collected presence and impact of all works of the creative imagination in every medium, as well as that body of criticism and philosophy which seeks perpetually to alter

From *The Annals of the American Academy of Political and Social Science*, March 1968.

or encourage or simply to explain the work with which it deals. It is not as easy to locate what we mean by "high" culture, and any definition will inevitably seem exclusivist to those more or less serious practitioners of an art, or their defenders, who cannot comfortably be placed within the magic circle, as it were. Acquiescently to extend the circumference of such a circle is no answer, however, for this would constitute an evasion of standards, and a sacrifice of that taste which it is the duty of every critic vainly to parade before his readers, as the badge both of his conviction and his fallibility. The serious literature to which I shall refer, then, will indicate my impressions of what is significant in contemporary culture. So that our focus will not be overly dispersed, we shall concentrate primarily on a few recent books of fiction which readily illustrate particular attitudes towards sex that I should like to explore.

To return, then, to the body — we having successfully, one would hope, mastered that inclination to be content with mere sex in the head which a no less renowned sexual reactionary than D. H. Lawrence could propose as a viable possibility for mature men and women — to that body which beckons to us, no longer sinful, nor even dirty, nor yet beautiful, but brimming nonetheless with promise, the promise of deliverance from all that is inauthentic or smugly innocent. What courses through our literature is this promise, rarely if ever kept, yet never wholly abandoned, as if all other frontiers had been reached, all other modes of knowing explored, and nothing left to do but plug on in search of that ultimate body which we plunder in our dreams, or that apocalyptic orgasm in which all barriers are magically removed, all connections passionately restored.

It is curious that a countertendency may be discerned in the literature of our high culture, though a tendency which similarly exalts the importance of the body. Among the writers of this second group, there is a conviction of the body as a limitation, a limitation which must be pursued. Here involvement with the body represents not a path to vitality nor a means to making contact with what is most real and complex in oneself. Instead, the body is seen as a mode of escape from painful realities, a mode of forgetfulness, in a sense a mode of a blessed nonbeing. In both tendencies, the body is cultivated as a means of redirecting energy and attention — in the one case, away from what is lying, hypocritical, convenient, inauthentic; in the other case, away from what may, in fact, be too utterly authentic, too much a pattern of experience in which one has been rendered the passive spectator of one's own inglorious dissolution.

SEX AS MAGIC

Probably the most talented, serious, and proclaimed champion of apocalyptic sexuality in this country is Norman Mailer, whose recent works of fiction have been received with howls of dismay and disbelief. *An American Dream* is a pop-art caricature of ideas which Mailer has held for some time, but which somehow never seemed quite so banal and ludicrous as they now largely appear. This is not at all to suggest what so many critics have insisted upon: that the novel is simply bad. Mailer can do more with a line of English prose than any man currently writing fiction. His imagination is teeming with invention, and his metaphors have the reach of genius. But Mailer's great gifts cannot conceal the fact that Mailer is a rather corny romantic who has been posing for years as a kind of big bad boy, obsessed by visions of brutality and voracious sexuality. As Elizabeth Hardwick has observed, "No heat arises from [the novel's] many brutal couplings." Through everything, one sees Mailer himself, sweating to make us feel something he himself cannot feel. His characters have no real lives of their own to which we can respond. They are plastic creatures, whom Mailer consistently fails to motivate adequately. Mailer is pathetically anxious for us to believe in his vision, and his earnest entreaties are frequently embarrassing.

Mailer's protagonist Stephen Richards Rojack is a war-hero, a former congressman, a one-time friend of Jack Kennedy, and an intellectual who compares the pain of a shrapnel wound to the "delicious pain clean as a mistress' sharp teeth going 'Yummy' in your rump." Clearly, an extraordinary character! In every way he appears to be a libertarian type, but in the first pages of the novel he gives himself away. His wife Deborah has committed five confessed adulteries during the eight years of their marriage, and Rojack recognizes each of these adulteries, with its subsequent revelation, as "an accent, a transition, a concrete step in the descent of our marriage." Rojack values fidelity as an index of love, in the most conventional way possible. For all his brutal frankness, Rojack is as puritanical as one might expect him to be, given his swagger and his panting insecurities. He speaks of the sexuality implicit in the act of murder, with its thrill of violent release, and Rojack indeed does murder his wife. But there is nothing erotic in the actual murder. The woman's neck is broken, and her corpse thrown out of a window, without any voluptuous emotions attendant upon the scene. In fact, the whole thing is not even titillating in the way one expects of a good horror story. Rojack is practically unconscious throughout the proceedings, moving from step to step almost in a trance. Nowhere is there a trace of passion or conviction.

Inevitably, he rushes to climb into bed with the German maid, whom he surprises, "all five fingers fingering like a team of maggots at her open heat. She was off in that bower of the libido where she was queen." They make violent love, Mailer permitting us to imagine for ourselves just how Rojack managed to pry those fingers from that "open heat." Rojack's bout with Ruta may best be described as a hysterico-comic exercise in advanced gymnastics. Back and forth Rojack springs, from orifice to orifice, fore and aft, "a raid on the Devil and a trip back to the Lord." Ultimately, full of guilt, Rojack drops his load at the door of the Devil.

It is appropriate that a book espousing apocalyptic sexuality should employ a reasonably flexible religious terminology. What is important for Rojack is making the correct connections during and as a result of his sexual transports. He views the sexual act as a kind of test in which he is gravely judged, not for his virility or endurance, but for his courage and profundity. Rojack's very soul is somehow at stake even in the most casual encounters. He worries over his commitment to life, and sees in each sexual lapse or crudity an acquiescence in that death-wish which laps at our very heels.

Rojack wants to be a Faustian type, but he is too much a victim of conventions that he thinks he has passed beyond. He wants to fly in the face of a civilization for which he would like to have righteous contempt. In identifying his stubborn reluctance to abandon anal intercourse with an attraction to the Devil, Rojack is passing a severe judgment on himself. For him, there is something sinful in following his own instinct or whim, for such indulgence denies man's fundamental responsibility to subject himself to a will more general and embracing than his own. In denying Ruta her orgasm, when she had every right to expect that Rojack would "think of her," he calls down a judgment upon his head. Rojack's happiness, or his right to experiment with human life, whether on a purely physical or emotional level, cannot be positive values in themselves, but must subserve the more basic requirement of preserving respect for the feelings and even for the gratification of others. In the light of Rojack's bowing before such an ethic, it is rather appalling to think how little he suffers over the murder of his wife. One can only conclude that, for Rojack, the taking of a life is a minor matter compared with the integrity of one's performance between the sheets.

There is something faintly touching and not a little bit absurd in attributing to poor coitus a burden of such momentous gravity. Indeed, Mailer's characters display the sort of elaborate, one might almost say literary, awareness of themselves and the symbolic significance of their every genital thrust which renders the possibility of their experiencing true passion or release highly unlikely. At its most intense, Mailer's characters seem to feel, sexual activity has the capacity of conferring on both participants an awareness of grace, of that still point in the midst of flux in which the sorrows of the world wash by, are lamented, but cannot really disturb the fundamental equilibrium so tenuously achieved. In *An Amer-*

ican Dream, predictably, Rojack falls in love, with a girl named Cherry, no less. Naturally the full magnitude and depth of their feeling for one another is understood during intercourse. Rojack and Cherry barely know each other as people, but there is something bittersweet in Cherry's juices which tells Rojack he has found the thing he has needed. Cherry is for Rojack a symbol of the eternal victim, a perpetual child in a world that plunders and corrupts and uses those who cling to their innocence. When Cherry spreads her mournful legs, it is consolation she seeks, not an electric charge. For Rojack and Cherry, sex is an activity which ideally takes one out of the body, and enables a communion with the diverse and determinedly unresponsive elements in the universe.

A reader must ask himself whether such projections can be valid. What the question really comes down to, of course, is whether Mailer has been able to make them appear, if not reasonable, then at least conceivable for us. It is difficult to consider Mailer's vision of human sexuality other than as symptomatic of a kind of pathological attempt to impose will on an experience which ought to be less a matter of will than of untrammeled emotion. Undoubtedly, there is something unpleasantly expedient, if not crude, in attempting to draw a distinction between aspects of human behavior which never function wholly independently of one another, and yet I think it is a distinction which must be drawn if we are to see what Mailer and other writers have done.

Rojack experiences a sexual gratification in which his partner is appreciated to the degree that she fits conveniently into a symbolic pattern which confers peculiar value wholly apart from any actual human qualities the partner may have. We are here in the presence of a phenomenon which is more than familiar, which may, in fact, be a predominating characteristic of western sexuality. Moreover, it involves a mechanism which is intrinsic to an understanding of the western love ethic that exalts marriage and fidelity as keys to fulfillment. In his deservedly classic work, *Love in the Western World,* Denis de Rougemont argues that marital fidelity is based upon a construct which has no particular merit of its own that should recommend it to lovers, aside from the fact that it is a construct which they have decided upon and determined to respect. In de Rougemont's own words:

I propose to speak only of a troth that is observed *by virtue of the absurd* — that is to say, simply because it has been pledged — and by virtue of being an absolute which will uphold husband and wife as persons. Fidelity . . . contradicts the general belief in the revelatory value of both spontaneity and manifold experiences. . . . It denies that its own goal is happiness. It offensively asserts first, that its aim is obedience to a truth that is believed in, and secondly, that it is the expression of a wish to be constructive.

In de Rougemont's view, then, the love ethic by which most men in the Western world have measured themselves, and according to which they have structured their lives, has not been supportive of untrammeled emotion, but has worked as a counterforce to passion. Marital fidelity is profoundly unnatural for any normal human being. Its capacity to gratify lies precisely in the opportunity it affords the individual of transcending the demands of his own ego, the demand, for example, to be happy on the most instinctual level. In marriage, there is a pride in renouncing what one would desire if permitted to do so, and a commitment to an alternative object which is viewed as more important — the willed making of a relationship, despite contingency, despite desires which would thwart one's project. The marital partners are permitted to grow only through obedience to the particular laws and requirements of the relationship that binds them, in a subjection to which they actively consent.

Rojack's view of human sexuality is closely related to and, one would suppose, derivative from this western love ethic. To the degree that sexual pleasure is purely or even largely physical, he considers it base and dehumanizing. He can have little affection for Deborah because "making love she left you with no uncertain memory of having passed through a carnal transaction with a caged animal." Rojack rejects carnal transactions in which he is unable to attach symbolic, even transcendent importance to his partner, and to their shared roles as part of some vast, if arbitrary, scheme. In his earliest sexual encounter with Cherry, Rojack is again disappointed: "We paid our devotions in some church no larger than ourselves." It is the prison of the self from which Rojack wishes to escape. He is embarrassed by the insistent demands, frequently perverse or sadistic, of his ego. For Rojack, sex is a means of replenishing the universe, of infusing the universe with the vitality of original creation. In its most authentic form, sex, like love itself, transcends particular personalities, just as there is a devaluation of particular sexual organs. All that matters is the vow to believe in the value of something which is, at its root, arbitrary and absurd. Rojack makes what one might properly term an extreme statement of this view, after discovering the authenticity of his love for Cherry: "Love was love, one could find it with anyone, one could find it anywhere. It was just that you could never keep it. Not unless you were ready to die for it, dear friend."

The nature of Mailer's apocalyptism has never been clearer. For Mailer, it is not sex itself which opens the gates to Paradise, nor is it the monumental orgasm which shatters forever one's allegiance to the shoddy and banal and mundane. He sees nothing liberating *per se* in the sexual act. In fact, there is almost nothing in Mailer's view of sex that one would expect of a sexual apocalyptist. For Mailer, authentic sexuality is a task, a difficult commitment, for it imposes a terrible burden upon both participants.

It is the burden of perpetually mythologizing the nature of an experience which could so easily represent nothing more than sheer forgetfulness and release. The apocalyptic element in Mailer's vision has to do with the liberating potential of any act of the creative imagination, the imagination which perceives the ostensibly crucial obstacles to harmony among men and things as basically superficial and capable of being transcended. As an activity which enlists the total energies and attention of participants, sex has the capacity to tap man's deepest resources of feeling and thought, which as an artist of considerable distinction, Mailer identifies with the imagination. Far from being an end in itself, sex is merely a kind of catalyst which releases a unique degree of zeal and energy that, in their turn, may alter man's pattern of existence. Moreover, not all or even most sexual activity can make such rewards available. Only sex in which the burden of consciousness is unrelentingly pursued, and in which the full weight of the beloved as an object of, in many ways, impenetrable density is accepted for himself, can promise the fulfillment which Mailer admires. As in de Rougemont's notions of marriage, what is important for Mailer is not happiness, nor the immediate gratification of instincts. Sex, like marriage, is a means to realizing qualities of the human personality which are resolutely unnatural, though qualities which the processes of civilization, and the refinements of culture, have conditioned responsible men to value.

RHETORIC AND WISH-FULFILLMENT

How utterly sophisticated all of this is, despite so much that is ludicrous and crude in Mailer's novel, when one compares it to the fiction of several other talented people who work from a related orientation. Jeremy Larner is a younger writer, whose first novel *Drive, He Said* contains passages of singular virtuosity and extraordinary humor. It fails, however, to give one a clear sense of what Larner really feels on various subjects, not least among these the question of human sexuality. The alternation of heavy-handed satire and an almost hysterical sincerity is handled rather sloppily, so that one cannot quite be certain as to what Larner wishes us to take seriously, and what satirically. Parts of the novel even strike one as patent adolescent wish-fulfillment, as mature, beautiful women permit themselves to be regularly ravished by young students who really have little to recommend them but their ardent desires and, one assumes, healthy erections.

There is considerable attention devoted in this novel to the possibilities of apocalyptic orgasm. The actor Tony Valentine, for example, is known as an orgasm man, who has "fuzzy intimations of how the orgasm might be just one feature of a hitherto unthought of psychic politics that could swing our desperate world into a new wild millennium of pleasure." Unfortunately, Valentine is a preposterous figure, whose intimations are deservedly bestowed with the epithet "fuzzy." Even more unfortunate, though, is that Larner never really tries to come to grips with Valentine's ideas, to which he is inexorably attracted, despite the satirical detachment he manages to affect. Larner's protagonist Hector Bloom takes his sexual transports very seriously indeed, and his friend Gabriel Reuben is driven insane by his inability to combine sexual passion with what he considers true feeling, something apparently distinct from passion in his view. Both Hector and Gabriel view sex in terms of instant revelation, though neither of them is clear on what it is they expect to have revealed. Proper orgasm is supposed to effect all kinds of remarkable transformations not only on a personal level, but in the social and political spheres as well, with attendant metaphysical vibrations. But it is all so much a matter of rhetorical indulgence that one is unable to discuss the ideas in Larner's novel seriously.

In a way, this should not be surprising, either with regard to *Drive, He Said* in particular, or to American writing in general. We have a great tradition of writers who have been consistently unable to deal seriously with sex, particularly with mature sexual relations between fully developed male and female characters. Leslie Fiedler contributed the definitive demonstration of this thesis in *Love and Death in the American Novel,* a book of criticism which perhaps says as much about the American psyche as any book of recent years. Even in the fiction of the 1960s, there is little or no evidence that Fiedler's thesis could not be easily extended. And it is not that we simply lack serious writers. Saul Bellow is a novelist of undeniable genius, but, as V. S. Pritchett has pointed out, his women characters fail to impress as real people. We cannot approach them as we are able to approach Bellow's male protagonists. There is in Bellow's entire fictional output no convincing illumination of the nature of normal sexual relations in American society. In *Herzog,* Bellow makes a valiant effort, but his sexual encounters are bathed in a kind of pathos, or a kind of dreary if occasionally quaint sentimentality which renders them almost ineffably idyllic. On the other hand, the female character who has most to do with the direction taken by the novel's protagonist is in the tradition of the all-American bitch-goddess, a figure whom we need never consider too closely, for we know she is a mere creature of those dire fantasies which we maintain to justify our inexplicable terrors.

To be sure, then, the rhetorical extravagance we have come to associate with most treatments of sex by American writers is understandable as an evasion of fundamental issues which they are still unable or unwilling to treat. It is almost impossible to conceive of an American novelist treating sex with the sort of spare, relentlessly analytic style of certain French

masters who can philosophize about sex without wallowing in sentimentality or yielding to grandiloquence. The one American writer of distinction
who, in her criticism at least, has managed to discuss erotics as a fundamental element in the consideration of any art form is Susan Sontag. Perhaps Sontag's distinction in this area is partially attributable to her profound absorption in European, and especially French, literature. In a
recent article entitled "On Pornography," Sontag dealt at length with
several pornographic novels, including one entitled *Story of O* by a pseu-
donymous author who is conveniently called Pauline Reage. This French
novel has had a wide distribution in this country, and has evoked rather
sober discussion in the more prestigious intellectual and literary publications — perhaps a sign of a new receptivity to the notion of pornography
as potentially serious literature.

There is no need at this point to go into *Story of O*, nor into its predecessors in the distinguished tradition of European pornography, in any
great detail; but it might prove instructive to suggest possible affinities with
works of American fiction which have been popularly characterized as lewd,
if not deliberately pornographic. According to Sontag, what one may justi-
fiably respond to and appreciate in a work like *Story of O* is the integrity
with which the author consistently pursues a largely diabolical vision. There
is no inclination on the part of the author to justify his vision, or the fantasies of characters, as in some way representative of a widely held position. The author is not primarily interested in impressing us with the universal implications of his work, but is more concerned with impressing upon
us the passion and singularity of his absorption in a vision which may be
uniquely his. Nor is the author worried lest we should think him deranged.
What is important is "the originality, thoroughness, authenticity and power
of that 'deranged consciousness' itself, as it is incarnated in a work."

What the more creative and original writers in the European tradition
have understood and accepted is that sex is not a normal activity. Sontag,
as we have learned to expect of her, makes the statement in the most extreme and yet most cogent way: "Even on the level of simple physical sensation and mood, making love surely resembles having an epileptic fit at
least as much, if not more than it does eating a meal or conversing with
someone." In American literature, even when sex is described in patently
brutal or perverse terms, one is almost always conscious of an attempt to
mediate the extremity of the vision to assure us that only very rare (if not
actually deranged) people are capable of a sexual response of inordinate
violence. Even Mailer's Rojack, whom one would not ordinarily expect to
make explicit confessions of inhibition, is driven to cry out in the extremity of physical and emotional passion, when his involvement with Cherry
has become consuming: "Let me love her some way not altogether de-

ranged and doomed. . . . Let me love her and be sensible as well." Unlike the author of a work like *Story of O,* Mailer is not possessed by a vision, but is instead the extremely self-conscious writer balancing several visions of possibility at once. Whatever Mailer says about the demoniacal energies inherent in sexual activity, his own understanding of these energies is mainly literary, and consequently limited in conviction.

PORNO-POLITICS

There is no lack of conviction in Ken Kesey's *One Flew Over the Cuckoo's Nest,* but neither is there an attempt to deal with human sexuality as a complex phenomenon. Kesey's novel is wholly successful as an indictment of modern society, and as an exploration into the kind of subtly repressive mechanisms we help to build into the fabric of our daily lives. Kesey's solution to our common problem is the opening of floodgates, the releasing of energies which have too long lain unused or forgotten. Chief among these are the twin resources of laughter and uninhibited sexuality, the linkage between which Kesey manages to clarify in the course of his novel.

The novel is set in a mental institution which is, in many respects, a microcosm of the society-at-large. It is to Kesey's credit that he never strains to maintain the parallel at any cost — it is a suggested parallel at most, and, where it suits his novelistic purposes, Kesey lets it go completely. His protagonist is one Patrick Randall McMurphy, pronounced psychopathic by virtue of being "overzealous in [his] sexual relations." His purpose in the institution, as in life apparently, is both to have a hell of a good time, and to defy "ball cutters," defined by McMurphy himself as "people who try to make you weak so they can get you to toe the line, to follow their rules, to live like they want you to." McMurphy is a truly monumental character — a gambler, a braggart, a fantastic lover, and a gadfly who insults and goads those who resist his charismatic injunctions. While he is something of a sensualist who dwells regularly on the ecstasies of sexual transport, and even goes so far as to bring his whores into the hospital to restore the vitality of his moribund fellow-psychopaths, McMurphy feels himself and his comrades the victims of women, not their lords and masters as his rhetoric would have it. His techniques of resistance and defiance are mostly pathetic, as they can achieve what are at best pyrrhic victories. One is never tempted to question the validity, the nobility, or even the necessity of McMurphy's defiance, but no mature reader will be convinced that his techniques can realistically accomplish what Kesey claims for them at the novel's end — the reclamation of numerous human beings who had grown passive and torpid before McMurphy's arrival.

At one point, McMurphy characterizes the inmates of the hospital as "victims of a matriarchy." In Kesey's view, modern society is a reflection of womanish values — archetypically responsible, cautious, repressive, deceitful, and solemn. One must look to the spirit of the whore if one would know what is best in women, and what can best bring out what is vital in men. There is no doubt that Kesey labors under a most reactionary myth, involving the mystique of male sexuality, which sees men as intrinsically better than women in terms of the dynamism and strength they can impart to the universe. Unable rationally to account for the disparity between such a projection and the puny reality of our male lives, Kesey waxes fatalistic, though never submissive, and sees "ball cutters" everywhere. It is a kind of paranoid, conspiratorial view of things, not without its measure of accuracy, but it somehow evades the crucial issues which Kesey and others have raised.

At the heart of Kesey's notion of what is possible for modern liberated man is a phenomenon which one may call porno-politics. It is a phenomenon which resides primarily in the imagination of a few thousand people, most of them young and bright, and which is occasionally manifested in the hysterical behavior of certain radical partisans of unpopular causes, a behavior which, by the way, many would call resolutely antipolitical, for all its pretensions to the contrary. Advocates of porno-politics are usually utopian socialists who lack the vision and patience to realize their goals politically: that is, they are youthful dreamers who are frustrated by the customary routines through which men achieve power or influence in order to alter the political relations which obtain in their society. Frequently, the retreat into varieties of porno-politics results from people relying too heavily on the flexibility of a given political system, and on the sheer magnetism of their own sincerity, which they and their associates had always considered irresistible. When the erstwhile utopian realizes how restrictive and closed the political structure of his society is, despite its aggressive disclaimers, and when he is made aware of the basic indifference to his ideals and to his attractiveness among the masses of people, he is suffused by a kind of anger and dread. As the society affords him virtually no outlet for these feelings, which rarely become specific enough to fix legitimate targets anyway, the befuddled utopian permits his vision of the possible to undergo a remarkable transformation. Unable to affect masses of men or to move political and social institutions, he transfers the burden of realizing a perfectly harmonious society to sex.

In Kesey's novel, we have what seemingly amounts to a *reductio ad absurdum* of familiar Freudian propositions. It is repressed sexuality which ostensibly lies behind every psychosis, and which is responsible for the acquiescence of all men in the confining conventions of western society. It is in the spirit of random and thoroughly abandoned sexuality that Kesey's McMurphy would remake men, and subsequently the world. What is a little frightening in a novel like this, though, is that such a projection does not at all operate on a metaphorical level. Sex is not here a mere metaphor for passion, nor for any positive engagement with one's fellow human beings. There is a literalism in Kesey's suggestions of sexual apocalypse, with its unavoidable ramifications into a political and social context, which cannot be lightly taken. Other talented people are caught up in such projections, and are delivering gospels of sexual salvation with a hysterical dogmatism that is, for many of us, laughable and pathetic. This is so particularly for those who have observed the failure of libertarian sexual experimentation and random coupling to affect substantially the pettiness and self-absorption even of those who are most easily committed to libertarian modes and who have no need perpetually to justify such commitments ideologically. How futile it is for intelligent people seriously to expect their sexual programs and practices to have a liberating effect on masses of men, when what these people want is to be left alone to enjoy what they have. What porno-politics essentially amounts to is a form of entertainment for a middle-class audience, which alternatively writhes and applauds before the late-night news, and welcomes the opportunity to indulge and express postures it considers intrinsic to its worth as modern men: tolerance and righteous indignation.

Kesey's brilliance is evidenced by his ability to be seduced by porno-political utopianism, and yet not to yield to it entirely. What save him are his sense of the ridiculous and his understanding of men as fundamentally dishonest and irresolute. Kesey wants to believe that the source of all terror and passivity is somehow sexual, that the liberation of sexual energies in the form of primal fantasies will enable men to conceive of themselves as more passionate and autonomous individuals. But his intelligence forces him, as it were, against his will, to tell a truth which is more complex and disheartening. He recounts a group therapy session which had taken place in the institution some years before McMurphy's arrival. Unlike the usual dispirited proceedings, this particular session stood out for the violent release of confessions that it evoked from the habitually desultory and tight-lipped inmates. Once the momentum is established, the inmates begin shouting confessions: "I lied about trying. I did take my sister!"/ "So did I! So did I!"/ "And me! And me!"

At first, all of this seems satisfying, at least from a conventionally clinical point of view: repressed memories are rising to the surface, where they can be handled therapeutically. But, almost immediately, we are shown that not only did such events never occur in the lives of these men; they do not even represent their fantasy lives. Such "confessions" have nothing at all to do with the wish-fulfillment that is a strong component of compulsive fantasies. What the inmates have done is simply to exploit certain readily available cliches issuing from standard interpretations of modern man as the perennial victim of sexual repression. The inmates are victims of something much more embracing and diversified than simple sexual guilt or repression, though the sexual element may be particularly significant in the case of two or three inmates among many. What is sickening is their desire to please the therapists by revealing what they are supposed to, rather than what is really inside them. Finally, they are shamed by the resounding announcement of helpless old Pete: "I'm tired," he shouts — a confession so simple and true that it puts an abrupt end to the rampant dishonesty of the others. Kesey loves McMurphy, and identifies with his aspirations — he wants men to be free, to laugh the authorities down, to refuse to be manipulated. He wants, moreover, to go along with McMurphy's sexual orientation, and to be as optimistic as McMurphy about the effects of sexual liberation on the reigning political and social atmosphere. But McMurphy is not a mask for Kesey, nor is any single character in the novel. In fact, as much as Kesey admires McMurphy's stratagems for outwitting the matriarch *par excellence* who goes under the title Big Nurse, we are never quite certain whether to laugh at McMurphy as well as with him. Big Nurse, as the personification of "the system" at its most callow, repressive, yet ostensibly enlightened, represents a tendency towards antiseptic desexualization which is abhorrent. We want McMurphy to bewilder her, to kill her with his charming nonchalance and boyish exuberance, and to parade his own aggressive sexuality before her. We want her to be teased and tempted so that she will be provoked to try to castrate McMurphy, if not actually, then symbolically, as she has successfully whipped the other inmates. We want to see McMurphy put to the test of the vitality and resilience he proudly proclaims, as if he could redeem us from any misgivings we might have about our own potency.

And yet, throughout this novel, we know that nothing McMurphy does, or encourages his comrades to do, will make any substantive difference to the system that we all despise. McMurphy, through an ideological predisposition, which in his case is more instinctive than learned, attributes to sex what even he knows it cannot accomplish. His is a heroic endeavor in every way, but McMurphy is at bottom a little lost boy who gets into the big muddy way up over his head. The picture of him, in bed with his whore at last, almost at the end of the novel, is utterly revealing: ". . . more like two tired little kids than a grown man and a grown woman in bed together to make love." McMurphy can behave as brashly as he likes, and speak with utter abandon of sex, but for him it has still an element of mystery, of vows exchanged, even if only for a brief duration. His libertarian apocalypticism is sincere, but in McMurphy's own character we can see that a libertarian sexual orientation ultimately has little to do with making men free as political and social beings. McMurphy needs no sexual swagger to be free, though, in his case, it is a believable accouterment of his personality. What is indispensable in McMurphy's character is his propensity to laugh, in his lucid moments to see himself as something of a spectacle, not wholly detached nor different from the other inmates who have failed to retain their resilience. When he loses his laugh, he grows desperate, and places upon sex that burden of hope for transcendence which the reality of sexual experience must frustrate. When, at the very conclusion of the book, McMurphy rips open Big Nurse's hospital uniform, revealing, for all to see, her prodigious breasts, we see where McMurphy's porno-political vision has led him. Unable to affect a world that victimizes him, a civilization which, in the words of the British psychoanalyst R. D. Laing ". . . represses not only 'the instincts,' not only sexuality, but any form of transcendence," McMurphy is driven to rape the reality incarnated in Big Nurse. In his fear and frustration, he does not see what, of all things, should be most obvious to him: that he cannot make another human being aware of his humanity by destroying or suppressing those elements of his own humanity that have made McMurphy a beautiful person. By his action, he demonstrates the original futility of his project, the necessary brutalization of his sexual ethic, and the dehumanization implicit in the act of invoking an *Eros* which is imperfectly understood and crudely employed.

SEX AS EVASION

Among writers who treat sex as a means of relief from painful reality, though not as a means of transforming that reality, several contrasting approaches are discernible. These approaches are largely a function of the individual writer's temperament, rather than a reflection of any ideological point of view. All of these writers are concerned with that crisis of identity which western writers have been engaging for forty years or more; all of them are cynical of the solemnity with which educated people customarily bow before conventions of thought and concern that they ought to have outgrown; and all of them view sexuality as a necessary evasion of issues which civilization has unfortunately encouraged us to confront.

John Barth is one of the most cynical, serious, and accomplished writers of this inclination. While his recent, extremely ambitious fiction has been given a great deal of attention, his earlier work is equally interesting, and especially rewarding for our present purposes. In particular, his 1958 novel, *End of the Road*, is a superb exploration of attitudes that we cannot overlook. Barth's protagonist is Jacob Horner, who fears he has no identity as a man, that he is, in fact, nothing more substantial than his moods, which are many and various. He adopts postures or roles, and holds on to them as long as they satisfy his requirements in given situations. A quack doctor who helps him in time of need strengthens his predilections towards what is an extreme relativism. All that is important for both the doctor and Horner is that man retain his ability to make choices, to act. There is only one wrong choice — the choice which leads to immobilization, an unresolved tension.

Such an orientation, of course, will lead a man to value noninvolvement, unless his character becomes so strong over an extended period of time that he learns to identify himself with a particular course of action which implicates every aspect of his being. Where Horner is concerned, the doctor advises against both marriage and love affairs, which are too complicated and might involve a man in painful tensions. Masturbation is recommended as a wise choice.

In the course of the novel, Horner pursues and goes to bed with two women, with whom we become familiar. In his sexual relations, the true ugliness of Horner's inclinations and aversions becomes gruesomely manifest. He is an inveterate son of a bitch, though he says some brilliantly witty things, and does manage even to suffer a bit. In his relations with poor Peg, who, in early middle-age, is desperate for a man, Horner's behavior is disgusting. He has always been uncomfortable, he confides, "with women who took their sexual transports too seriously." Moreover, he sincerely exalts sexual relations in which he is not thought of as a human being, so that it does not become incumbent upon him to consider his partner as human.

Barth is not Jacob Horner, but Barth's attitudes towards sex and towards human involvement in general emerge rather clearly in *End of the Road*. These attitudes emerge in the form of a tension established between Horner and his opposite number, a fellow named Joe Morgan. Joe takes himself very seriously. He is a brilliant young professor, hard at work on a book. His relations with his wife Rennie are terribly self-conscious and absorbing. They are, in a sense, each other's project, and their pride in what they accomplish in their relationship spills out into their communications with others, and, in fact, dominates their secondary relationships.

At first, Horner can do no more than sneer at Morgan, but his aversion quickly turns to admiration, then to jealousy, and finally into a compelling desire to expose Morgan's integrity and discipline as essentially dishonest. Convinced that no one can be genuinely decent, or devoted to another human being as he is devoted to the gratification of his own needs, Horner has an affair with Joe's guilt-ridden wife, and grows curious as to how the inordinately generous and open-minded Joe Morgan will respond to the revelation of his cuckoldry. But before they have a chance to apprise him, Joe is caught literally with his pants down, or at least with his zipper opened. What Barth gives us is an unforgettable tableau which can stand as an image, complete unto itself, of what Barth thinks of high-mindedness, total commitments, and pretensions of having transcended the demands of the diabolical self. Joe Morgan is observed by wife and friend executing military commands, mugging ridiculous faces at himself in the mirror, then, finally, simultaneously picking his nose while masturbating. It is one of the funniest scenes in all of literature, heightened as it is by Barth's sheer stylistic virtuosity, but it is not at all poignant. We are not shattered by this revelation of Joe, for we knew all along somehow that Horner, and even Barth, would have it this way. Morgan was too good to be true, too much an obstacle in the ready flow of cynicism that pours like syrup over Barth's fictions, and sticks to everything it touches.

Barth's attitude towards sex, then, as one might suppose, is very much bound up with his total view of things. A line of Horner's says it rather succinctly: "Maybe the guy who fools himself least is the one who admits that we're all just kidding." One requires a great deal of irony and a great deal of courage to feel this way about oneself, as about men in general, it seems to me. But perhaps when one grows sick enough of man's pervasive hypocrisy, and tired enough of one's own inability to commit one's self to anything beyond one's own pleasures, perhaps then the defensive irony and detachment come easily, and the cynicism grows into a mask not readily removed. What we are left with is the image of man as masturbator, mechanically satisfying his needs, unwilling to romanticize those needs in terms of suggesting that they might be more profound or consuming than, in fact, they are. And Barth, to be sure, sees nothing demonic or even obscene in the various expressions of sexuality. Nothing in his universe is sacred or taboo: it is a landscape with which we have suddenly become all too familiar.

VARIETIES OF EVASION

In the hands of lesser writers than Barth, such materials and attitudes are worked on more casually, and more superficially. Barth's fiction has an energy and a relentless logic which is truly remarkable, given the bizarre creations that are the very texture of his work. In a writer like James Purdy, one cannot but feel that we are dealing with a man who has attitudes at second hand, and who writes novels with the express purpose of having a platform from which he can crudely denounce the popular deities. The attitudes are not all that different from Barth's, but their expression is puerile and lax by comparison with Barth's presentation. *Cabot Wright Begins,* to select but one example, is a novel about a rapist, and incidentally about everything in the modern world — everything, that is, that Purdy can think of, which are usually the most apparent things. I mention him at all only because his reputation is very high among some responsible critics, and because he has managed to treat the problems of human sexuality with some maturity, if not with precision.

The crux of Purdy's "message" is that, for all the abandoned talk of sex, for all that liberalism has accomplished, "there isn't a stiff pecker or a warm box in the house." Of course, Purdy may be right, but I doubt it — I doubt even the sense of his character's assertion. What is more important, though, is that it really does not matter very much, for, in Purdy's view, sex is an experience which suggests an extreme impoverishment of other faculties that might instill vigor into the personality. Characters in Purdy frequently resort to sex almost as a last resort, and the novel challenges the very notion of sex as closely related to passion. Cabot Wright is a prodigious rapist not because he is in thrall to his passion, but because he has tried everything else and has been bored to distraction. Finally, of course, the sex fails adequately to satisfy, and Purdy can attribute to it nothing more than minimal significance, which is perhaps as much as it deserves. As one of Purdy's main characters engages in a casual homosexual affair, he is politely set straight by his partner: "A little pressure here, a little pressure there lifts the weight of the world from the heart, but no need to celebrate it by way of explanation." It is difficult to argue with so temperate a statement.

It is not at all surprising that the point of view with which we have here been dealing tends to consider both masturbation and homosexuality as not in any way deviant, nor especially different in the satisfaction they can afford, from "normal" heterosexuality. Some of our better writers, of course, retain a more traditionalist position, though this, too, has its complexities. In a recent story entitled "Whacking Off," Philip Roth recounts an adolescence and a young adulthood tainted by the spectral presence of masturbation and the fear of exposure. For Roth's character, who speaks in the first person, "My wang was all I really had that I could call my own!" Beset by a world which has destroyed his confidence in his ability to make choices for himself, which has instilled in him a fear of life itself, he escapes into the privacy and sanctity of his room to work variations on his monomaniacal obsession. What is unfortunate in the story is Roth's need to explain the bleak and cowardly world view with which he has been impressed as a peculiarly Jewish phenomenon. How frayed and worn the "Jewish mother" gambit has become, with its images of the perennial nag, neurotically concerned to prevent diseases and see to it that the members of her family eat appropriately. One wonders whether Jewish writers like Roth do not believe that Irish mothers frequently express such concerns, and that Irish sons sometimes resort to masturbation as a means of evading a depressing environment.

In any case, what is important for us is that Roth's character implicitly harbors a view of "normal" sexuality as potentially satisfying to the degree that it represents adjustment to the world, engagement with its realities, and the ability to overcome a heritage of petty fears. Masturbation he views as a necessary mode of disengagement in which the masturbator ceases to recognize the unreality of the fantasy that grips him. Roth's character is compelled to reside in the realm of the imagination, but he is fundamentally dissatisfied because he cannot stave off the encroaching reality that surrounds him. The dream of omnipotence is shattered by his social instincts, which advise him to join the world and to consider his evasion immoral and cowardly.

THE OUTER LIMITS

It is perhaps difficult to conceive that there is anything new left to say on the subject of sex. To be sure, our avant-garde writers, including artists as well as social scientists, have more or less exhausted considerations of the possible varieties of sexual experience. What is remarkable, though, is the degree to which emphases have been shifted and primary allegiances reexamined. This is largely the work of a few influential neo-Freudians, including Herbert Marcuse and Norman O. Brown, though it would be misleading to suggest that such men work from a common orientation or proceed in similar directions. What Brown is especially responsible for is a criticism of sexuality as essentially a matter of genital organization. In *Life Against Death* and the more recent *Love's Body,* Brown has articulated an elaborate, if largely fragmented and incoherent, theory of the body as the proper medium for mystical experience, and has tried to move beyond our notions of the genital orgasm either as central or indispensable to human sexuality. To reach his conclusions, Brown has exploited and extended familiar Freudian concepts, particularly Freud's observations of polymorphous perversity identified in the behavior of infants.

Brown has been widely read and discussed in recent years, and his work has been praised in all quarters of our high culture. Even where Brown's proposals have been questioned or vilified, he has been taken seriously, and ideas which we associate with him and with other influential people have become part of our circulating intellectual currency. This influence is reflected in the way that many of these ideas arise in the creative work of some of our best young writers, who cannot ignore their fascination even though they may be repelled or dubious. One example is the novel *Beautiful Losers* by a Canadian writer named Leonard Cohen. The book has been so popular in the literary community as well as among generally literate readers in the United States, and it is so pervaded by a tone which is undeniably American, that we need not apologize for treating it as a product of American culture. Cohen speaks as one of us, alternately bemused, bewildered, and appalled by the dimensions of experience which our writers and artists have tempted us to explore.

Cohen's is not a balanced vision. The tone of *Beautiful Losers* is shrill and hysterical, reflecting Cohen's conviction that we have become inured to so much that we have almost lost the capacity to feel the numbness that creeps over us. Cohen's pessimism is so embracing as to leave almost no loophole for the soul. He is driven, as it were, to extreme positions, but these do not seem tenable once they are considered in real terms, rather than as abstractions. Cohen's characters exalt playfulness, but they are determinedly unplayful. They are attracted to Brown's theories of the adult body as fundamentally erotogenic, but in describing their participation in various erotic rites, Cohen lapses into a parody of Brown that ultimately suggests Cohen's skepticism. Cohen presents a series of hysterical passages in which characters make love by stuffing their index fingers in one another's ears, to the amazement and dismay of a conventionally jealous husband: "You did it to each other? With your bare fingers? You touched ears and fingers?"/ "You begin to learn"/ "Shut up. What did her ears feel like?" /"Tight."/ "Tight!"/ And so on. Notions of orgasm are to be expanded to include a wide range of sensation: "All flesh can come! Don't you see what we have lost? Why have we abdicated so much pleasure to that which lives in our underwear? Orgasms in the shoulder! Knees going off like fire crackers!"

In fact the range of human sensation may be extended by a conscious and habitual application of such principles to one's experience, but what this cannot do is counteract other tendencies in experience which tend to desexualize human beings and to detach them from the roots of human behavior. The industrialization of Cohen's native Canada involves a destruction of the primitive cultures that Cohen associates with the American Indians. "They are pouring roads over the trails," his character cries, and later, "I've poisoned the air, I've lost my erection." For Cohen, one cannot separate existence into discrete categories of things which do not interact. What Cohen wants, but knows he cannot have, is a reassertion of the possibilities of love among men, but he feels that such possibilities must remain remote so long as we commit ourselves to them only tangentially. What Cohen ideally envisions is a humanity prostrate before all varieties of experience, yet still somehow able to discriminate, to make choices based on a perception of what is most authentic.

Sexuality will involve a thrust towards an impossible, because complete, engagement with the love object, which may be a real person or an imaginary projection of various ideal qualities. What matters for Cohen is the individual's willingness to accept immolation as a necessary concomitant of genuine engagement. All distinctions between subject and object must cease to be operative, as one becomes what he envisions through the act of willing and naming the terms of his immolation. Sexual activity is an enabling agent in this process, for as it gratifies, it also makes one receptive to the possibility of harmony among things. For Cohen, however, one does not achieve this purely on an imaginative level, through a passive receptivity potentiated by the release of sexual energies. Unlike Mailer's, Cohen's is an activist ethic, in which sexuality must ideally bring one back to the world, and back to the body, but a body which is loved to the degree that it incorporates qualities of all bodies, and is a pathway to the love of all men. Cohen's activist ethic has a communal basis, and sexual activity, as part of this ethic, must implicate masses of men in a process which renews them as individuals and unites them as a collectivity.

In *Beautiful Losers,* Cohen's protagonist is thrown against a girl in the midst of a swarming political rally. Without a word passing between them, they grope for and find each other's sexual organs, as the frenzy of the crowd begins to mount. As Cohen puts it, "We began our rhythmical movements which corresponded to the very breathing of the mob, which was our family and the incubator of our desire." For Cohen, sex is gratifying insofar as it directly involves men in the task of rebuilding their society. It is a beautiful thought, and if it ignores what we have come to take for granted in human behavior, perhaps it is time that we began to envision possibility in the image of our desire.

In any case, what our best writers and artists have demonstrated is that the engagement of the creative imagination with the materials of sexual experience can be a fruitful process, both for art and for our appreciation of the range of human resources. Though it has been impossible here to do more than suggest certain broad tendencies, it is clear at least that, for our most gifted people, human sexuality cannot be considered apart from other essential elements of the human personality. Where the vision of sexual encounter has been reducible to the grating of organs, at least we have been made aware of our impoverishment as men. We can say with gratitude that we have not been taken lightly.

II

THE AMERICAN
POETRY SCENE

SEVEN

A VERY SEPARATE PEACE: ON ROETHKE

Iris Murdoch has written that the greatest art "invigorates without consoling, and defeats our attempts to use it as magic." The poetry of Theodore Roethke constitutes an artistic achievement of a very high order. It
is a poetry suffused with magical transformations suggesting the fluidity
of human experience and the metamorphic facility of the creative imagination. It is, moreover, a poetry which invigorates precisely in proportion
as Roethke insistently attempts to console both himself and his readers.

Roethke's *Collected Poems** may be described by one of the poet's
favorite metaphors, that of the journey. From his earliest published verse
to the final posthumous volume, Roethke strove to recapture both the
remembered childhood past of peace and organic security, and the archetypal past, the slime and torment of the subconscious. He grasped for
these not as absolute ends in themselves but as means to accepting the in-
evitabilities of change, the dying of passion, and ultimate finitude. It is his
triumph that his best poems permit us to embrace the principle of change
as the root of stability; that his best poems, through rhythm and syntax
and diction, so evoke passion that we are able actively to sympathize with
his sense of loss; and that we can feel, with him, how "all finite things
reveal infinitude."

Whoever wishes to write of Roethke is faced with multiple problems.
It is not that Roethke is as diversified in his concerns as other poets, or
that his language presents obstacles to the rational intellect. Rather, it is
his shifts of mood that weary us, though they never cease to fascinate and
please. Just beneath the surface of the love poems lurks an almost obses-

From *Kenyon Review*, November 1966.
*The Collected Poems of Theodore Roethke. (Doubleday and Company, 1966).

sional concern with death; for every step toward the primeval sources of existence, there is a shuddering retreat toward the daylight world. Even in the middle of that magnificent "North American Sequence," published in *The Far Field* after his death, Roethke is uncertain of how far he wishes to go, how great a journey into his murky interior he is willing to undertake. In "The Long Waters," he moves confidently toward "The unsinging fields where no lungs breathe," but cries at last: "Mnetha, Mother of Har, protect me/ From the worm's advance and/ retreat, from the butterfly's havoc/ . . . The dubious sea-change, the heaving sands, and my tentacled sea-cousins." In such poems, there is a powerful tension between Roethke's desire to explore the depths of his sensibility and his natural reticence before the specter of hideous possibilities which may be revealed. The demands of the poet's nature seem to vie with the projects of his imagination. Fortunately, the projects are not ultimately scuttled in the interests of safety, and Roethke goes as far as his imagination can take him.

Roethke's major concerns and metaphorical staples have been competently, even superbly discussed on occasion. I can think of no better introduction to or map of what we may call the Roethkean landscape than the one provided by Stanley Kunitz in *The New Republic* a couple of years ago. What I should like to do here is to suggest the peculiar limitations of Roethke's vision, and to draw close attention to those particulars in which he especially excels. We all know that, with the possible exception of Yeats, our poetry has not for some time produced a more melodious singer than Roethke. Nor, I think, need we dwell on the wonderful, quick humor which so distinguishes Roethke's lighter poems and permits him to get such rare effects as he manages in a love poem like "I Knew a Woman," in which the lady's "choice virtues" are to be articulated by "English poets who grew up on Greek/ (I'd have them sing in chorus, cheek to cheek)." Roethke's own choice poetic virtues are too well established to require constant repetition.

A basic approach to Roethke's work should question the direction of his consoling qualities. Roethke was profoundly conscious of impending death, but perhaps even more concerned about the ineffectuality of old age, the fragrance of life and passion lingering in the nostrils without any ability to affect or rouse a benumbed sensibility. In other poets such a fearful premonition might be construed as a nervous apprehension of the loss of imaginative daring and insight. Wordsworth and Coleridge shared this orientation with the approach of middle age. Roethke's nostalgia for youth is a complex element which somewhat resembles the longing of the nineteenth-century Romantic poets. The child's fundamental innocence is a common factor, though Roethke embraces this not as a universal principle. Rather, he sees it as unavoidably attendant upon the benevolent circumstances in which he spent his childhood. In the poem "Otto," named for his father, Roethke recaptures the sense of pride he felt in a parent who controlled a rural environment immersed in the sounds and stinks and inconsistencies of nature. Roethke's fond remembrance amounts almost to hero-worship: "Once when he saw two poachers on his land,/ He threw his rifle over one hand;/ Dry bark flew in their faces from his shot,—/ He always knew what he was aiming at." The natural man who "does not put on airs" is also a crack shot!

Roethke's childhood, spent in the environs of his father's greenhouse, becomes for the poet an emblem of an intimacy with the elements that he knows he must maintain. It is not reality in a naturalistic sense that he values, in which he wishes to be immersed. He covets the limited detachment that permits contemplation, and finally imaginative projection beyond the boundaries of the patently real. He strives to cultivate in a distinctly Wordsworthian sense "a wise passivity." In such tranquil receptivity, as he reports in "The Abyss," "The Burning lake turns into a forest pool" — the violence at the heart of all creation is resolutely transformed into an acceptance of flux and perpetual restoration.

Many poets feel victimized by civilization, which is supposed to put us out of touch with what is most genuine in ourselves. Roethke's is an essentially anarchic personality, thoroughly amorphous and shifting. In his poems he associates himself most completely with water, always changing in the intensity and direction of its internal movement, always rhythmic in its perpetual ebb and flow. The aridity of conventional life, the expedient veneer called civilization, is effaced by the poet's ability to get out of himself, the self which has been erected as a mask between his nature and his awareness. In "The Song," first appearing in *Words for the Wind*, the poet retreats from an image of a "ragged man" whom we associate with Roethke himself: "I stared at a fissure of ground/ . . . The old house of a crab/ . . . I sang to whatever had been/ Down in that watery hole/ . . . And the sweat poured from my face/ When I heard, or thought I heard,/ Another join my song/ With the small voice of a child,/ Close, and yet far away./ Mouth upon mouth, we sang,/ My lips pressed upon stone." The terrible, because impossible, longing for identification with the child, or the crab, and ostensibly other creatures of the deep, is nowhere more poignantly evoked than in those last two lines.

Roethke was not unaware of his inability to achieve union with "the other" which is the lost self, and it is his awareness which makes the perpetual longing so noble and moving. As in the philosophy of an absurdist like Camus, the absence of faith in an external power capable of ratifying the value or correctness of our actions is not sufficient motive for abandoning commitment. If there is something vacuous in commitment to commitment itself, such an orientation does enable the organism to retain its sense of vitality and purpose. For Roethke, where there is song there is life. The negative possibilities that beset us are to be at least temporarily dispelled by the singer's continuing desire to articulate them and sing them into oblivion. On occasion, the singing may resemble the chanting of a would-be conjurer, and the optimistic resolution may be unconvincing, but we are prepared to forgive the poet his lapses in gratitude for his successes. The nervous strength of Roethke's best work disposes of most notions of easy resolutions. It is rare that the poet mistakes moral platitudes for moral revelation, as in an inferior poem like "All the Earth, All the Air," with its "What's hell but a cold heart?"

In the poems of Roethke's maturity, written during the years of his marriage (he married relatively late in life), the other becomes identified with his wife. The subject of Roethke's love poems is interesting largely because of the anachronistic reticence before eroticism displayed in many of them, despite the full-bodied frankness of his memorable work. The reticence is nowhere clearer than in an early poem like "To My Sister," in which the poet becomes virtually hysterical. The movement is nervous and halting — there is a shuddering apprehension of irremediable loss and even sin in lines like "Keep faith with present joys refuse to choose/ Defer the vice of flesh the irrevocable choice." The surrender implicit in the sexual act, the abandonment of what Roethke calls "the proud incredible poise," is a frightening prospect for him at this early period, though it is transformed into an absolutely ruthless self-revelation in the later work. This peculiar strain, peculiar especially for a passionate singer of erotic love, never quite disappears. In "Love's Progress," the warm expectation of sexual union and the eager call to action: "Love me, my violence,/ Light of my spirit, light/ Beyond the look of love," dwindles to the plaintive note of "Father, I'm far from home," and finally, "I fear for my own joy;/ I fear myself in the field,/ For I would drown in fire."

It is rather strange to find such a progression in the poems of a man who often wrote with lyrical abandon and hysterical warmth. Of course, the combination of opposites is an integral feature of Roethke's work. As M. L. Rosenthal has noted, the laughter which rings in Roethke's voice is most frequently "the pathetic hilarity of the unbearably burdened." His assertiveness is neither defiant nor forced, but a natural expression of his need for release from an introspection which often verges on the obsessive. Roethke is not unintellectual — one is aware of ideas revolving in his brain and crossing the page. At the same time, it is his ability to intoxicate with sound patterns and to make his images pirouette and dissolve without any concomitant exhaustion of clarity that first arrests our consciousness. With what energy and passion Roethke drives forth lines like

"I could love a duck./ Such music in a skin!/ A bird sings in the bush of your bones./ Tufty, the water's loose./ Bring me a finger. This dirt's lonesome for grass./ Are the rats dancing? The cats are" (from "Give Way, Ye Gates"). Poems like these, intensely playful and reverent of life, soon become more erotic, more focused on the promise of sexual embrace and the transference of energy from the self to the beloved. There is only the slightest vestige of that reticence previously discussed. For the most part, Roethke rollicks freely in unabashed sensualism, as in "Words for the Wind": "I kiss her moving mouth,/ Her swart hilarious skin;/ She breaks my breath in half;/ She frolicks like a beast;/ And I dance round and round."

What is involved for Roethke in the surrender to sensualism, in the willingness to lower his guard, is the refusal to intellectualize his condition. He opens his arms to existence and lets it wash over his sensorium. In the last poem quoted from, Roethke reports that "She kissed me out of thought." There is a lightness in such an assertion which is not to be confused with flippancy or whimsy. Roethke truly yearns for the passivity of the observer who feels involved but profoundly unconcerned: "Fingering a shell,/ Thinking:/ Once I was something like this, mindless" (from "The Far Field"). Death becomes an acceptable prospect for the romantic feeding his imagination on visions of transcendence and reconciliation with the nature from which he is sprung. The frenzy characteristic of Roethke's reminiscence is replaced in his later years by a serenity that reflects the poet's confidence in his vision, as in "The Rose": "And I stood outside myself,/ Beyond becoming and perishing/ . . . And I rejoiced in being what I was."

Roethke's love poems frequently reflect the poet's desire to get beyond himself by achieving identification with the beloved. In "The Other," he wonders aloud: "Is she what I become?/ Is this my final face?" And in "Four for Sir John Davies": "Did each become the other in that play?/ She laughed me out and then she laughed me in./ . . . We played with dark and light as children should." One thinks of the child and his eagerness to pass rapidly from role to role in play, his wondrous ability to project himself into realms of giants and fairies and sparkling elf-like *Wunderkinds*. The image of the self is as yet marvelously flexible, and the newest role can demand a sincerity of absorption unknown to the average mature personality. It is this kind of absorption that Roethke wants to achieve in his maturity, but he eventually discovers that the love of woman is not the ultimate mode for him. True, the speculation evoked by erotic involvement becomes less and less draining, more and more spontaneous and improvisatory, but there still remains a level of self-consciousness that is unsatisfactory. Roethke gropes towards an imaginative ambience in which all significations seem tentative, in which the will is no longer operative, anxious to achieve an intense pleasure which may constitute an evasion of its true destiny. In "The Longing," written near the end of his life, Roethke wonders "How to transcend this sensual emptiness?/ . . . And the spirit fails to move forward."

The mechanism of the transcendence is not, strictly speaking, clear. It is not "put over" on us by dexterous manipulation or surface cleverness. There is no question of sincerity. Still, the satisfaction Roethke is conscientiously able to express at the end of his climactic "North American Sequence" seems to be in excess of the facts as we are able to understand them. Roethke's denouement does not meet the demands consistent with his initial poignant evocation of the human predicament. The pain implicit in his awareness of old age — "the darkness of falling hair," "An old man with his feet before the fire,/ In robes of green, in garments of adieu" — appears to have shaken him into an affirmation of peace that is both imaginatively and intellectually unconfirmed and undeserved. It is, I suppose, the problem of the tiresome but inevitable objective correlative. The context in which Roethke launches his rhapsodic incantations makes us respond — the largeness and generosity of the verse disposes us to be generously receptive. We enter his world as willing if slightly intoxicated hostages. There is none of the coercion of spellbindery which we associate with the work of Dylan Thomas. Nonetheless, the intellect may in the end withhold its approval of Roethke's resolution. If the appeal is not predominantly directed towards the intellect, it must be conceded that cultivated people cannot always expeditiously stifle their developed inclination to analyze and judge. For the trained reader of poetry, emotional assent must remain fundamentally incomplete as long as intellect withholds recognition of validity.

Roethke finally affirms the primary importance of accepting experience on its own terms, without evasion. When we are free, he says in "Journey to the Interior," we can be "Delighting in surface change, the glitter of light on waves," "Unperplexed in a place leading nowhere." There is an element of static resignation here which is somewhat unsavory. Roethke wants to stand solidly rooted in the earth he loves, gathering everything to him, all sensation, every trace of loveliness, like the rose "Rooted in stone, keeping the whole of light,/ Gathering to itself sound and silence —/ Mine and the sea-wind's." We must learn to be explorers of the knowable, the finite, the perishable, if we "would unlearn the lingo of exasperation." Such resignation is neither ignominious nor unpleasant in itself, but the implications are likely to seem unsatisfying to a modern audience still smarting from the rigors of Robert Lowell's latest sequence.

It is perhaps gratuitous to refer to Robert Lowell at the conclusion of a piece which has deliberately restricted itself to Roethke, and yet I find the reference unavoidable. There are qualities in Lowell's best work that seem to me essential elements of modern poetry, and these are clearly lacking in Roethke. One is not surprised to discover this absence in the later verse, for the object of Roethke's strivings often seemed rather inane and impossibly idyllic, particularly in the early volumes. Roethke soars happily when he beholds "The cerulean, high in the elm,/ Thin and insistent as a cicada,/ And the far phoebe, singing,/ ... A single bird calling and calling." The landscape is exotically rural. His vision is landscaped with images out of the poetic past. He refuses to make himself intimately conversant with the materials of the modern world, which is, after all, an urban universe. It is one thing to speak of a timeless ambience unconstrained by a devotion to the particularisms of specific times and places. It is another thing to write as though all times and places were alike, and as though the tone of the atomic age were interchangeable with that of the nineteenth century. From our vantage point, we are in a position to know more about the horrors of the human heart than has been possible at any previous time. Our nightmares are in no respect perfectly equivalent to those of our fathers, whether in scope or ferocity. Surrounded by a gaudy affluence, we are beset by intimations of global disaster and the pitiless exploitation of millions of men. The appalling apathy and lobotomized drift of the average man are specters as frightening as any that have clouded the poet's vision.

That a poet like Roethke can "overlook" such undeniable elements of the human condition is lamentable. I do not call for commitment to a political position, nor for a resolute determination to reform the state of the world. Robert Lowell would properly indict such strictures as blatant, vulgar, and irrelevant to the poet's true function. I do feel justified in demanding that the poet tell what he knows, what we all know. How he tells it and from what orientation constitute the texture and framework of his uniqueness, and ultimately the test of his validity. We can sympathize, in purely human terms, with a poet's inability to maintain an indefinite spiritual militancy, but his exhaustion must not be tantamount to repression. The attention Lowell pays to particular varieties of the human experience enables him to bring a more comprehensive perspective to his exploration of the human heart. Roethke's speculations appear to be of the defiantly hothouse genre by comparison — they are carefully cultivated, rather lush in themselves, but somehow lacking the vitality of context. It seems to me that the surrender of the modern sensibility to things as they are, to Experience in the archetypal mode, must be preceded by a thorough acknowledgment of precisely what such acquiescence involves. Otherwise, the resignation is disappointing in its insignificance.

One admires and is moved by the energy of Roethke's struggle to get beyond morbid introspection, but one is not convinced that the battle was
fought along spiritually fruitful lines, at least insofar as we are concerned.
There is irony in the strange spectacle of an ostensibly "universal" poetry
impressing us with the basic privateness and limitation of its relevance.

EIGHT

THE ROETHKE LETTERS*

Reading the letters of a poet like Theodore Roethke, one will almost inevitably be tempted to remark upon the strange relationship between works of art and their creators. If it is true, as some have said, that an intensely moving and compelling body of work need not be useful as an index to the personal dynamism and attractiveness of an artist, it is nonetheless disturbing to be reminded of how greatly at variance these may be. In the case of Roethke, one has special reasons for the uncomfortable feelings evoked by the publication of his letters, for many of us had to overcome considerable misgivings in order to respond positively to the broad corpus of his work, and it is still with some hesitation that we allow ourselves to think of him as a major figure in our poetry. A major figure he does still seem to me, even after reading this presumably representative selection of his letters, but I do not think I shall ever again regard him as an attractive figure. How can one feel, after all, about a writer most of whose correspondence covering a period of more than thirty years might have been turned out by any number of literary hacks, and which exposes its author as alternately petty, manipulative, self-indulgent, and desultory, a life punctuated only by infrequent moments of genuinely profound emotion. Were the letters more intellectually bracing, perhaps we should feel less dissatisfied with Roethke as a man, turning our attention primarily to the poet's reflections on his fellow artists, and on the tradition out of which he painfully emerged into the unique poetic voice we know as his alone. But the intellectual content of the letters is at best

From *Georgia Review,* December 1968.
**Selected Letters of Theodore Roethke* edited by Ralph J. Mills, Jr. (The University of Washington Press, 1968)

shallow, the scope of the poet's interests appallingly narrow, facts not without importance in coming to terms with the obvious limitations of the poetry, whatever its beauty and vigor. One does well in reading these letters to take Roethke seriously when he laments over Auden's poems: "Oh, why am I not smart like Auden?"

Roethke was not uneducated, having earned a Master's Degree at the University of Michigan in the mid-thirties, and he taught at a variety of colleges during his life. He admits, though, that he read very little of Freud, or Jung, two men whose work figures prominently in Roethke's verse, and one recognizes how very different a man was Roethke from Auden, whose familiarity with Freudian materials has so much more to it than mere breezy acquaintance. Just a few years before his untimely death, Roethke was awarded a Ford Foundation grant for the purposes of reading in such areas as philosophy and religion about which he felt he knew so very little. Kenneth Rexroth has written lately of the intellectual thinness of our recent poetry, though in most of our best writers, like Lowell and Jarrell, one would be hard put to locate such a deficiency. And of course, Roethke's finest poems are proof against any suggestion that an elaborate, sophisticated intellectual apparatus is what poetry is all about. Still, there are indications in the letters, which one may deduce from a number of off-handed comments, that Roethke was less than an accurate judge of poets like Lowell, and of Wallace Stevens, from both of whom he might have learned a good deal had he been able, and willing. There is a repetitious quality in much of Roethke's imagery, particularly in the later poems, as well as a quality of timeless abstractness which ignores much of our desire to be addressed by a man we recognize as one of us, a contemporary of exceptional sensibility yet driven by the self-same specters that haunt our common nightmare. How one would like to know what Roethke felt about nuclear weapons, whether he thought often of such things, whether his view of humanity poised permanently on the brink of extinction had anything to do with, or was conditioned by, his awareness of the bomb. A fleeting reference to Dr. Edward Teller, the nuclear scientist, near the end of the volume of letters, tells us something, but not, somehow, nearly enough. I suppose we must wait for the biographies and memoirs of friends and associates to find out all we would like to know.

Nor, for that matter, do the letters, any more than the poems, tell us about Roethke's lady loves, nor of his relationship with his wife Beatrice, a former student whom he married when he was well into middle age. Such matters are both interesting and important, for Roethke's attitudes towards love and towards erotic involvement are highly ambiguous as they are developed in the poems. The letters written ostensibly to former mistresses, letters which are now available to us for the first time, are hardly impassioned, and while it would hardly be fair to demand that the author of poems like "The Sensualists" and "I Knew a Woman" be passionate in everything he wrote, one does have a right to wonder about the degree to which the pose of sensual singer was nothing more than — a pose. For if it were truly that and little else, we should be in rather a better position to discuss the imagery and symbolism of a volume like *The Lost Son,* with its intimations of masturbation fantasies and more overtly developed theme of entrapment within the confines of a self anxious for connection with another, whatever or whoever it might be. These are the kinds of things we hope better to understand by studying the letters and personal papers of our great writers, but the present volume thwarts such expectations at every turn. At most we get faint glimmers, such as the line "I (we, how hard the plural comes!)" in a letter written shortly after Roethke's marriage in 1953.

What does emerge more clearly from this volume of letters is a portrait of the poet, not as the sum of his opinions and attitudes, which are notoriously insubstantial and contradictory, but as a man for whom different views seem primarily a kind of hard currency which one uses to maintain a usually precarious position in the tempest that is the modern literary community. The atmosphere almost invariably evoked by Roethke's letters involves interminable petty conflicts and disappointments, savage backbiting directed against some of Roethke's better established peers, and a persisting resentment against an older generation of professional authority figures Roethke never seemed able to ignore or forget. In these letters, self-definition is always mounted in terms of the relation of one's ambitions and achievements to those of Eliot, or Yeats, or Lowell, or some lesser man. Once Roethke even acknowledges that his resentment of Eliot is more in the nature of a necessary, possibly healthy love-hate relationship, but it is hard to interpret some of Roethke's other letters from such a benign perspective, as when he writes: "Christ, Eliot in the Quartets is tired, spiritually tired, old-man. Rhythm, Tiresome Tom. Is my old lady tired? [Referring here to Roethke's "Meditations of An Old Woman" sequence] The hell she is! She's tough, she's brave, she's aware of life and she would take a congeries of eels over a hassle of bishops any day. (2) Not only is Eliot tired, he's a [. . .] fraud as a mystic — all his moments in the rose garden and the wind up his ass in the draughty-smoke-fall-church yard."

It is necessary in considering such a performance to remember that Roethke's letters were not written for us, but for his particular correspondents, and that he rarely showed such form in his many public utterances and published reviews of his contemporaries, though Roethke was never notorious for his verbal restraint. What is curious, I think, is that

Roethke rarely took pains to tailor his letters to the person to whom he was writing. Expressions of disgust and self-pity abound in letters to virtual strangers, and there is a perfunctory quality even in letters addressed to those one would have thought Roethke anxious to impress. One can hardly wonder what Roethke expected Mr. Mills, the editor of the letters, to think when he received the letter addressed to him containing the passages on Eliot I have quoted. I suppose such sentiments as Roethke expressed, and his unusually vigorous manner of expression, might prove amusing to some readers, perhaps even to Mr. Mills, but the pervasive ego-involvement and self-advertisement which characterize these letters are likely to make for an attenuation of any modest pleasures evoked by isolated passages.

Judging from these letters, it is in fact remarkable that Roethke was able to cultivate as many loyal friends and associates as he apparently could boast. To his fellow poets he regularly complains that he's unproductive, "mindless and barren," stupid, a disseminator of "inane crap," and when his mood is better, he sounds off on his more sensitive critics as "limp pricks" and "damned earless asses," and on his students as "these little bitches," though he tried as hard as he could to commit himself to their needs. The truth is that Roethke suffered almost without remission from a serious illness, which he would refer to as his "bed-rock neurosis," and the letters reflect a rather constant fluctuation which we associate with the cycle of manic-depression. Through his life Roethke would refer to his previous and imminent sojourns in one mental institution or another, and to some of the professional problems occasioned by these lapses in his routine commitments. Relatively early in his life he lost a teaching job as a result of a few months in the hospital, and he would allude to this not without some pique in letters to friends. Many of these friends remained devoted to Roethke, and one is hard put to know to what influences we can attribute their steadfastness, often in the face of persisting emotional and professional demands. No doubt, in certain cases one will feel disposed to interpret demands as the justifiable requisites of genius, but I confess I do not quite understand how Roethke's associates became convinced of his genius during the early years. Certainly the early poems, spirited and intelligent as they are, hardly give promise of great things to come, and the conventionality, even starkness of the verse could not have suggested the wild eccentricity and meditational intensity that distinguish Roethke's mature creations in all their diversity and freshness. I have found myself wishing, in reading these letters, that at least a few of the relevant communications written *to* Roethke by his correspondents might have been included in this volume, so that we might better understand the dynamics of important relationships, as those between Roethke and William Carlos Williams, Kenneth Burke, and Stanley Kunitz. One would like to know, for example, whether Roethke simply assumed he could count on the devotion of his friends because he could not imagine their abandoning him in his need, or whether they gave him to believe from the first that his genius, though still latent, was manifestly certain in their eyes, and because of this they would not abandon him. It may seem a small matter, but the impact of circumstances on our few creative geniuses cannot be considered without taking into account such seemingly minor questions. After all, Roethke had a great deal to overcome, both in his personality and in the direction of his art, to forge the kind of poetry we respond to so warmly, and while it would be foolish to insist any more than necessary upon particular factors in Roethke's development, one cannot overlook them.

In this regard, it is important to remember that Roethke sent early drafts of his poems to many associates, and he was terribly fearful of his poetic blunders going unchallenged. He was always mistrustful of his ability to be clear about what it was he wanted to say, though he went on and on about writing rings around Eliot, or going beyond the skills of Robert Lowell, whom he both admired and envied. It is common practice, of course, for poets to send parts of their work in progress to peers for comments and advice, though to many casual observers of the literary scene it may seem disappointing to imagine poets resorting to anything but their own inspiration. I have heard a number of otherwise intelligent persons complain about Eliot's "unpoetic" reliance on Pound in determining a completed form for *The Wasteland*. An excellent remedy for such a response is an attentive reading of Roethke's letters, for here, as in the letters of other artists, the profession and craft of the writer is unmistakably differentiated from that inspirational ecstasy which is too often confounded with the severe discipline the serious artist can never know too well. For those who are intimately acquainted with Roethke's verse, the various early drafts of poems that the editor of this volume has seen fit to include with the letters are extremely revealing, for the fact of continual revision stands behind so many of Roethke's pieces we have come to love. Of course, we shall have to wait for the appearance of the workbooks and journals in order to understand precisely how Roethke revised his work, and what were his goals aside from the usual poetic virtues of conciseness and simultaneous richness of phrasing. Mills has also included in the present edition the texts of several previously unpublished poems, originally enclosed with letters to particular correspondents. None of these can properly be described as gems, but fragments of several of them were later incorporated in a number of successful poems, improved by Roethke's concerns with loosening his rhythms, banishing dryness, and minimizing poetic mannerism, imperatives to which he alludes with great urgency in the course of his letters.

Perhaps the most terrible, and the most consistent, note to be sounded in Roethke's correspondence is his expression of anxiety about the presence or lack of originality in his verse, an anxiety which remained at the root of Roethke's professional insecurity, and which was not wholly without foundation. As early in his career as 1937 he wrote to Stanley Kunitz about one of his newer poems: "The shadow of Yeats is on the page, but is it too heavy? In other words, is it my poem or a series of echoes?" It is all rather remarkable, and depressing, when one considers that as late as 1959, just four years before his death, Roethke was haunted by the same shadows, anxiously beating his wings to ward off just such intimations, in one instance reacting angrily to W. D. Snodgrass's suggestion of Yeatsian influence in the famous love poems, on other occasions growling at John Crowe Ransom: "I am nobody's Dylan [Thomas, of course]," or lamenting to Selden Rodman: "Only thing that saddened me was that derived-from-Williams business. I do owe him a debt for jibing me in conversation and by letters to get out of small forms; but his own work I don't know as well as I should." I cannot think of any other important writer, at any time, who allowed himself to be so bothered by such charges, especially when it was clear to everyone, including the poet himself, that his best work transcended any and all influences, whether acknowledged or not. Indeed, the picture of Roethke locked in dire, if only intermittent, struggle with these largely spectral notions is extremely moving, and finally pathetic. To be sure, Roethke's working out of his perhaps dangerous fascination with a poet like Yeats, in the eloquent sequence "Four For Sir John Davies," is a bit too Yeatsian for comfort, whether in its rhythmic modulations, or in its tonal qualities. But Roethke had nothing seriously to fear in this, and he signaled his readers within the poem itself of his concern to "assimilate, not to imitate," as he put it in one of his letters. And certainly, what Roethke referred to as his "fart-beat" developed sufficiently in the course of his career as to leave no doubt that he had found a voice that could be mistaken for no one else's. The progress of this voice, culminating in Roethke's North American Sequence published posthumously in *The Far Field,* and more recently in the *Collected Poems,* is as much attributable to Blake as to Yeats, to Davies as to Eliot, to Mother Goose as to Williams, but was finally made possible by an imagination that in the end was sufficient unto itself. It is gratifying, at least, to know that Roethke suffered in the service of an ideal which he was able to reach, and that the achievement must have reduced the anguish of his many painful memories. While he still felt the need to sign a letter "I-love-me Theodore," he had to be consoled by the impressive accolades he had begun to collect, even from those like Ransom, who had resisted his enchantments.

As Roethke developed his art, he became increasingly wary of the various pitfalls which were to be resolutely avoided, not only by himself, but other artists, and by younger writers who turned to him for advice. There is little evidence in these letters that Roethke was ever able to get much beyond his concern with himself and with the advancement of his own career, a fact that is not surprising given the nagging doubts and emotional turmoil to which he was subject, partially as the result of a largely unappreciative response to the more innovative and experimental work which he began to publish in mid-career. Yet he could prove helpful on occasion to less gifted practitioners, and while he did not organize anything like a coherent aesthetic, as Stevens did for example, he knew what he did not like, and the intensity of his antipathies was surely of benefit to his students, if not to more mature correspondents. The source of Roethke's occasional epistolary intensity is not certain, but there would seem to me to be in it a strong admixture of jealousy, at the very least, and one finds that Roethke's critical strictures are always identified with particular poets, in itself not an unworthy critical practice. Some of the remarks are amusing, as well as insightful, such as the advice he directs to John Ciardi: "be careful of the 'big theme,' the I-have-the-sense-of-infinity sort of thing out of Auden via MacLeish or vice versa." Yet on the whole, Roethke is untrustworthy as a critical guide, for some of his remarks would seem attributable to the sort of psychological projection that can pollute the discourse among artistic peers, and Roethke was apparently not above writing one thing to one correspondent and something quite the contrary to another. Ought one to be disturbed by such things, or is it a better policy simply to be grateful that the poet was fallibly human and demonstrated as much in his letters? I am not sure which is the preferable view, and while I am skeptical about the claims of genius to ethical purity and critical generosity, I believe we have a right to hope for a greater abundance of these qualities than we find displayed in the Roethke letters. No doubt it is crucial to recognize the role of the competitive drive in directing and energizing the thrust of an artist's career, and we know that resentments frequently run high among creative people, despite the usual pretenses of civility and selfless commitment to the higher life. Nonetheless, it is difficult to deny the conclusion that Roethke's views on most issues will matter to us less than they might were he somehow a less interested observer. The suspicion grows that not only are artists poor judges of their own work, which has been noted on many occasions, but that they are often far from reliable observers of any work produced in their own time, for reasons that have little to do with sensitivity or intellectual competence. The "dirty little secret" of unsavory ambitions and limited generosities among artists and intellectuals is not as shocking and unfamiliar as a few of our current literary mandarins suppose, but it has still to be adequately explored by cultural historians.

What *was* largely unexpected in Roethke's letters is the extraordinary lack of stylistic distinction. Most of them are flat and fragmented, and it is distressing to recall how regularly Roethke apologizes for the unremitting shoddiness of his responses, whether of a personal or literary nature. To be sure, one had no reason to expect something masterful. Obviously Roethke was no Keats either as poet or as letter writer, and far from valuing epistolary communication as a means for enlarging and clarifying his views on different matters, Roethke seems to have resorted to letter-writing only when he was too exhausted to manage anything else. Nor was Roethke, apparently, in love with language for its own sake to the extent that any setting of pen to paper constituted something of an adventure. Leon Edel has written in his introduction to the James letters that "Henry James was incapable of offering a thought without pinning a flower in its buttonhole," and one cannot deny that to think of the James letters is to be aware of how fundamentally colorless are Roethke's. Even on matters of finance a writer like James was able in his letters to project a vivid impression of his overriding concern, which was the health of literature and the absolute right of the artist to pursue conditions favorable to the uninhibited exercise of his creative faculties. By comparison, Roethke's epistolary transactions are without dignity and, somehow, small, and the smallness is in no way related to modesty, as we have seen. What we have in Roethke's letters is a man who wanted to love himself, to believe himself a spokesman for the poetic tradition he embraced, and despite himself, represented, but who stood in constant dread of finding himself unloved, uncherished by those "others" for whom he was rarely capable of conceiving an eloquent, sometimes justifiable scorn. The consequent dabbling in varieties of literary log-rolling does not in itself impress us as unrighteous, but it shares with other examples of the species a certain tawdriness that we must find distasteful. It is safe to say that such imperatives as Roethke found it necessary to conceive are never such as to engage one's noblest instincts. A great proportion of the thoughts Roethke had to communicate to his many correspondents were not of the kind to warrant embellishment, and if they were not quite worthy of oblivion, they were certainly less than a suitable testament to the imagination that could stir us so deeply. The Roethke letters may stand ultimately as a grave reminder to us of the great price extorted in pain and unsatisfied longings by the life of art. It is with sympathy more than with charity that we must think of a poet like Roethke, for his commitment to his art, to his excellence, was somehow redemptive if his poems can better enable us to imagine a life more noble, more intense, more beautiful than his. It is our experience that they can.

NINE

ON ROBERT LOWELL

Decidedly, we do not live in "The Age of Lowell," despite what critics and others have recently said. Nor would it seem appropriate even to bestow the name of a lesser poet on so inglorious a period in man's history. Let us make no mistake about it: ours is the age of the Johnsons, the Nixons, a period in which what once seemed extraordinarily brutal or shoddy or banal now seems almost normal, certainly tolerable to most people. That is to say, we live at a time when it is remarkable that men of intelligence and compassion should bother to write poems at all; and that one or two should insist on creating great poems is a fact that imposes an unusual burden of gratitude on those of us who still care about such things.

It is difficult to know how anyone actually relates to a man like Robert Lowell. Certainly, for many of us, he is more than the sum of his poems, more a palpable presence than a tissue of convictions and doubts. We are aware of him always in his role as poet, but our notions of this role have distinctly expanded under the influence of his example. If Robert Lowell would not presume to accept Shelley's designation as "unacknowledged legislator of the world," he might lay claim to the office of unofficial spokesman to that small portion of the human brain we manage somehow to preserve against the clamor and violence that wither consciousness. Steadily, Robert Lowell has shown us not what it means to be a man in our time, for this we can know all too clearly by looking at ourselves, or at those around us; no, he has given us a portrait of a sensibility in retreat, in part from the world, but chiefly from the self he has become in response to that world. What we have come to expect from Robert

From *Salmagundi,* Summer 1970.

Lowell in his poems and in his appearances before us as a man is a rather graphic demonstration of how little we have left that we can try to preserve. It may not be that what diminishes us as men is very much worse than what ordinarily diminished others in the past, but there is nonetheless a terror peculiar to our time. We know for certain now what diminishes us, and how, and perhaps even we know why, and still we cannot resist. How awful to know one's enemy, indeed to recognize him almost in every face one sees, to lack the grace and charity to turn one's cheek, and to want that faith and will which would permit one to strike back. There was a time, Lowell tells us in a poem, "when God the Logos still had wit/ to hide his bloody hands, and sit/ in silence, while his peace was sung./ Then the universe was young." Now, as free as gods, though unable to decide how to use our freedom, and self-conscious to a fault, we fear our own potentially bloody hands, and mock the futility of our few commitments. Our prime gift, it would seem, is what Lowell has called "inexhaustible fatigue." Happy those growing multitudes of the sensitive and gifted whose negative capacities have not been thus limitless, and who have gratefully "dropped out" by whatever means they found available.

Those who have sought in Lowell's poems for strategies to ward off intimations of disaster, or metaphysical dread, have no doubt come away disappointed. When a fine poet-critic like Robert Bly complains about the failure of Lowell and his friends to achieve "a clear view of modern literature or politics," and about "their insistence on the value of alienation," he betrays expectations which measure the great distance between his own view of what is possible in the modern world, and Lowell's. In the view of Robert Bly and the gifted people around him, one decides either for or against alienation. One's poetry is either reducible to or suggestive of a program. One's emotional commitments are firm, rather than ambiguous, and doubts will disappear at the behest of will. Really, it is a most attractive way of looking at things, only of course it is but one way among many, and it is in the nature of human experience that those who believe such propositions as Bly's viable, will have an inordinate capacity for self-deception, or dishonesty. These are qualities conspicuously lacking in Robert Lowell, as even his severest critics have had to agree. And their absence has not made him or his work more appealing. Candor can become offensive when manifested at the expense of one's cherished illusions, and we are learning that it is possible to engage on behalf of human values while certain that on that field where battles are fought, values are as nothing, and engagement a hopeless gesture.

What is it then that has so drawn a generation of literate people to Robert Lowell? Certainly he has not courted favor as a hero, and the odd combination of hesitation, commitment, regret, disgust, reminiscence, and weariness one finds in his poems and public utterances does not give promise of heroic stature. Or does it? It may be that we have lately conceived another kind of hero than we once worshiped or imagined, not exactly an anti-hero, nor a proletarian everyman, but a victim, one who has not learned to cope to the degree that he has refused to compromise the clarity of his perceptions. His tragedy, if you will, is not that seeing clearly, he must lose his eyes, or wander friendless, but that he continues to see, to grow bored, and to be unable to turn away. Robert Lowell has been "our poet" because he has had trouble getting through each day, and told us why. We do not identify with him, we envy him, foolishly, sentimentally, but definitively. He sees, and suffers, and we would suffer with him if only we could convince ourselves there were something in it for us. Ultimately, we decide, it is enough that Robert Lowell sees and suffers for us all, a distinction we might have permitted him to share with Sylvia Plath had she lived to a riper age.

It is an extraordinary relationship for a poet to have developed with his audience, and to maintain this relationship, Lowell has had to violate the integrity and unity of his personality. For some people, whether great or ordinary, a posture is a strategy which is followed or abandoned according to the exigencies of a given situation. In the case of Robert Lowell, the man has become the posture, and nothing in the poems or utterances rings false — but it is a posture that addresses us, a role, not a man. So perfect has been the assumption of this role that we rarely notice how it dictates gestures and commitments wholly at odds with the man's temperamental indisposition to indulge such things. What most of us applaud when he publicly insults the President of the United States, or counsels young men to resist the laws of their country, or storms the Pentagon, is his temerity and conscience. What we are less likely to consider are the doubts, the irony that are so much a part of the commitment, and which in fact call into question the very meaning of the various enterprises. But then, nothing has become more paradigmatically demonstrative of purity of intention in our time than failure, and those of us who have found even the lesser failures a bit more costly than we are willing to allow ourselves must often have silently thanked Robert Lowell for permitting us to deplore and pity his. He is our truest victim, for we have together cast him in such a way that he can only assuage, never goad. And if he has been a witting and willing accomplice in the entire operation, by so much has it been the worse for him. To be aware of the mechanism by which one is appropriated by an audience is to understand how little that audience can deserve.

As it is, Lowell's generosity towards his audience, and towards those one could not ordinarily expect to distinguish between his poetry and any other body of work, is nothing less than a wonder. For it is not the kind of generosity that consorts with mere flattery or muddle-headedness. What it reflects, instead, is a terrible and unceasing sense of the poet's own complicity in the brutalities and casual cruelties to which his poetry bears constant witness. His latest volume, *Notebook 1967-68,** is in this regard a continuation of earlier volumes even as it introduces a whole number of considerations we have not encountered before in Lowell's work. He has, after all, always been concerned with varieties of victimization, as he is still, but such concerns are no longer mounted with such obsessional ferocity as they once were. The rage, the disgust, the self-loathing are still present, but a note of philosophic detachment has crept in. The grotesque particulars continue to abound, including apocalyptic blue-black flies, the corpse of Che Guevara "laid out on a sink in a shed, displayed by flash-light-," and the embitteredly neurotic harangues of the aging William Carlos Williams. But these particulars work in the service of a vision that has somehow relaxed as its perspective has broadened. Lowell was always a rather learned poet, but the range of his language and the variety of his references in this new volume are an extension of what has come before, and where personal experience had always been evoked against the background of particular failed cultural institutions and inherited family hang-ups, Lowell here paints upon a canvas of limitless dimension. I am speaking, then, of a momentous shift in Lowell's entire conception of necessity, the consequences of which we can only begin to perceive in the present volume, but which clearly do not involve a reduction of those human sympathies Lowell has managed to retain despite great personal pain and loss. This shift is perhaps best examined in connection with a passage from one of Randall Jarrell's essays on another poet, W. H. Auden:

"He [Auden] is fond of the statement *Freedom is the recognition of necessity,* but he has never recognized what it means in his own case: that if he understands certain of his own attitudes as *causally* instead of logically necessary — insofar as they are attitudes produced by and special to his own training and culture — he can free himself from them. But this Auden, like most people, is particularly unwilling to understand. He is willing to devote all his energies and talents to finding the most novel, ingenious, or absurd rationalizations of the cluster of irrational attitudes he has inherited from a former self; the cluster, the self, he does not question, but instead projects upon the universe as part of the essential structure of that universe . . . it turns out that the universe is his own shadow on the wall beside his bed."

Now there are all sorts of assumptions implicit in Jarrell's remarks

---

*Notebook 1967-68 by Robert Lowell (Farrar, Straus & Giroux, 1969).

that we really have not the time to dwell upon in their generality. What seems clear is that Jarrell was largely right about Auden as a particular instance of a projection that in Auden's case was illegitimate because insufficiently understood as what it was, by the poet himself as well as by the majority of his readers. What is questionable at the very least is Jarrell's notion that to see attitudes as *causally* rather than as logically necessary is to have a lively possibility of freeing oneself from them. That it were true, is all one can say by way of general response. Who better than Lowell has seen the specifically *causal* necessity of his debilities, and how many among our poets of major stature in this century have had a more impossible time freeing themselves from the attitudes and anxieties causing them? Lowell has of course avoided the projection Jarrell attributes to Auden, a projection that has allowed for "rationalizations of the cluster of irrational attitudes," and the subsequent quietude that has made Auden seem so removed from many of us. Where Lowell has even suggested a necessary relation between the failures of culture and the despair of the self, he has done so with a vital sense of ambiguity, an awareness of the perpetual tension between that self as source of the world's miseries and the self as victim of forces beyond its control. The freedom that Lowell's verse has always managed to nourish as a possibility is the freedom to see everything in its unrelieved complexity. The tightness and organization of his idiom has testified to the urgent complication of materials the contemporary artist must deal with, rather than to any desire to get away from the complexities of life.

The *Notebook* represents a shift which would seem to promise just that freedom Jarrell conscientiously refused to acknowledge as possible under such circumstances. For as Lowell's perspective has opened out, as he has learned to dwell upon a woe that is in no way time-bound or culture-bound but truly universal and for all time, his heart has lifted, his energies throb toward life as we cannot remember them doing in any previous volume going all the way back to *Land Of Unlikeness* in 1944. At the center of *Notebook* is still the self, its manifestation the peculiar speaking voice whose inflexions reverberate in the mind, all unmistakably resonant with echoes remembered from dozens of earlier poems. It is even in some sense an autobiographical volume, its pages filled out with many poems on Lowell's marriage, his daughter Harriet, even on the father whose memory Lowell clings to guiltily like the shadow of a debt never to be paid. But what is most impressive here is the poet's desire to deal with the history of his time, in this case the history of a single year, on its own terms. This is not a portrait of a sensibility in retreat, either from the world or the anguish of the stricken self. He can say in honesty and with relative confidence, knowing what he is about, "Still, it's a privilege to enter the bullring." For the first time in reviewing Lowell's volumes the reader has a sense of the poet as somehow equal to everything he describes, no matter how grisly. Though none of us including the poet is ever very far removed from the prospect of pain, he will have us understand that we ought to survive it, that we will. There is nothing especially brave in this — the tone is more quietly resolute and humbly human than we could have expected from the author of *Lord Weary's Castle,* and though one of his recent critics calls him a "magnificent curser," the presence that speaks through the pages of *Notebook* is better approximated by such lines as: "'Better to die, than hate or fear,/ better die twice than make ourselves feared or hated-.'" Gone for Lowell are the days "when hurting others was as necessary as breathing,/ hurting myself more necessary than breathing."

In charting a path away from the morbidly obsessional preoccupations with his own psyche, Lowell has had to project a vision of necessity much closer to what Jarrell claims was the undoing of Auden. But Lowell refuses ever to indulge anything like evasive rationalization, as we have suggested, and to the extent that Auden has found it possible to justify withdrawal from the arena of politics and history, Lowell has found it more and more possible to participate both actually and emotionally, though his awareness of attendant ironies and miscastings has in no way diminished. To the extent, that is, that Lowell has been able to see himself as a man among other men, subject to the temptations and disorders of an Agamemnon, a Napoleon, a Kennedy, a Robert Frost, rather than as a being peculiarly unsuited to vital existence by virtue of specific disorders associated with his own very special inheritance, he has been able to acknowledge and be grateful for those goodly dispensations that have come his way.

The freedom to dwell upon his own strength and relative happiness, then, is a function of Lowell's hard-won recognition of necessity as the sign under which all men live, not some men, and there is in *Notebook* a very special awareness of the dangers implicit in the enjoyment of good fortune, in the cultivation of one's own health and resilience. The necessity that often encourages us to deal cruelly with one another need be no mere outgrowth of neurotic debility, but a certain unstable dynamic that enforces our radical isolation from others even as we reach out to touch them. One does not, under the force of such an impression, thereby cease to reach out, but one does so with a measure of hopeful resignation that might have amused Lowell twenty years ago. The almost gratifying tension is clear in lines from one of Lowell's poems on the Charles River: "the Charles itself, half ink, half liquid coaldust,/ testified to the health of industry—/ wrong times, an evil dispensation; yet who/ can hope to enter heaven with clean hands?" The particulars are all in place. Lowell is writing about his own time not as though it were simply reducible to those abstract universals by means of which men escape all sense of necessity as the density of circumstance crowding the subjective consciousness, pressing it for dominance in a constant dialectical interplay. But the detachment from sheer necessity, the sense of the self's contingent potency is nonetheless proven in the generalization ". . . who/ can hope to enter heaven with clean hands?", which, if it is not a logical culmination of preceding particulars, is hardly in the nature of an afterthought, or a mere wishful projection of private need onto the structure of the universe.

The 274 "fourteen line unrhymed blank verse sections" that constitute *Notebook* are tremendously varied, but a number of impressions would seem valid for the sequence as a whole. For one thing, the structure of the sequence itself cannot but generate tensions of a peculiar sort, for while Lowell tells us that "the poems in this book are written as one poem," a number of them are so complete, so self-contained that one is loath to admit them into the jagged contours of the whole, to see them thus swallowed and perhaps obscured. The impression of the *Notebook* as a unity is bothered by pervasive discontinuities not so much in tone or language as in the levels of reality evoked, and these discontinuities are as present within the confines of single poems as they are in the sequence. One thinks for example of the piece called "Che Guevara," which swings from the gaudy reality of Che's mutilated corpse laid out on display, to a casual love-tryst in, perhaps, New York's Central Park overshadowed by towering and unfeeling skyscrapers boding ill to human relationship, and finally to some ancient image of exiled kings hiding out in trees. It is all very colorful, and not a little pregnant with apparent significance, only the reality of Che is lost completely, and the feelings mentioned seem so impermanent, so arbitrary in the poem's structure that one cannot know what to make of them. We know very well what Lowell means when, in addressing his fellow poet in "For John Berryman" he writes: "John, we used the language as if we made it./ Luck threw up the coin, and the plot swallowed,/ monster yawning for its mess of pottage." Surely the marvelous richness of texture and virtuosity of metaphor in *Notebook* is a reflection of this compulsive originality in Lowell, his desire to preserve the mystery inherent even in the surfaces of events and things by avoiding the easy presentations we associate with prose accounts. But we may be permitted to wonder whether sheer chance ought legitimately to govern not only the concerns of a poem, but their concrete poetic manifestations as well. If in reading Lowell's "Che" we suspect the poet might have little difficulty in justifying the progression of details were he set upon to do so, we have certainly no reason to believe that he could not do as well justifying wholly disparate particulars.

Most of the poems in *Notebook* are, however, considerably more coherent, and many rank with the very best things Lowell has written. Underlying everything is this relatively new, unanticipated concern with health, strength, animal vitality, and their reflection on a political level in the perpetual exercise of power. We see it operating at once in the volume's opening sequence of four poems entitled "Harriet," concluding with the lovely and troubling reflections on what a parent ought to wish for his only child.

> The child of ten, three quarters animal,
> three years from Juliet, half Juliet,
> already ripens for the night on stage —
> beautiful petals, what shall I hope for,
> knowing one choice not two is all you're given,
> health beyond the measure, dangerous
> to yourself, more dangerous to others?

And we confront such notions again in the deeply moving poem on "Robert Frost," which concludes on the following exchange: "And I, 'Sometime I'm so happy I can't stand myself.'/ And he, 'When I am too full of joy, I think/ how little good my health did anyone near me.'" The political consequences of power are too often dwelled upon in our culture to require that we rehearse them in their abstract potentiality still again — as Lowell himself acknowledges in an earlier poem from *For The Union Dead*, we frequently open our eyes to realize that "we have talked our extinction to death," there referring to fears of nuclear calamity.

But what is new in *Notebook,* beyond the concern with power and health, the relation between personal vigor and political commitment, is the relative delight Lowell is able to take in things, in people, in the procession that is history, replete as it is with murder and disaster. He no longer seems to want to turn away from the gaudy spectacle, and the boredom that is consequent upon the turning in of all experience upon the relatively static responsiveness of the self has largely disappeared. There will never be anything remotely playful in Lowell's work, we may suppose, nor could we ever desire such a thing. But the degree to which he has here given himself to the contemplation and vivid evocation of realities beyond the twistings of his old self surely speaks optimistically of Lowell's own health and satisfaction with the fact and manner of his survival. If anything, his poetry has become a more comprehensive and essential document of civilized consciousness in the twentieth century, and its registration of fluctuations in conviction and hope is surely testimony to the relentless honesty of Lowell's work. If he can say at one point, "it's the same for me/ at fifty as at thirteen, my childish thirst/ for the grownups in their open car and girls . . ." we know that he has won to better conclusions. What the critic F. W. Dupee wrote of Lowell's *Life Studies* upon its appearance ten years ago may perhaps be said of *Notebook,* but one would not, somehow, have Lowell any other way. "But given their [the poems'] intense response to what they describe, they suffer a little from being inconclusive as to the meaning of it all. Where, Henry James would inquire, is your denouement?" Well, Robert Lowell is not Henry James, and perhaps it is not amiss to suggest that in the vision of life's possibility we share with Robert Lowell, and to which he is our most intelligent and consistent witness, we cannot find anything like the denouement James would have required. Surely it is not anything about which we can now afford to worry. There is a sense in which motion, process, the will to keep going, is all we have, very likely all we shall for some time need to have.

TEN

SYLVIA PLATH: THE TREPANNED VETERAN

The poetry of Sylvia Plath's *Ariel* is a poetry of surrender, surrender to an imagination that destroys life instead of enhancing it. Nowhere in our literature has a finely wrought art proven so subversive as hers, so utterly at odds with those designs, those structures within which we customarily enclose ourselves to hold experience off at a distance. Emerging from encounter with her poems, as from the murky, subterranean depths of a well, one feels not so much emotionally raped as simply breathless with weariness and confusion. It is as though we had been flung into hideous contact with another order of being, suffocated by a presence too driven and hungry to be supported by the thinness of the air we breathe, a presence thrashing about, taking no notice of us, poor mortal creatures, a presence, finally, reaching, touching, shrieking on a scale that dwarfs into insignificance the familiar scale of our activities. It is with caution and humility that we must approach her art, for it is vaporous with potions that do not intoxicate, but depress and confound. If we listen humbly, there are insistent voices trembling beneath the surface of the poetry, voices which beckon to us, suggesting that we lift our heads from the page and answer the poet in kind, assenting to manipulation by that imagination which has taken everything around it for its own, wringing experience to satisfy its hungers.

In spite of the voices, in spite perhaps even of his own sympathies, the reader will relate to Sylvia Plath's poetry largely in aesthetic terms. The poetic surfaces are bristling with the energy and design of a craftsman, and one will frequently be tempted to remark the virtuosity of the phras-

From *Centennial Review*, Spring 1969.

ing, or the subtle variations of rhyme, or the arrangements of words in lines which permit her perceptions to come upon us in sharp thrusts, rather than as a flood of continuities which surround and finally drown the reader. There is a rush of associations, but they are somehow detached one from the other, though firmly contained and related by the context which gives them life and meaning. It is all a matter of phrasing and syntax. Units of meaning are at once self-contained and yet open to the influence of other units. They are never arbitrary, but the sequence of correspondences is not always clear. This absence of apparent sequence serves as a goad and a challenge to the reader, drawing him into the dense networks of the poet's imagination, tempting him somehow to understand the principles of selection operant in that sensibility, and thereby to acquiesce in those principles. This is a poetry fraught with implicit dangers.

How little present were the luminous qualities that distinguish her *Ariel* in the pages of her first collection, entitled *The Colossus* (1960). Here and there, of course, a line, a phrase, something grotesque, a weird juxtaposition, a flash of wit or self-parody, would perhaps suggest a mostly latent propensity that might spring to fruition under appropriate circumstances. One may be permitted to smile — how appropriate the final years of that horribly brief life, how propitious the suicidal hysteria and absence of all defenses. She has left us a legacy.

Ariel points an implicit accusatory finger at the critical language we habitually employ to describe the poetry we love. Indeed it is doubtful that one ought even to assay an explanation of his strange love of these poems, with their repellent details and anguished evocation of insufficiency and dread. Perhaps one can be content merely to locate the major sources of our fascination, wherever possible refusing to dilute the tensions which constitute the very fiber of the poetry. The late R. P. Blackmur has described literary criticism as the resolute creation of "a fiction to school the urgency of reading." It is possible to take issue with the word "fiction," which in application to criticism may evoke pejorative connotations. It should not. Clearly, any attempt to generalize, to abstract patterns from a veritable maelstrom of seething particulars, will involve the reader in falsification. To comment is in its nature to falsify, to give less than the thing in itself. And if this is true for criticism of any poetry, how much more applicable must it be for a poetry which is the very embodiment of that divine preternatural madness which has ever been the bane of critics who would mediate between the inspired and the anxiously normal.

The notion of pervasive victimization is a convenient "fiction," if you will, a skeletal structure around which a reader may weave a varied tissue of lesser fictions, all related, and which may finally constitute an organism of sufficient complexity to convey some impression of the poetry. The victimization, of course, entails a fundamental opposition, in Plath's case an opposition between life and art, between reality and the imagination that appropriates it. Almost always in Plath's work it is the imagination that wins. The poetry is generated at the expense of life, as the rigors of selection overwhelm the comforts of a more benign pluralism. The poet selects in such a way that the diverse aspects of her experience are fixed into immutable categories. Locked within these relatively static structures, they participate in mythic interaction with elements of a different order, an order deriving from broader cultural perspectives, which function similarly as categories holding their peculiar elements in recurrent patterns. Always in Plath's poetry we are aware of the functional paradox, in which the most literal transcriptions of painful reality, down to gross particulars, only serve to point to a level of experience which is defiantly abstract, mythic, "fictional." The subject of these poems is not a woman, not a life, but the way in which one woman consents to participate in the transformation of the particulars of her life by an imagination which cares nothing for life except as it provides materials for the play of metamorphic virtuosity. In *Ariel*, art is not a means for resolving conflicts, but for heightening them to a degree of glowing intensity in which all extraneous superficies are burned away, until finally nothing is left but that dreadful image of ash which litters the surface of several poems in the volume.

To close in, as it were, on individual poems, is to see how wilful Plath's imagination can be, how it insists, sometimes petulantly, on what it knows it should not want. Conflict is intermittently apparent in a poem like "Poppies In July," in which the poet struggles to see natural phenomena in such a way that they will validate her despairing perception of violence and suffering everywhere. The opening four lines of this brief poem are instructive:

> Little poppies, little hell flames,
> Do you do no harm?
> You flicker, I cannot touch you.
> I put my hands among the flames. Nothing burns.

In these lines the speaker is surprised to find that the objects of her attention are at least neutral in their effect upon her. "Do you do no harm?" she asks, as though the poppy were some noxious weed or ghastly augur which might be expected to injure or frighten. But the poet will not be satisfied by a perception of neutrality, and strains her imagination to appropriate the poppies as symbolic validations of the violence that smolders within her. The more ugly and menacing they grow, the more the poet wishes to identify with them, to become the thing she watches and poetically imitates. From the image of "a mouth just bloodied," which she forces the flowers to evoke, it is but a brief step to "If I could bleed, or sleep! — If my mouth could marry a hurt like that!" Such yearnings are, of course, suicidal, for they indicate the gradual dissolution of those barriers which separate the ego from the objects of its concern. Time and again in these poems, Plath becomes the thing or person imagined and described, so that cumulatively the poems evolve an image not of a single human victim, but of a monstrous, abstract victim whose condition is general and unavoidable.

Plath's most ambitious and successful poems are those in which she effects a conjugation between the concretely personal and the specifically cultural. Such a poem is "Cut," which I quote in full:

What a thrill—
My thumb instead of an onion.
The top quite gone
Except for a sort of a hinge

Of skin,
A flap like a hat,
Dead white.
Then that red plush.

Little pilgrim,
The Indian's axed your scalp.
Your turkey wattle
Carpet rolls

Straight from the heart.
I step on it,
Clutching my bottle
Of pink fizz.

A celebration, this is.
Out of a gap
A million soldiers run,
Redcoats, every one.

Whose side are they on?
O my
Homonculus, I am ill.
I have taken a pill to kill

The thin
Papery feeling.
Saboteur,
Kamikaze man—

The stain on your
Gauze Ku Klux Klan
Babushka
Darkens and tarnishes and when

The balled
Pulp of your heart
Confronts its small
Mill of silence

How you jump—
Trepanned veteran,
Dirty girl,
Thumb stump.

It is in every respect a remarkable poem, which works out its meanings on a level that wholly transcends simple logic. No principle can be said to order the progression of associations which issue from the poet's obsessive focus on her injured finger, but one is never disposed to question the essential structure of the poem. Perhaps this acquiescence in the idiosyncracy of her progression is attributable to the thin sequential principle which dictates the extremities of the poem, that is, the beginning and the end. Clearly, the poem begins with the moment of incision, followed by the inevitable flow of blood, and proceeding finally to the dressing and bandaging of the wound. These inevitable steps define the contours of the poem and lend to it an aura of order and unity which is responsible for guiding and controlling the diverse impressions evoked by particular lines or images.

Plath is always aware of herself as a spectacle, aware also of the morbid curiosity that so frequently attracts people to the outcast, the freak, and the mad. She does not cringe before the glare of attention, but performs, forcing herself into the most macabre postures, chastising in the extremity of her gestures the voyeuristic exploitations of her life and work. This component of performance and spectacle is largely subdued in "Cut," but it is an element of the poem's opening line, which is a giddy exclamation, almost light-hearted and playful. The poet savors the pained sensation which sends a thrill coursing through her veins, alerting the nervous system to an impending release of energy. She anticipates the prospect of working her virtuosic variations on a theme. In this poem, as in so many others, a sharp sense impression provides the necessary occasion for a devastating display, in the course of which the poet locates the sources of her convulsive anxieties. The poet employs the word "celebration," and it is well taken, for poems like these are celebrations of the creative imagination and the urgencies of the poet's vision. All is colored and transformed by the context, so that the "bottle/ Of pink fizz" functions naturally on two levels, simultaneously mercurochrome and champagne. In creating such identities, the poet destroys all separation between the literal and the visionary, for neither can exist fruitfully without the other in this poetry. Jarring juxtapositions fail to jar, and we are left to wonder at the more permanent and serious effects these juxtapositions conspire to produce.

The poem is in itself so strange, the occasion for a comprehensive cultural statement so unorthodox and unexpected, that one may not notice the nature of the cultural references Plath makes. For the most part it is an accumulation of clichéd references which in themselves might call forth nothing more than a show of lassitude or irritation. Set alongside the vivid reality of the bleeding thumb, however, and the stricken sensibility which is able to collect and unite such material, the references assume a relevance and insistence that may chill the reader. What the succession of cultural references calls forth are notions of constant violence and persecution, from America's genocidal destruction of the Indians to white America's more recent brutalization of the Negro. The various examples of institutionalized violence, violence which is manifested in modes of behavior and policies practiced by an entire culture, are not identified merely as counterparts of the more intimate varieties of aggression we can find in our own private lives. Plath is locating sources for her malaise in the history of western culture, drawing on particular moments in time to have them stand for pervasive tendencies which are apparent to those who will have eyes to see and read. The history of the West as it appears in Plath's poetry can with little difficulty be accommodated within the rigid framework of violence, injustice, and betrayal, within a single category, that is.

Such knowledge is debilitating in the extreme, necessarily making for a relativity of values. Brutality is indivisible. "Whose side are they on?" Plath asks, contemplating the line of soldiers advancing like the blood cells pouring from her finger. Alliances will be formed not by mutual commitments to an informing value system, but will be dictated by the exigencies of the cultural moment. Suffering and retreat are normative under such conditions, and there is no need any longer to wonder why the specter of victimization haunts these pages. In the poem, of course, there is pleasure in following the trajectory of Plath's projections, a pleasure which in no way diminishes the effect of what she is saying. The effect is, after all, achieved by the mode of saying, and in Plath we can never properly extricate our awareness of content from awareness of form and expressive language, for it is the processes of her imagination that lure us, beyond the materials it employs. And so we are fascinated by the rapid metamorphoses the thumb undergoes. But more gripping still is the poet's shifting of allegiances and identifications in response to these stereotyped purveyors of violence. By the middle of the poem, she has accepted her victimization at the hands of these agents of darkness, and she turns to "a pill to kill/ The thin/ Papery feeling." The thumb with all its metamorphic propensities has become her enemy, her tormentor. But in Plath, hatred and resentment are never very far removed from their opposites, and the poet can as well project one potential as another. Ultimately the bandage stain strikes the poet as a kind of head-wound sustained by the enemy-thumb, and the personified finger becomes nothing less than an equal, a fellow sufferer. The final three lines are not description, but total identification. They are united, the "trepanned" veterans of the world, the put upon, the feeble, left alone to contemplate, perhaps, the "Hiroshima ash" and murderous "radiation" evoked in "Fever 103°."

The extraordinary transformation of the thumb from oppressor to victimized comrade in retreat from the world is explicable in terms of the archetypal oppressor-figure which dominates Plath's imagination. Sylvia Plath was born in Boston, but her parents were of German descent, both of them teachers. Her father was the dominant figure, though he died in 1941 when his daughter was only nine. He is remembered as an impressively powerful man, a supporter of the Nazi cause, possibly an anti-Semite. There is even suggestion that Plath's mother was partially Jewish, retrospectively providing the mature poet with a familial pattern that perfectly parallels and enforces the basic dichotomy which controls her thought, in which men are conceived either as victims or persecutors. As a child, of course, Plath could not have understood the cultural parallel implicit in daily confrontations between an anti-Semitic father and a Jewish mother. She loved her father when he was alive, but always tended to see him as a god-figure, sublimely authoritarian and efficient. This family background, taken together with the poet's need to see everything in terms of symbols and peculiar connotations, quite effectively accounts for Plath's compulsive practice of moving rapidly between contrary sensations, between love and hate, between weakness and manic strength. The strange love-hate relationship which she carried on with the memory of her father became a pattern which she imposed on practically every aspect of her experience as it was expressed in the poetry.

The major symbolic identities around which several of her better poems revolve include the Jew as victim, and the German as Nazi or oppressor. Frequently the cultural setting within which such identities are appropriate is lightly sketched, suggested by no more than a word or phrase. A poem like "Lady Lazarus" raises interesting questions about the legitimacy of certain stereotypes as literary symbols. After all, much has been made of Pound's and Eliot's use of the Jew as Shylock, a stock figure who has been a source of great resentment among many literary intellectuals. Since World War II, however, the Jew as victim has been a far more characteristic figure in western literature, though frequently the identity has been deliberately ambiguous. One thinks of a novel like Saul Bellow's *The Victim*, in which the Jew serves as symbolic victim and potential avenger of his own malignant destiny. Bellow's victim cannot wholly dispel even from his own mind the ancient blight, the heritage of the Shylock out for his pound of flesh. What distinguishes his novel from others on similar conflicts is precisely that Bellow's stereotypes work to enforce ambiguities, rather than to suggest that there are absolute distinctions among men which are permanently irreconcilable. Plath's racial stereotypes are in this tradition and confirm our impression that what is chiefly important is how the stereotypes are managed. The stereotypes are neither good nor bad in themselves. In Plath, they are successfully employed because their juxtaposition within the context of other themes and a variety of concrete details permits the reader to tie together apparently diverse, even unrelated elements. By the time "Lady Lazarus" moves towards its apocalyptic climax, we are prepared for Plath's reference to her tormentor as "Herr Doktor," "Herr Enemy." In the course of the poem it has become acceptable to view any victim as a Jew and any enemy as a German. This does not represent a political judgment but a commitment to particular expedient categories which are functional within the poem alone. They are acceptable and functional because the poet needs to see her suffering as emblematic of a more widespread affliction, and because she is able to draw upon a wealth of concrete details from the Nazi debacle, details which for the moment at least are capable of releasing tremendous rage and pity in most of us.

"Lady Lazarus" presents the poet in the midst of her final, successful suicide attempt. She marvels at her ability to stay alive: "A sort of walking miracle, my skin/ Bright as a Nazi lampshade." Right away, the strategy is clear, though one feels that for Sylvia Plath it was more a habitual mode of confronting her life than a temporary strategy. The details which permit her identifications continually to exert effect include: "A cake of soap,/ A wedding ring,/ A gold filling," all summoning concrete images associated with the great holocaust. When she howls such lines, summons such visions, we know she speaks as the Jewess, and who would tell her to be rational, to respond normally, to get hold of herself? Who would tell her that there is no need to call upon "Herr God," that the manifestly various authorities before which she has cowered all her life have not been such as to evoke terror? And finally, who will tell her that madness is not the most authentic response to the human condition as we now see it?

The ambiguity of Plath's identifications is nowhere more evident than in "Daddy," a thoroughly devastating performance which A. Alvarez calls a love poem, and it just might be possible that he is right. M. L. Rosenthal reports the poet's description of it as a poem about a girl with an Electra complex, whose father died while she thought he was God. In this poem, Plath becomes an absolute victim, the Jew confined by barbed wire in the concentration camp, unable to explain to herself the reasons for her persecution at the hands of faceless, omnipresent authorities. But there is nothing pathetic about the spectacle, for here the poet has refused to be merely the victim. In desperation, and with hatred for the role she has consented for too long to play, she forces herself simultaneously to assume the contrary role of the avenger, fierce and unyielding. An incredible tension is established, in which the associations dredged up by the poet are at odds with the passionate defiance that rings in the poet's rhythms and language. While the image of the inexorable "roller/ Of wars, wars, wars" stalks her consciousness, she defies any power that would roll over her life, trampling her right to be what she would be. The bruising "You" which falls like a sentence of execution at the end of so many lines in "Daddy," points up the tension and ambiguity which is the very life of the poem. It is at once an accusation, a challenge flung in the teeth of tormentors everywhere, and an admission of weakness and subordination. "Ich, ich, ich, ich" the poet cries, struggling to assert that she exists, an "I," a subject in fundamental opposition to that "other" which is the world and its multiple embodiments in diverse authority-figures.

"Daddy" confronts, as no other poem has, the problem of retaining one's individuality, that is, humanity, in the face of a repression that threatens literally to obliterate all distinctions among men. In exploring with deadly precision the manifestations of this problem, the poet creates a fluid language which permits her to pass back and forth from the level of personal experience to vast cultural moments, so that finally it is impossible to extricate one from the other. The internal repression which prevented her from communicating meaningfully with her father becomes simultaneously the more general barriers to communication which traditionally have kept victims and oppressors apart: "I never could talk to you./ The tongue stuck in my jaw./ It stuck in a barb wire snare." So completely do the two levels of repression fuse in this poem that there is no possibility of the speaker's personal problems diminishing the obvious magnitude of the political situation. In the course of establishing these identities, the poet suggests the peculiarly modern aspects inherent in such repression. The barriers to communication are not simply superficial obstacles imposed at various points upon the flow of discourse, obstacles which can be removed at will. Rather, they must be understood as per-

manent features of conventional discourse which one cannot hope to
evade, totalitarian language structures which render genuine communication virtually impossible. George Steiner has written at length on the obscene corruptions of language which lay at the heart of the totalitarian
prose employed in Germany during Hitler's ascendancy. I do not know for
a fact that Sylvia Plath was familiar with Steiner's work, especially his
controversial essay, "The Hollow Miracle," originally published in 1959,
but in "Daddy" she gives poetic expression to a perception which no one
has articulated with greater understanding and concern than Steiner: "A
language shows that it has in it the germ of dissolution in several ways.
Actions of the mind that were once spontaneous become mechanical,
frozen habits (dead metaphors, mock similes, slogans). Words grow longer
and more ambiguous. Instead of style there is rhetoric. Instead of precise
common usage, there is jargon . . . the language no longer sharpens thought
but blurs it . . . it loosens and disperses the intensity of feeling." With
normal modes of expression helpless to convey feeling, there is an inclination to scream for attention, to indulge the extreme gesture in an effort to
transcend the clotted verbal matrix. And such impulses are not limited to
inhabitants of totalitarian dictatorships. They represent a frustration of
which citizens in the western democracies must be more and more aware.

For one who has screamed and stamped and pointed to no avail,
whose extreme gestures have been chastised or ignored, there are few
available options for maintaining contact with the world. There is a feeling
of smallness, of that utter psychic alienation from which there is rarely
any return. In "Daddy," the poet feels that the common language is
simply inadequate for any reasonable communication of her needs. Her
infrequent attempts at regaining her foothold in the world are easily repulsed. Always she feels she has been disposed of, a mere nuisance who
can but barely be tolerated. And finally she develops the language of the
permanently *aliéne*, the madman, the Jew forever denied grace:

> And the language obscene
>
> An engine, an engine
> Chuffing me off like a Jew.
> A Jew to Dachau, Auschwitz, Belsen.
> I began to talk like a Jew.
> I think I may well be a Jew.

The language of the hopelessly victimized is not without its expressive
richness, but it is a dangerously narrowing instrument. It perpetually
justifies its myopic determinacy by taking relish in its own peculiar dynamics, by tending to turn more and more in on itself, ultimately, and

most disastrously, with neither reference nor recourse to anything beyond its own defiantly detached and self-sufficient matrix. "Daddy" does not open onto visions of experience, but engulfs fragments of experience and inflates them into wholes, forcing them to stand as general statements rather than as indications of merely contingent necessities. As Sylvia Plath speaks of adopting at least the accouterments of Jewish discourse, with its built-in defense mechanisms and pervasive negativism, one thinks inevitably of Kafka and his unforgettable aggregations of victim-characters. One thinks of the imaginary Siberian self-exile of George Bendemann in "The Judgment," of his pathetic self-sentencing and execution.

Both Kafka and Plath demonstrate a psychotic attraction to forms of brute power that tend towards extermination of their victims, inducing paroxysms of self-contempt and complicity in their own destruction. *Ariel* presents the poet in the final throes of a heroic but doomed effort to preserve that self through the assertion of its own violence and desires, an assertion Kafka was never able even to attempt. The magnitude and strain of Plath's effort is evident in the pervasive hysteria of these poems, some of them containing the hysteria beneath the surface in latent though potentially explosive forms. In "Daddy," the poet attempts to purge the violence which threatens to tear her and everyone around her to pieces, to purge it by allowing it expression in that sublimation which is the poem. The poet conjures up an image of herself as a group of villagers, enacting some primitive ceremony which in its ritualistic order and communally sanctioned mode of unfolding can cleanse the soul and satisfy:

> There's a stake in your fat black heart
> And the villagers never liked you.
> They are dancing and stamping on you.
> They always *knew* it was you.
> Daddy, daddy, you bastard, I'm through.

In so many of Plath's poems, the cyclical recurrence of words and phrases, and the hammering, static regularity of syntactical arrangements help to provide a ceremonial atmosphere, evoking images of a hideous black sacrament in continual progress. But nowhere in her poetry are such intimations given explicit sanction as they are in "Daddy." The symbolic murder is, of course, nothing more than that — symbolic. But the poet's concluding "I'm through" may suggest either an acknowledgment of failure or a determinedly unrealistic wish-fulfillment. Needless to say, as long as she lived, she could not be "through." The word is best taken to refer to her imminent death, towards which perhaps she could look more hopefully, having at least imaginatively settled the score once and for all.

Clearly though, the father-figure who is stamped upon in "Daddy" is no more than a convenient and intimate representative of something so general and powerful that it cannot be abolished or forgotten, except in the moment of our death. Unless, of course, we consent to be permanently drugged, to settle for "the black amnesias of heaven" which the poet is unable to retreat into in "The Night Dances." Remarkably, Sylvia Plath demonstrates a positive contempt for those who have not eyes to see and delight in the beauties of the created universe, despite the admixture, even the predominance of suffering that is certain to dilute or extinguish pleasure. As she stares with pleasure in "Poppies In October," she notices around her "eyes/ Dulled to a halt under bowlers," and she exclaims in wonder that beauty should persist, beset as it is by indifference or malignity. Always she projects the familiar imagery of destruction and creeping numbness, the "forest of frost," the "slow/ Horse the colour of rust," the "dolorous bells." We are grateful for her sake at least that those final months were not wholly grim, that once, perhaps, the light of stars, "these lamps," fell "like blessings."

ELEVEN

MORE ON SYLVIA PLATH

It would seem that those possessed by the Sylvia Plath legend will have to do some fancy stepping to accommodate the volume of her poems recently issued here and in England. *Crossing The Water** is an extraordinary book, not promising merely nor dazzling as one might have expected of a poet who was later to write the poems in *Ariel,* but perfectly satisfying in the way that only major poetry can be. That her achievement here may be spoken of in terms more orthodox than one could legitimately apply to *Ariel* is but one of the facts the promoters of the legend will have to deal with — how distressing it must be, for some of them at least, to confront a Plath largely in control even of her most terrible associations, and deliberately fashioning a voice by working through the poetry of Stevens, Frost, Lowell, Roethke, and others. The figure of the demon-lady with red hair eating men, and everything else, "like air," is considerably attenuated in the perspective of this new volume. Though one was always grateful for the dozen or so magnificent poems in *Ariel,* one may now be grateful that they can be read in a broader perspective wherein we shall more resolutely attend to the poems themselves rather than to the figure of the poet haunting the margins.

The items included in *Crossing The Water* were written, or so at least the dust-jacket of the volume informs us, "in the period between the publication of *The Colossus* (1960) and the posthumous book *Ariel* (published in England in 1965)." A number had appeared in periodicals before the poet took her life in 1963, but very few writers and critics had

From *Salmagundi,* Winter 1973.
* *Crossing The Water* by Sylvia Plath (Harper & Row, 1971).

taken notice of them in discussing her career. It was as if, with *Ariel*, one had all one needed to reach some proper estimation of the poet, and the intricacies of idea and language were so great in *Ariel* as to provide hungry critics with all they needed to keep busy on Sylvia Plath.* We see clearly now that *Ariel* was by no means enough, that we wanted some assurance of substantiality and permanence in our impression of such poems as "Tulips," "Lady Lazarus," and "Daddy." Already too many of us had come to think of these poems we have so often read aloud and heard recited to us as instances in some peculiar event we had lived through and wondered over, but which seemed more and more remote from conventional poetic experience. In part, of course, it is the propensity of our youth and literary cultures to convert disturbed people into heroes that was responsible, but the *Ariel* poems themselves had no small hand in encouraging us to think of them as extraordinary primal events without antecedent or analogue. *Crossing The Water* may be discussed less feverishly, and one does not hesitate to describe it as a book with a number of great poems, a number of less ambitious but beautifully realized poems, and several immature pieces each of which calls to mind a particular poetic voice imperfectly assimilated.

One need only be familiar with the work of a few poets to speak of Plath's failures in *Crossing The Water*. In poems like "Who," "Dark House," "Maenad," and "The Beast," the hand of Roethke is unmistakably heavy on the page. To read the following lines in a Plath poem is to have our attention forcibly turned *from* the intrinsic relations among the poem's constituent elements *to* a mode of comparison that has little to do with Plath, but a great deal to do with Roethke's compelling ingenuity and uniqueness:

> Pebble smells, turnipy chambers.
> Small nostrils are breathing.
> Little humble loves!
> Footlings, boneless as noses,
> It is warm and tolerable
> In the bowel of the root.
> Here's a cuddly mother.

(from "The Dark House")

Or how is one to avoid the inevitable comparison with such Roethkean lyrics as "Love's Progress," "The Other," or "She" as one reads:

---

* As one of those "hungry critics," I should know. See my essay "Sylvia Plath: The Trepanned Veteran" in this collection.

This mouth is fit for little.
The dead ripen in the grapeleaves.
A red tongue is among us.
Mother, keep out of my barnyard,
I am becoming another.

(from "Maenad")

The presence of Stevens is ordinarily less obvious in Plath, whether one examines *The Colossus* or the present volume, but how startling it is to come upon these opening stanzas in a poem called "Black Rook In Rainy Weather":

On the stiff twig up there
Hunches a wet black rook
Arranging and rearranging its feathers in the rain.
I do not expect a miracle
Or an accident

To set the sight on fire
In my eye, nor seek
Any more in the desultory weather some design,
But let spotted leaves fall,
Without ceremony, or portent.

It is as though Plath had sat down to write the poem fresh from an intensely involving session with "Thirteen Ways Of Looking At A Blackbird" and a few shorter lyrics in the *Opus Posthumous*, such as "The Course Of A Particular." Again, one draws attention to these things not to score points on Sylvia Plath but to suggest emphatically how thorough was her absorption in the poetry of her time and how difficultly she forged what is by all accounts an original voice. In her memorable work one hears that voice practically alone — nothing alien clings to it, nothing interferes with its inwardness and that special resonance which is the imprint of a driven and strangely passionate sensibility.

It is not especially challenging to compile a list of the best poems in *Crossing The Water,* though one can always find disagreements if he tries hard enough. So fine are the best poems that they cannot fail to impress a trained reader with their distinctive authority and linguistic abundance. I speak of the following, in no special order: "Candles," "Widow," "Leaving Early," "Ouija," "Wuthering Heights." Less wonderful but surely finished and moving poems include "Parliament Hill Fields," "Blackberrying," "Insomniac," "Magi," "Two Campers," "Last Words," and "A Life." In these poems the Sylvia Plath whom we have learned to speak of as a case, a clinical item in a running catalogue of the century's abuses, has transformed her character into a fate, an emblem of the singular personality gorgeously projecting itself into a universe of alien things allowed their otherness. Though the project of *Ariel* involved an insistent appropriation and evisceration of this otherness, this peculiar thinginess in the object and human universe through which the poet moved like a devouring angel, the project of the major poems in *Crossing The Water* falls short of so encompassing an enterprise. What we so admire in the present volume is the formal verbal apparatus which makes possible the evocation of a conflict without altogether dissolving the initiating elements in that conflict. The ardor of immediate perception coexists here with the hunger to use that perception and transform its objects into something that they are not, but the tension is manageable, and the objects retain their identities. In *Ariel*, a poppy observed had inevitably to be changed into something it could call to the mind only of a furious and distracted sensibility, into a bloody mouth, in fact, or "little bloody skirts." A warmly upturned smile in the concerned face of a loved one would turn to a fish hook, ominous and seductively sinister. There are conversions of this sort in a number of poems in the new book, but they are relatively few, and they seem almost out of place here. Frequently the poet will play with the far-flung association or the grotesque extension of an already unpleasant image, but it is the original image itself she cares for here, its special character and irreducible resonance. In the poem "Widow," to take but one instance of the poet's resolute cultivation of the tension we have described, the opening stanza threatens to overwhelm us and to work an unhappy magic on the ostensible subject:

> Widow. The word consumes itself —
> Body, a sheet of newsprint on the fire
> Levitating a numb minute in the updraft
> Over the scalding, red topography
> That will put her heart out like an only eye.

"The word consumes itself —" immediately we suspect the poet of contriving an occasion for a display of hysteria such as we have known in *Ariel*, a display in which a series of wondrous metamorphoses will tell us a great deal about the processes of an intelligence conceived almost abstractly, as if it were nothing but process devoid of determinant content. We see though, in succeeding stanzas, that this is not to be the case in "Widow," for it is carefully directed towards the establishment of a vital tension between the reality of the widow, the essence of the condition the word itself traditionally invokes, and the poet's emotional relationship to that condition as dictated by her own needs. What she does here is to imagine what the condition must really be like, to insist upon a mode of imaginative relation, in fact, in which the needs of the self will be deliberately restrained. To speak in such a context of responsible imagination is not at all misguided, nor ought it to invite critical reprisal, as if the merest mention of responsibility were to introduce into a specifically aesthetic domain a moral dimension not at all warranted or conceivably welcome. One may speak of responsible imagination, after all, without any reference to realities external to the poem. The question of propriety here refers exclusively to elements set in motion within the poem itself, and the loyalty to experience one feels moved to comment upon in reading *Crossing The Water* is a loyalty to a particular experience whose dimensions the poem initially describes or suggests. Consider the following lines from the middle of "Widow":

> The moth-face of her husband, moonwhite and ill,
> Circles her like a prey she'd love to kill
> A second time to have him near again —
> A paper image to lay against her heart
> The way she laid his letters, till they grew warm
> And seemed to give her warmth, like a live skin.
> But it is she who is paper now, warmed by no one.

Or these concluding stanzas:

> A bodiless soul could pass another soul
> In this clear air and never notice it —
> One soul pass through the other, frail as smoke
> And utterly ignorant of the way it took.
>
> That is the fear she has — the fear
> His soul may beat and be beating at her dull sense
> Like blue Mary's angel, dovelike against a pane
> Blinded to all but the grey spiritless room
> It looks in on, and must go on looking in on.

How extraordinary that concluding image, spun out really over two entire stanzas, how substantial the condition it evokes, and yet how general and, one is inclined to say, conventional. How unafraid the poet is to inhabit this almost otherworldly dimension of the widow's loss, to give expression to a grief anachronistic in its single-mindedness. The relative simplicity of the phrasing in no way mitigates the striking clarity and interest of the condition as it is developed.

Often in going through *Ariel* one thought of the late R.P. Blackmur's reflection on Robert Lowell's earliest work, to the effect that in it there is nothing loved unless it be its repellence. Blackmur never really understood what Lowell's first volumes were about, and just so does his observation miss the mark if too rigidly applied to Plath. Still there is some truth in the observation taken in relation to *Ariel* where one necessarily thinks of *Crossing The Water* in other terms. If Sylvia Plath does not love the widow she describes, her compassion for and insight into her condition are at least considerable. Always, of course, the impulse to cry me me me is present, but the determination not to clearly masters any such impulse, and one must be moved by the drama the poet enacts among her warring desires. In the poem "Two Campers In Cloud Country," she and a companion camp in the woods, and the poet notices at once what poets have frequently recognized in similar circumstances. Looking up at rocks and clouds, she reflects that "No gesture of yours or mine could catch their attention,/ No word make them carry water or fire the kindling/ Like local trolls in the spell of a superior being." This is all rather familiar, though finely observed in a manner uniquely Plath's. But what one trained in the excesses and hungers of *Ariel* would not expect are lines like these:

> It is comfortable, for a change, to mean so little.
> These rocks offer no purchase to herbage or people:

How restrained the sentiments in such assertions and yet how tense the voice that utters them, how unlike comfort are the attendant emotions. If from nothing else in the poem, a reader would know for sure of the tension that rings just in the background of every utterance by listening to the final words:

> Around our tent the old simplicities sough
> Sleepily as Lethe, trying to get in.
> We'll wake blank-brained as water in the dawn.

For Sylvia Plath it was no easy matter to love what did not openly include her or that did not yield to her will, and she did no doubt court repellence precisely so that she might justify her poetic and personal excesses. The image of her acquiescently pondering a blank-brained awakening is then no emblem of an easy regression, but the expression of a determined wish to be, occasionally, nothing at all, and thereby to inhabit a various universe according to the principle of a negative capability. "The horizons are too far off to be chummy as uncles," the poet observes, and the line may stand in a sense for the impression one takes of the entire volume. It measures the poet's capacity to endure limited distance and otherness, to resist the temptation to suffocate everything in her fervent embrace.

That readers coming to the new volume from *Ariel* may find this tension very difficult to appreciate we have already suggested, and the reception it has been given by Helen Vendler in The *New York Times Book Review* demonstrates just how great the problem will be. She writes that "Plath would like, in distrust of mind, to trust nature, and yet she ends in the volume, by refusing nature any honorable estate of its own." And later in her review, "the poet's eye bounds the limits of the world, and all of nature exists only as a vehicle to her sensibility." To which one wants to reply, go back to the poems themselves, and study them even as the *Ariel* poems resound in the inner ear, and consider again whether the former work upon you exactly as do the latter. That the Plath of the present volume would like to trust nature and cannot, we do not deny, but that she permits it some authentic and uncompelled expression in the dozen best poems is a certainty. As one reads through the *Ariel* poems one is taken not by any sense of mystery but by a sense of inevitability that grips one by the throat, occasionally perhaps by the fingers of the hand, and drags him along to an ending that was never really in question, no matter how dazzlingly circuitous the route. There is an element of mystery in *Crossing The Water* that is very different indeed, and one may locate its source at just that point where the object refuses to yield in its intransigent otherness and insists upon a range of potential meanings or associations that lead not in a straight line but in several directions at once. And this mystery is no mere rhetorical affair, but at least equally an affair of a spirit which can still afford a limited generosity. Suffused as so many poems in this volume are by this genuine current of mystery playing over the surfaces of objects and persons, it is no wonder that even ritualistic enactments incorporated by the poet are touched with a gentleness, a tentativeness one will hardly identify with *Ariel*. One need look no further than the poem "Candles," in fact, to see a perfectly glorious manifestation of this gentleness, this tentativeness, an alternation of somber sentiment and delicate perception that constitutes a fabric as fine as anything Sylvia Plath has given us:

> They are the last romantics, these candles:
> Upside-down hearts of light tipping wax fingers,
> And the fingers, taken in by their own haloes,
> Grown milky, almost clear, like the bodies of saints.
> It is touching, the way they'll ignore
>
> A whole family of prominent objects
> Simply to plumb the deeps of an eye
> In its hollow of shadows, its fringe of reeds,
> And the owner past thirty, no beauty at all.
> Daylight would be more judicious,

Giving everybody a fair hearing.
They should have gone out with balloon flights and
    the stereopticon.
This is no time for the private point of view.
When I light them, my nostrils prickle.
Their pale, tentative yellows

Drag up false, Edwardian sentiments,
And I remember my maternal grandmother from Vienna.
As a schoolgirl she gave roses to Franz Josef.
The burghers sweated and wept. The children wore white.
And my grandfather moped in the Tyrol,

Imagining himself a headwaiter in America,
Floating in a high-church hush
Among ice buckets, frosty napkins.
These little globes of light are sweet as pears.
Kindly with invalids and mawkish women,

They mollify the bald moon.
Nun-souled, they burn heavenward and never marry.
The eyes of the child I nurse are scarcely open.
In twenty years I shall be retrograde
As these drafty ephemerids.

I watch their spilt tears cloud and dull to pearls.
How shall I tell anything at all
To this infant still in a birth-drowse?
Tonight, like a shawl, the mild light enfolds her,
The shadows stoop over like guests at a christening.

How pleasant to be able to say of such a poem that the Lowellian echoes are unmistakable, and that they do not matter a bit, that so totally has the poet taken possession of her materials and transformed them that the life and breadth of all she has touched are enlarged and enhanced. And as to the craft that makes such a poem what it is, how just it is to observe that mere quotation is nearly sufficient — analysis of dynamics may well take a back seat to a mode of pleasure we may not have thought possible where Sylvia Plath was concerned.

TWELVE

TO CONFRONT NULLITY: THE POETRY OF BEN BELITT

Ben Belitt is a poet who has written at least twenty exquisite lyrics, perhaps half of which appear in his most recent volume, *Nowhere But Light*
(University of Chicago Press, 1970). That he has been largely overlooked
by critical commentators in the course of a thirty-year career is not surprising really, nor cause for very much concern. The poems survive, and
are readily available. What is alarming, though, is that fewer and fewer
people, even among devout readers of poetry, seem any longer inclined to
pursue the kinds of pleasure that a poetry like Belitt's can provide. There
is an almost elegiac quality even in the appreciations of his admirers, as
though they were honoring something passed or passing, but surely not to
come. The late Henry Rago, editor of *Poetry* magazine for many years,
wrote of Belitt that "[his art] is rich in ways that seem lost to most of his
contemporaries." And indeed, the phrase "lost to most of his contemporaries" seems to say precisely what the situation has been for this poet.

Belitt extends and enriches a tradition that includes Wallace Stevens,
John Crowe Ransom, and Marianne Moore. It is a tradition in which the
eccentric particular flourishes, and in which the line between will and
fancy, on the one hand, and responsible imagination, on the other, is consistently challenged though rarely obscured. We experience in reading
Belitt's verse, as with Stevens's, "the fascination of what's difficult," to
borrow the title of Howard Nemerov's 1964 review of Belitt*, but what is
difficult in Belitt seems also necessary, if not perfectly inevitable. That is
to say, the texture of Belitt's work is characteristically dense in a way that
compels strict attention to details even as those details beckon towards

From *Sewanee Review*, Fall 1973.
* See *The New Leader*, June 22, 1964, pp. 23-25.

others which seem not so much predicted by their earlier counterparts as waywardly implied. We are not tempted, really, to stop at particular images for very long, for we believe the poet knows just where he is going and where he can confidently take us, and we feel we ought somehow to let ourselves be guided. We learn gradually to anticipate not the inevitable, but the relevant particular, the word or image that surprises us by revealing a significant pattern we had not expected but only minimally apprehended. Rarely in Belitt, or in the work of his distinguished predecessors, does the extravagant detail disturb the reader's developing or retrospective experience of the poem as a whole. Always the function of the vivid metaphor, the strange idiom, the rare and chiseled phrase, is to enlarge the context of a poem, or to clothe an abstraction in the flesh of an unmistakable object. Verbal feeling, an at least partial reliance on the sound and texture of words in themselves, does not in Belitt vie with sense, with the content of the poem, for as in Stevens, the processes of the poem's composition are very largely what the poem deals in. What we value above anything else in our experience of the poetry of a Belitt, a Stevens, a Ransom, is the pleasure of making our way through the obliquities of syntax and imagery and diction, for we recognize throughout that the obliquity is no evasive stratagem contrived to throw us off the trail of meaning, whatever that may be. We accept in reading this sort of work that poetry evokes a complex state of consciousness of which ideas and reductive meanings are a very limited part.

All this by way of introduction may seem an elaborate invocation and exaltation of an empty formalism, but that is not at all what I have in mind. Only a very inexperienced reader of poetry will take such an impression from an encounter with Belitt's work, to say nothing of Stevens's or Ransom's, though I confess that is just the initial impression I have to deal with as a teacher of undergraduate classes in contemporary poetry. Students complain that heightened language and gorgeous images are "insincere" regardless of how they are made to operate in a given poem, that an unfamiliar vocabulary is precious under any and all circumstances, that the sort of conscious elegance we find in a Ransom or a Belitt may have served some purpose at an earlier date but is hopelessly out of touch with the realities of our present moment. To speak to such students of the special intensities of Belitt's work, of the very specific dangers it invites and proves itself equal to, is to ask to be told that the dangers are not dangerous enough, are not sufficiently real and visible to warrant much concern. One senses early in one's pedagogical exertions how hard it will be to convey a sense of Belitt's commitment to writing as craft, to poetry as a means of testing and celebrating the energy and invention of the race, of which the poet is the type of the creative individual speaking on behalf of the universe we commonly inhabit. Perhaps it is necessary to say that certain poets require to be read only by a certain kind of reader, to be confronted by an intelligence for whom the idea of an equilibrium perilously approached and maintained continues to be beautiful. Belitt's is the ripe signature of a matured style, and though his poetry is hardly plain in Horatian terms, it is clear and exact and orderly, and full of teasing substance, to those who can submit to the conditions upon which each piece is predicated.

Just what it is Belitt wants his poems to get at, and in the process to become, we can identify by looking at his recent poem "The Orange Tree," surely one of the most lovely and persuasive poetic credos we have had in our time. I quote it in its entirety:

The Orange Tree

To be
intact and unseen,
like the orange's scent
in the orange tree:

a pod of aroma
on the orange's ogive of green
or a phosphorus voice
in the storm of the forge and the hammer:

to climb up a ladder of leaven
and salt, and work in the lump
of the mass, upward and down
in the volatile oils of a wilderness heaven:

to sleep, like the karat,
in the void of the jeweler's glass,
yet strike with the weight of the diamond —
perhaps that is to live in the spirit.

So the orange tree
waits on its stump as the wood of its armature
multiplies: first, the branch, then the twig in the thicket
of leafage, then the sunburst of white in the leaves, the odor's
epiphany.

All burns with a mineral
heat, all hones an invisible edge on the noonday, while the
orange's scent
speaks from the tree in the tree to declare what the holocaust
meant:

to be minimal,

minimal: to diminish excess, to pare it
as a child pares an orange, moving the knife through the peel
in a spiral's unbroken descent, till only the orange's sweat,
a bead of acidulous essence, divides the rind from the steel:

perhaps that is to live in the spirit.

Analysis cannot really touch a poem so wonderfully controlled and precise, though it is the business of the critic to try his hand at it, to wrest some trophy from an ultimately futile enterprise. One thinks, confronted by such a poem, of the words of the late French poet Paul Valéry, who wrote that "literature attempts by 'words' to create the condition of an absence of words." Well, perhaps that is what Belitt means when he speaks of his intention "to live in the spirit," but I do not think Valéry's formulation really tells us as much as we need to consider. What is, after all, an absence of words, and what would constitute a permitting condition? Surely Valéry is not speaking of the poet's yearning for death, for the transfiguration into the pattern of perfect silence, for it is not permanent extinction that the poet makes us think upon. He is much more involved in the evocation of what Dylan Thomas called "that momentary peace" which is brought about by and finally indistinguishable from the poem. And if it is not death that Valéry has in mind, the poem as harbinger of extinction, can we suppose he intends something akin to death yet not quite final or physical in the sense the word "death" conveys? With some confidence, I think, we can say that for Valéry, the idea of "an absence of words" expresses a commitment at once perilous and exhilarating to the void, to a self that refuses to be anything in particular. Valéry's commitment, and to some degree Belitt's, is to a "lucidity distilled and purified of all complicity with objects and events," to take the resonant words of the critic E. M. Cioran. The question we must ask, of course, is to what degree the inclination to dwell on one's own mental operations necessitates commitment to a metaphysical void as stringent and embracing as we find in Valéry's vision. Belitt's "The Orange Tree," with the weight it lays upon the word "minimal," is more modest somehow, more generous in its affection for the things in themselves rather than as paraphernalia in an exotic intellectual apparatus. Belitt's object is not to abolish the materials of his vision nor primarily to test his creative faculties against them, as though the materials were wholly alien objects existing only to be taken apart and exposed for their essential superfluity. In this respect, the spirit of Belitt's enterprise lacks the almost compulsional thoroughness and lofty severity of Valéry's poetry. Though he tells us rather little of himself, Belitt is a poet we feel we might want to get close to.

What is it, then, to live in the spirit, and why should it be so important to a poet, like Belitt, for whom the things of this world are not
wholly inimical and for whom the celebration of his own intense relationship to them is continuously gratifying? Surely it is no sudden or whimsical notion that Belitt develops, for it clearly underlies most of his best
work, and yet one senses that what is spiritual for Belitt may not be at
all what one calls to mind as he ponders other poets whose aspirations are
even vaguely spiritual. Would it seem fruitful to speak of reducing one's
physical needs, one's gross desires, in a quest for some spiritual essence
that is presumed to lie just beneath the surface of the object universe we
familiarly identify as the real world? Probably not, it would seem, for
Belitt's is no moral vision, no saintly pursuit, no trance-like reduction of
self to a still point stripped of instinct and content with waiting for
some ultimate deliverance. For Belitt, the line of poetry may be a stroke
of incantation, but it does not banish opposites, it invites them, even as it
invites the irreducible surd to a festival of intellect in which it must consent to be modified in tenuous juxtaposition with other figures. Belitt
neither fears an acquiescence in things nor is tormented by the inconsistencies of a mind bent on occasionally appropriating them for its uses. His
are confident appropriations, neither ecstatically fierce nor solemnly
detached and philosophical. To live in the spirit is to lend oneself to
things, to be open and unafraid rather than grasping, and to seek always
"that momentary peace" which is the emblem of an equilibrium precari-
ously achieved in the face of all that resists it. This is the crux of Belitt's
project, a project that is not merely facilitated by poetry as a medium,
but that is really indistinguishable from the life of poetry as an exercise
of will and discipline.

For Belitt, then, to live in the spirit is a very special sort of thing,
nothing less really than the conception of a poetic idiom so finely modulated that it constitutes a system of notations far removed from practical
language. Again, this is in no way to suggest that the raw materials with
which the poet works are to be discounted, or tolerated only so that they
may be transformed. What Belitt loves are the things *and* the transformative urgency he must at once yield to and control. What we wonder at
in reading Belitt is that he transmutes his raw materials, the stuff of reality
as we generally acknowledge it, as completely as the grape is transmuted
in its conversion to a fine wine, and yet the original elements remain. In
fact, they are felt with greater force and clarity than they were before
their translation into the specifically poetic medium. Belitt's "The Orange
Tree" speaks of "the sunburst of white in the leaves, the odor's epiphany,"
and we may perhaps be instructed in attending closely to such a line. We notice surely the non-visual associations of a phrase like "the odor's epiphany,"

and ask what such associations can generate. Are they essentially abstract associations — that is to say, can they generate anything like a substantive emotion? Do we know how such associations work in the poem as a whole? What seems all but certain is that a phrase like "the odor's epiphany" is essentially abstract, but that in combination with other such phrases and a number of different items its impact can be concrete, which is to say felt and specific. Take, for a moment, just "the sunburst of white in the leaves." The dominant word in that phrase is obviously the "sunburst." As a word taken strictly in a literal sense it calls to mind only the shadow of a visual impression. It is this shadowy quality that Belitt is after, and that he identifies with the word "minimal." What he courts is that essential impression which upholds the integrity of the observed and alien object even as it seems to whisper, "Change me, shape me, relate me." The "white in the leaves" of Belitt's poem is a whiteness momentarily apprehended and on its way to becoming something else. Now we may not expect the leaves or their white flowers simply to evanesce, and we are not concerned with their mortality. In this poem they are neither emblems of life nor harbingers of death. They bespeak rather a quality of light modified in the process of being considered. Belitt's concern is for the explicit object (the tree), its organic accouterments (the branches, leaves), and the inexplicable qualities of the object that describe an unseen order of reality. The commitment to process is inevitable in the light of such concerns, though Belitt more suggestively describes process as the longing of the poet for contradiction and for the created exigency. Speaking to an interviewer of "The Orange Tree," Belitt reports: "I can't assume that I have, in any idealistic or stylistic way, arrived at what readers would call minimal discourse. You've already said that, quite to the contrary, I am impelled to the baroque, which is the reverse of the minimal. Maybe that represents the longing of the baroque creature to be reduced and to achieve something that is sparing, the longing of the person who is committed to his own physicality to achieve invisibility — merely as a longing — and the hope that through the mediation of poetry, the two modes of being can in some way be reconciled, or at least dreamed of."*

What is so marvelous in Belitt's best work is its evocation of dreamlike longings without the accompanying fuzziness of patently poetical dream-states. Occasionally the mind is made to boggle a bit before it can get at the sense of a poem, but such disorientation as a reader may experience has more to do with the laxness of conventional discourse than with the excessive rigors of Belitt's. The late R. P. Blackmur once wrote of Stevens that his ". . . ambiguity is that of a substance so dense with being,

---

* See *Midway*, Winter, 1970, "Antipodal Man: An Interview with Ben Belitt," pp. 19–40.

that it resists paraphrase and can be truly perceived only in the form of words in which it was given." It is the sort of thing one feels compelled to say of whatever seems inscrutable or at least resistant to paraphrase in Belitt, and Howard Nemerov was no doubt correct as well when he wrote: "This predilection for what is not only odd but also oddly right may have been nurtured in him by his many years' work at translation, that desperate double-entry book-keeping where you get the word exactly matched at a price you hope isn't always extortionate, the momentary perfection at the risk of stopping the discourse while everyone says Ah! —." And so, Belitt's longing to be minimal in "The Orange Tree" is not confusing but tantalizing, the longing to be intact and unseen a function of the poet's capacity to abide in language as a notational system founded upon the dream of what is merely possible. That condition of possibility is no universe of patent weirdness such as we may expect in less responsible visions, visions whose linguistic trappings have no basis at all in verisimilitude. For Belitt, possibility is evoked by means of that tenuous equilibrium which the words of a language conspire at once to establish and to unsettle. To be minimal, to live in the spirit, as Belitt's poem clearly tells us, is not to be "a bead of acidulous essence," but to participate in a process by means of which an essence is conceivable: "to diminish excess" in accordance with our gifts may be sufficient "to live in the spirit."

What a reader will want to know, of course, if he takes all of this to heart, is what constitutes excess, and how the poet comes to make the necessary decisions. He will not want to handle the knife, to move it through the orange peel that is an aspect of his vision, without knowing just how much he ought to cut, after all. That there are no simple solutions to matters so complex as these we all know, and yet we harbor some vague anticipation that in any given instance, confronted by any poem with an air of competence and the demeanor of authority, we will surely know what ought to go, and what to stay. We read "The Orange Tree" and proclaim, as though insensible to contradiction, "nothing may be cut, no word but is essential." And while it is hardly recommended practice to pick words out from the poem, to isolate them from their fellows, as it were, there seems no substitute for such a stratagem if one is to make this sort of point. We take a word like "karat," for instance, and ask why it should not be discounted and removed. The figure to which it belongs conveys well enough what it means to be intact and unseen, but that has already been conveyed in three preceding figures. Why, then, still another? We might fish for an answer by speaking of the karat as an element of poetic texture, and of this texture as by definition a tissue of logical irrelevancies. To do so would be at once to claim for our argument the authority of Ransom's formulated poetics, and to banish the question.

I do not think this is necessary, for even if Ransom is largely right about texture, there are other ways of discussing what constitutes poetic excess. If we look at the word "karat" by itself, we are apt to think not only of its definition as a unit of weight for precious stones, but of the precious stones themselves in all of their hard-angled surfaces and glinty facets. We will be drawn within the consideration of a single word from an abstract to a relatively concrete apprehension, and in the process we will recognize just how much that is specifically referential can be condensed even in an abstract term. Then to replace the word in the proper context to which it has been assigned by Belitt is to see much more, to see how thoroughly the word elaborates its context, not merely enhances but enlarges it, and that is not a function we can easily dismiss. Having spoken earlier of the poem as a notational system, we begin to see "karat" as systematically related to other words and phrases which it either modifies or strengthens. These other items include "scent," "pod of aroma," "ogive of green," "phosphorus voice," "volatile oils of a wilderness heaven," and so on. What "karat" does is to extend the quality of what are fundamentally nonvisual associations and to modify our sense of each item by introducing simultaneously the notions of hardness and a weight consciously impressed. That the karat can "sleep in the void of the jeweler's glass,/ yet strike with the weight of the diamond" is crucial in whatever it is Belitt wishes to convey. To wish to be minimal, he would have us see, is not to desire self-effacement, but to aim at moderation and precision. If Belitt writes, as one critic noted, "with an unabashed sense of the grandeur and theatricality of the English tongue," he would have us discriminate between mere rhetorical pomp and a somewhat more chastened splendor. This splendor in the language, and this inextricably related weight of concern with precision and impact, is not to be mistaken for any incidental volatility in the poetic fiber, any presumed lightness of gesture as whimsical in its origins as it is likely to be ephemeral in the character of its impression. Without the word "karat" and the poetic figure to which it belongs, Belitt's reader might well be taking his primary guidance by emphasizing words like "phosphorus," "leaven," "volatile," and "epiphany." In so doing, the reader would surely miss the full significance of the poetic process as Belitt conceives it, and of the range of experience that process potentiates.

There are some things the poetry cannot actually accomplish, of course, though the poet can dream all he wants, and draw us in as fully as his skill allows. Belitt's figure of "The Loco-Bird," in the poem of that title, is an unsettling and charming phenomenon in this respect, for it casts a sharply ironic eye on the poet's tricks and that shortness of breath which signals his awe before mysteries the bird can scan more or less unmoved.

As Belitt reports, "All my need/ for the marvelous, my awe/ at the slant and equivocal — all/ I have stood on its head in behalf of the wonder/ that sharpens the bat's wit and tightens his decibels/ to portents and sounds from down under,/ is undone by his stance." Belitt's more hard-nosed readers may of course reply, well, why shouldn't this so-called "need for the marvelous" be undone? Why shouldn't the poet simply take us to the things of this world, without making them seem more than in fact they are? The answer, for Belitt, would have to be that he cannot quite manage such a stance, that he can only admire and dislike it at once. This poet must deal with the fact that for him the continuous stream of flux into which all things ultimately topple and fade is a nothingness which he can only identify with the presence in the world of the devil. Confronted by this specter, the poet is moved to the rigors of his creation, so that he may mitigate the sting of this intolerable condition. That the loco-bird "has no answers" is predictable, for it is "the bird/ of the abjectly ridiculous." That is to say, it is subject to none of those distinctions that permit men to speak seriously of what is beautiful and wondrous. It is all very well to prattle about poetry as an instrument uniquely capable of bringing us to the things themselves, but the course of a particular as reflected in a poem will be strongly tainted by need and sentiment. In a characteristically marvelous idiom, Belitt tells us admiringly that the loco-bird "knows how it feels/ to look into the billy and badge/ of the actual/ and veer out of range on his wheels/ without ruffling his daily sensorium," but we cannot be expected to opt for such a knowledge, and neither can Belitt. It is safe to say that those of us who continue to be interested in poetry will not mind having our daily sensorium ruffled from time to time, even if we lack the confidence we shall be able perfectly to get ourselves together again. To live in the spirit, as Belitt shows us, is not simply to acquiesce in things, but to dream of their possible transformation, to abide our longings with measured praise for the actual we seek to get beyond.

On occasion, we know, the transformative urgency the poet brings to experience threatens to distort that experience and to propose an occultation of reasoned perception which both poet and reader alike must resist. In Belitt's "Chipmunks" we have an evocation of the animal as a really various and exotic creature who alternately calls to mind a "sweet playfellow," a "safecracker," even a ballerina with "eyes/ sootily bowed back/ as for *Swan Lake,*/ dancing the word for surprise." But Belitt proceeds to still another, clearly less acceptable association, for he cannot decide "what draws love to its object, unlike to like, impure to pure,/ as my eyes to this?" Surely, one wants to proclaim, this should not be so very difficult to answer, for the poem early captures the vivid gestures and suggestive features even of so unlikely a creature as the chipmunk. One is drawn to the object both for the sake of the object in itself and for the release of creative faculties in ourselves which it presumably facilitates. The dire temptation, however, is to use the object as if it could legitimately be made to assume any shape at all, to forget its intransigent integrity. As Belitt ponders just "what draws love to its object," he returns to the chipmunk, and observes as follows:

> The chipmunk, balancing the spike
> of the acorn on prayed paws,
> knowing the stations of the rodent,
> finds kernel and meat
> with his nose,
> like any other rat . . .

The reader is intrigued, no doubt, by Belitt's flirtation with what is clearly an irresponsible, a tritely fanciful, association, and his almost immediate reversal of direction. The poet's visionary probing of the object is corrected by the density of his observation, by his regard for the object. ". . . Like any other rat" is the phrase that definitively reminds Belitt, and if need be his reader, just how silly it would be to assimilate the chipmunk to any singularly human context. The chipmunk does not pray, and to speak of "the stations of the rodent" is to seek to impose a spurious dignity and elevation on an object which is sufficiently wonderful to be loved without any impositions. What Belitt decides finally is that love must be content with what is different, the ambivalent imagination satisfied on occasion with the spectacle of pure animal instinct going about its grubby business, only marginally qualified by the poet's transfigurative zeal.

Throughout his career, Belitt has taken pains to remind us that it is the essential otherness of things we must respect and ponder, that our appropriations whether slight or immodest must be achieved by means of what can only be termed an art style. Only such a style, precisely nuanced, highly associative, frequently magnificent in the quality of its texture, can enhance our sense of nature's otherness and seal our conviction of some finally unknowable essence in the direction of which the poet's words can only motion. We are not speaking here of the art style as necessarily adequate to every kind of object, nor of its attraction for every poet. Obviously, as we have only to examine a representative contemporary anthology to conclude, most readers and poets hardly take it seriously any longer. It is assumed that the sheer quantity of life, of things, is inadequately represented in art poems, that the pure speculative interest in the action of words upon one another is an artificial, even effeminate preoccupation. In Belitt, as we have indicated, the focus on texture ultimately eclipses any other concern. An underlying honesty of observation is always apparent, but the reader's attention nonetheless is drawn towards the poem's internal chimings, allusive relationships, partial echoes. For a Belitt, what we have called the otherness of things consists precisely in their static qualities, those perfectly obvious elements which in themselves generally affect us very little, except as we anticipate just what it is they conceal. The static particular is enhanced in the art poem by the occasion it invests with necessity, and that occasion is nothing less than the poetic moment, the moment in which the poet's energies and gifts are mobilized to create the tension and temporary peace we earlier invoked. Belitt is not one for whom the world is a terrible place, a fact that bears repeating in a study of a poetry about which one has unfortunately to be defensive. There is nothing escapist in Belitt's poetics, though clearly the work is little engaged in the burning issues of the moment. The poems quietly contend that only a lethargic spirit would insist that we abandon a rich and versatile poetics in favor of that direct, natural, unartful style we have heard all too much about in recent years. Such a style cannot possibly evoke otherness, for its underlying assumption has to do with an equivalence between the raw materials of a vision and their mode of presentation, between the poet and his object.

The sort of assumed equivalence Belitt rejects is very much a hallmark of contemporary culture, and his poetry is therefore in profound conflict with a great deal we have almost learned to take for granted. A culture as detached as ours has been from the roots of mythic consciousness cannot suddenly decide to alter its direction and recover the spirit of the past, and Belitt to be sure never indulges an easy nostalgia for simple truths and religiously sanctioned identities. He wants to believe the heart can palpitate from time to time, if not in response to its own immensity, then at least in response to its unpredictability and occasional intensity, but he is too skeptical ever to settle for the wilfully generated ecstasies of the spirit-cultists. His is the modern critical spirit at its most profound and thorough remove from solutions of any kind, at home only in the cultivation of tensions. What he abhors is slackness, nullity exalted as nature, authentic conflict dissolved in the role-playing of amateurs. And as one would expect of an intelligence so fine as Belitt's, it is not violated by mere ideas, nor absorbed in the polemical engagement with trifles, no matter how influential those trifles may be. Belitt's best poems confront nullity by insisting that there are yet better things to do than lament one's losses, better even than counting one's blessings. Here is a poem entitled "Fat Tuesday" which calls upon the example of the great Spanish poet Antonio Machado to tell us what it is the poet must continue to cultivate, and why such poets will always be rare among us. A note to the poem tells us that Machado taught French in a provincial high school and lived out his life as an exile in France during the Spanish Civil War.

Fat Tuesday
(Homage to Antonio Machado)

Yesterday's
seven-thirty still clots the band-stand
clock. A child sleeps near the tinsel and papier-mache
in a kerosene ring under the wavering flies.
The lovers embrace on the grand-stand

as slowly
the machinery of celebration engages
its spokes and wheels around the incandescent center
of their pleasure. The plazas sparkle like stages
with a blind bicarbonation, and the masquers enter.

How simply
their dangerous reversal
is accomplished, the permutations of concealment
turning the cheese-cloth and the mica of their disguises
into the dramatis personae of a dress rehearsal

and showing
the eye-hole's razor edges framing the double ovals
of the masquer's eyes, like buckets rearising in a well, glowing
with vagrant spontaneities, the amateur's surprises
caught in the act of his improvisations.

Knowing
those Tuesdays of the flesh, reptilian
in their hungers, Antonio Machado, dragging his horse-hair
great-coat, his *Irregular Verbs for French Beginners,* the chalky
bastinado of his calling,

through the parched
Castilian school-day, in ear-shot of a parish's explosion,
scribbled a maxim in his Marginalia:
"Not to put on one's mask, but to put off one's face: that
is Carnival; the face alone in the world — that is appalling!"

And watched
from a cindery tussock how the masquers circled
a fountain in Baeza, putting off his cheekbones, eyes, the sensuous
underlip, emptying his skull of what it held
under the make-believe regalia,

leaving only
the arm-band of the widower's long deprival,
the school-teacher who had "studied under Bedier and Bergson"
counting martlets between the bell-tower and horizon,
intent on the apocryphal and lonely.

And noted:
"The poet is a fisher in time: not of fish
In the sea, but the whole living catch: let us be clear about that!"
He put off his face, facing away from Madrid; the Tuesday of the
                                        guns grew fat;
he crossed the border into France, put on his mask, and died into
                                        his wish.

This is a poem that might almost be said to aim at making a statement, and as such it stands somewhat outside the range of Belitt's characteristic productions. The language is clearly Belitt's, the attitudes not at all in contradiction of anything earlier encountered, and yet the organization of materials is surely unusual for the poet. In reading even a poetic credo like "The Orange Tree," or a deeply moving, lengthy autobiographical poem like "The Orphaning" (in five parts), one has the sense that the subject is important to Belitt as means rather than predominantly as ends. This is not to suggest that the poet is not really interested in his subject matter, for that is something any poet would find it difficult to counterfeit. Belitt is, though, interested in his subject no more than he is interested in his poem, since the poem allows him to possess his subject as he could not under any other circumstance. With "Fat Tuesday" we confront something else. It is a poem that does not strike us in any sense as having structured itself. It progresses according to the requirements of a determined two-part structure which is to impress upon us a firm distinction. Nowhere in Belitt's work do the poet and his function emerge so clearly in contrast to everything else, though the flavor of Belitt's generosity is in no way impaired. The poet Machado is presented to us as the type of the true poet, lonely, detached, not quite of this world though clearly attracted to it as to a gaudy spectacle. He sees clearly what others can see but vaguely if at all. Where he is given to what is rare and mournful, the others are readily manipulatable, committed only to pleasure and novelty and ease. The two-part structure of the poem roughly corresponds to the two-part distinction Belitt wishes to draw. The masquers in "Fat Tuesday" seek easy equivalences, dissolving old identities mechanically by putting on disguises and assuming new ones, but the poet resists the temptation to participate, and so retains his integrity as observer and artist.

Such an explanation is surely reductive, and it little suggests how moved I am by Belitt's poem. It is a lucid and poignant tribute to the life of poetry, after all, and puts in their proper place foolishly sentimental notions about the crucial value of inspiration and improvisation as determinants of the creative imagination. All the same, the poet does organize his materials here according to conventions we identify with other writers. The eccentric particular seems here considerably subdued, and even a line like "the plazas sparkle like stages/ with a blind bicarbonation" is less adventurously suggestive than one might expect it to be, were it located in another poem. What is absent in "Fat Tuesday" is the sense of the chance configuration, the happy juxtaposition of apparently disparate elements which surprises a reader and promises revelation. Though we know Belitt is not the poet to leave details to chance, to the happy accident, most of his structures seem at least open to an occasional "vagrant spontaneity" of the sort one comes upon in Stevens or Moore, though not often in Ransom. The child paring an orange in "The Orange Tree" is as close to such an unanticipated touch as anything in that poem comes, but we have seen how effectively playful tensions are evoked in "Chipmunks" and elsewhere in Belitt. Why this quality should be absent in "Fat Tuesday," why in fact Belitt's poem should actually disparage it as it is manifested in the masquers, we can only surmise. I see the poem as Belitt's definitive rejection of the amateur's surprises, of that radical imperfection contemporary poets and prophets of the authentic passion cultivate for all they are worth. Limiting ourselves exclusively to poetics, we might say that Belitt here evokes and dismisses what R. P. Blackmur in an essay on Lawrence called "the plague of expressive form." In that most important piece, Blackmur stressed "the operative principle, that the chaos of private experience cannot be known or understood until it is projected and ordered in a form external to the consciousness that entertained it in flux."

It seems reasonable to assert that expressive form, plague or not, has its strengths, and even Blackmur responded warmly to some of Lawrence's poetic excesses. But the masquers in Belitt's poem are not poets, and it may not be altogether fitting that we consider their vagrant spontaneities in the way we consider loosely associative, vaguely inspirational improvisations within the context of a poem. In fact, though, I do not think Belitt dislikes the masquers, or wishes to have us dislike them. What he dislikes are the uses that may be made of them, the frivolous conversion of the local carnival into a general spirit, a cultural ambience which Belitt associates with cheap trickery and self-deception. That the poet should ultimately be taken in by such a spirit is for Belitt unthinkable, and so he contrasts to the masquers not any man of sense and self-respect, but one of the very great poets of this century. For Machado, the poet must deal with "the whole living catch," the most exalted eminence as well as the mundane. No less might be said of any other modernist poet of stature. What the poet must not do, however, is to acquiesce in what he sees, to project his own selfhood as inevitably a reflection of what it is he observes and treats. Such a refusal is hardly characteristic of the poetry we hear most about these days. That circumstances may reduce the man who studied with Bergson to "counting martlets between the bell-tower and horizon" we cannot deny, but the poet with whom Belitt can identify will remain "intent on the apocryphal and lonely." It is an aspect of the minimal that Belitt here once again invokes, though in unique terms, and we know he speaks of living in the spirit when he describes its opposite as "those Tuesdays of the flesh, reptilian/ in their hungers." And as if this were not enough to tell us what we need to know, Belitt enlarges the dimensions of the poem to take in that basic political reality which the poet may only be able to mourn as from afar: the "Fat Tuesday," the "Tuesdays of the flesh," become at the poem's conclusion "the Tuesdays of the guns." The masquers, those who know only how to put on their masks and play without conviction of consequence, can be too easily led to those carnivals of riot and bloodletting that have so long absorbed men in the West. Such carnivals are the fruits of that vagrant vacancy Belitt refuses simply to smile at.

Belitt's is no moralistic perspective in "Fat Tuesday," and the poem never yields to the enticements of polemic or outrage. It is composed almost entirely in a minor key, one might say, a little unhappy with its knowledge, determined to make its discriminations without malice or overweening pride. What clinches the poem for us, though, is Belitt's clear reluctance to give in to the temptation of his own habits of language, at least in the sense that his verbal texture often dictates the structural progression of his poems. If in most of Belitt's memorable pieces a resonant word or phrase will set up an entire field of effects, a veritable chain reaction of brilliant and related images held together musically rather than logically, as if the poem were an abstract notational enterprise, the poet must reverse his direction in a poem that explicitly rejects excesses often associated with his characteristic practice as it is found in other poets. Since the subject matter of contemporary poetry has increasingly become the sheer chaos and disorientation of the poet's inner life as it is reflected in the chaotic surfaces of his lived experience, and since the form in which the poems are cast is increasingly diffuse and frivolously associative, Belitt feels he must resist both the substance and form of such a poetry. In "Fat Tuesday," then, he turns to a logical rather than to a musical structure, if the distinction may be made so unambiguously. He resists not only expressive form, with its implied equivalence between form and consciousness, but the compositional mode to which he has always been committed. Howard Nemerov described the mode as writing "by a kind of radar," wherein "a relevant sound is assumed to be a relevant sense." Surely no such procedure is operant in "Fat Tuesday," though one might argue over an expression like "blind bicarbonation," perhaps. Clearly sense alone dictates the contours of the poem, though here and there the eccentric particular continues to raise its head, unmistakably determined by the statement to which the poem is directed.

I have dwelt, perhaps to excess, on "Fat Tuesday" in part because it is an attractive poem, but more especially because it points up by contrast what we may generally expect of Belitt. If most writers achieve universality by sticking to the local particular, the particular that has been wrenched from some intimate experience whose redolence is somehow retained even in the unfamiliar, rarefied atmosphere of the poem, Belitt's universality is somewhat different. He opts for a kind of universal particular: the most eccentric detail or startling idiom rings with a sense that transcends any one place or moment. The detail is never really local, in the sense that it will often be in Ransom, never referential in the sense that it will condense and focus the visions and anxieties of an entire culture, or subculture. And Belitt does not generally set spiritual symbol against mundane effect, as though to reconcile levels of vision variously available to us. The function of Belitt's universal particular is to make process substantive, to render the experience of process, of dynamic creation as concretely as possible. That this is not the core of the matter in "Fat Tuesday" we have seen, but the poem does surely correct any misapprehensions we may have had about the nature of that process Belitt conceives. It is not a process we need worship, and to the degree that it dissolves the detached poetical faculty, or threatens to absorb it, it must in fact be resisted. What more fitting tribute to that process can we find in Belitt than the earlier mentioned five-part poem entitled "The Orphaning"? A resurrection of and coming to terms with the past, the poem memorializes the poet's mother, but while we would be mistaken to speak of this as merely an ostensible subject, the poem does operate on another level as well. It celebrates, in fact, itself, its commitment to that process wherein nothing is finally unthinkable or inhibiting, not even the painful fact and circumstances of a mother's blindness and death. Cumulatively the poem has the effect of a wondrous release, for it rehearses in an idiom at once elusive and explicit memories both nostalgic and painful, and permits the poet to emerge at last with neither pain nor nostalgia. This is no willed resolution — indeed, one has the sense that the poem resolved itself, that the poet allowed his art to function restoratively if it would. By the poem's end, the figure of Belitt's mother has become an emblem of all that makes us what we are, a universal emblem of influence and energy. What Belitt comes to cherish as the poem concludes is not the stone monument to the dead, but the poem as monument to life as ongoing process:

> Now I would reckon
> the whole cost of our greed,
> who would have the dead with us—

alive to us only in the indecent duress of their breathing—
because they still work in our pulses.
How much better that the lost and unseeing
should see through our need, in the end, foretell
our heart's changes, pass on to non-being,
knowing all would be well with us?

All is well with me, Mother.
Holding the great shell of your heart
in my hands, I hear the whole power of its passion
move through my fears, with its buoys and its bells
in a tilting horizon of undertow:

your blood and your milk still encompass me;
you walk through the gums and the leaves of midsummer,
first at the gates of my Sunday, with a paper
cornucopia under each hand:

There is nothing to own or disown,
nothing left to commemorate,
as now, in the year of your wish,
filling the sky like a birth-mark or a ripened placenta,
knowing the rite to be good,
I bend toward your death with this stone.

And what is that ongoing process but a succession of commitments to re-member, to create precisely in the face of what is difficult to celebrate. Belitt's poetry, as a medium uniquely adapted to reflecting and controlling that process, keeps us gratefully in mind of such commitments and is itself a most worthy occasion for celebration.

THIRTEEN

ALAN DUGAN: THE POETRY OF SURVIVAL

The poet Robert Graves in a memorable lecture series once criticized Ezra Pound's unabashed ambition of writing great poems. For Graves, it is more than enough simply to try to write good poetry. Such a view may perhaps be too easily explained by the fact that it represents the advice of a minor poet to a great poet. Alan Dugan is a good poet who has in his own peculiar way proven what Graves was getting at. By cultivating what is by any standard a confining style, and by exercising his caustic intelligence on a relatively narrow range of subjects, Dugan has created a significant body of work that speaks with authority to a variety of modern readers. One does not get terribly excited about Alan Dugan's work, but one nevertheless returns to it with increasing regularity, for it successfully inhabits that middle ground of experience which our best poets today seem loath to admit, as though to do so would somehow in itself constitute a denigration of their talents and a disavowal of intensity.

In Dugan, at least, if one is able to hope at all, he hopes to endure rather than to triumph. If one feels trapped, he will strive not for ultimate freedom and total independence, but for the sensation of freedom, temporary, imperfect, illusory. Dugan's spirit is best expressed in the conditional, which is to say that nothing he feels or thinks is very far removed from regret for what might have been, what the speaker might have thought, or done, or said. He asks nothing more of himself than he does of the hermit crab in "Life Comparison," that he do ". . . what is appropriate within his means, within a case," though even within these terms he is a failure. In short, Dugan's poetry succinctly conveys what most of us

From *Salmagundi,* Spring 1968.

perennially feel—that even genuine commitment to a life of inconsequence fails to silence the persistent anxiety that we might be somehow less human than even we agreed to be.

It has been generally accepted that Dugan is something of a moralist, and I suppose it is possible to go along with such a view if we understand a moralist to be someone who experiences convulsive fits of nausea from time to time, whenever, that is, he remembers who he is, what he has consented to become, and to what he has given his approval if only by means of undisturbed acquiescence. But then, it might just be that public demonstrations of nausea, a kind of communal vomiting, is all we have left in the way of genuinely viable expressions of response to the modern world. Dugan's is an intensely private, almost a claustrophobic vision, but the poetry is accessible to any kind of sensibility. In this sense, I suppose, most poetry is fundamentally communal if it enlists imaginative participation on the part of readers in whatever it is the poet describes. Dugan's poems do not threaten us as do the poems of writers like Plath and Lowell. At his best, Dugan communicates small perceptions appropriate to the lives of small people, and we listen not because of any glittering eye, but because we feel we should. The voice that apprehends us is as earnest as any we might hope to encounter, and the combination of brittle surfaces and an underlying warmth is relentlessly imposing. I am not sure that Dugan "is exactly what we need," as one observer claimed, but he shows us why we have little right to expect anything more.

To date, Dugan has published three collections: *Poems, Poems* 2, and most recently, you guessed it, *Poems* 3. In the latest volume, nine of the poems are entitled, simply, "Poem," which should not be terribly surprising to readers of Dugan's verse. His poems have variety, but they might all be drawn together as a single long poem. The same alert but static sensibility is operant in all of them, and the speaker rarely indulges the sort of emotional extremism which might distinguish his more inspired from his more characteristically quotidian utterances. Generally speaking, a Dugan poem begins by positing a problem, often representing a conflict between what the poet would like to think or imagine, and what he must in fact acknowledge as he looks about and within himself. Which is to say that Dugan's poems deal more or less with an extremely limited range of subjects, any combination of particulars in his work being easily reducible to an elementary abstraction in which polarities are anxiously opposed until, under the wry focus of Dugan's imagination, they somehow coalesce. Alternatives become merely matters of perspective, and the wise man gradually learns that as between one choice and another, we had best avoid choices altogether. If there is to be found in Dugan's verse a notion of what is good, one may be sure that it could be a lot better, and if Dugan occasionally permits himself the luxury of criticizing others, one may be certain that these others are only slightly worse than the poet can imagine himself. In Dugan, reticence is not just strategy, but a way of life. If you say too much about someone else, you will find his features growing disconcertingly familiar.

A poem like "Adultery" from Dugan's most recent book is particularly instructive. It is one of those poems in which Dugan's compulsive honesty is manifest to a degree that makes a reader almost as uncomfortable as Dugan must regularly make himself. I quote it in full:

> What do a few crimes
> matter in a good life?
> Adultery is not so bad.
> You think yourself too old
> for loving, gone in the guts
> and charms, but a woman says
> "I love you," a drunken lie,
> and down you go on the grass
> outside the party. You rejoin
> the wife, delighted and renewed!
> She's grateful but goes out
> with a bruiser. Blood
> passions arise and die
> in lawyers' smiles, a few
> children suffer for life,
> and that's all. But: One
> memo from that McNamara and his band
> can kill a city of lives
> and the life of cities, too,
> while L.B. "Killer' Johnson And His Napalm Boys
> sit singing by their fire:
> The Goldberg Variations.
> So, what do a few crimes
> matter in a neutral life?
> They pray the insignificance
> of most private behavior.

The poem is at once impressive in purely formal terms, for its construction is considerably more elaborate and careful than in most of Dugan's poems. There is the opening rhetorical question, repeated with slight but highly significant adjustment towards the end of the poem. There is the self-conscious wordplay working under conditions of great concentration: "can kill a city of lives/ and the life of cities, too." And finally there is the curiously logical if distinctly circular patterning of observations which permits the reader to savor the subtle modification of the poet's point of view which the poem has effected. I confess to what is perhaps a disproportionate admiration for poetry in which the dynamic process by which the poem unfolds is capable of forcing a shift in the poet's original intention. This is an essential element of our response to the work of a great poet like Sylvia Plath, and it is not without its rewards in Dugan's "Adultery," so different in both texture and authority from anything Plath wrote.

The conflict in "Adultery" is, as suggested, between what Dugan would like to assert, and what he must in fact discover as an honest man. On the one hand is Dugan's intention of contrasting the relative innocence of the average man with the calculating murderousness of "L.B. 'Killer' Johnson And His Napalm Boys," who institutionalize violence and blithely proclaim its wonders to the world in "The Goldberg Variations." On the other hand is the poet's discovery, in the interests of accuracy, that the "few crimes" of the private life can produce their own peculiarly terrible results, and that the diminutive scale of one's activities is not always assurance against an anxiety which ideally ought to afflict only the patent monsters of our civilization. At the poem's beginning, Dugan is relatively certain of what he has comfortably believed for some time. The opening lines are genuinely rhetorical. The average life is a good life, not glorious, but modestly decent. The adulterous foibles of the middle-aged are nothing more serious than ... foibles, testimony to the weakness of flesh and the unreality of righteous presumptions. Only what emerges in the scope of a few lines is not merely the ugliness of the pattern, but its utterly predictable contours. The question that must form at the lips is, how is it possible that even the most modest of men should allow such a circumstance to develop as far as it frequently does? Dugan's morality does not counsel him to condemn an action out of hand, but he retains enough sense of our common dignity to demand, quietly, that we be somewhat accountable for what we do. What Dugan calls into question in this poem, as in so many others, is not so much what we do, as how we do things without considering them. Adultery does not present the problem of controlling passion, but of doing something about drift, heedlessness.

The irony of ". . . a few/ children suffer for life,/ and that's all" is unmistakably a bitter irony. How dreadfully skillful we have become in our rationalizations of what we do. After all, we argue, it is foolish to expect perfection of mere mortals. But then, it is the characteristic sickness of our age that we wear our flawed humanity as a coat of armor, humbly displayed, as protection against any charge that we might be less than we ought. In the course of Dugan's poem, the "good life," gratefully unexamined before, becomes the "neutral life," which is quite different. The notion of neutrality suggests a refusal or inability to commit oneself in any particular direction. Where it is deliberate and considered and

contingent, neutrality may be useful. Where neutrality hardens into a comprehensive ethic or a life style, the individual ceases to think of himself
as fundamentally responsible for the things he does. In Dugan's poem,
while the speaker would like to plead neutrality and evade guilt, his
sincerity and intelligence block his way. The precision with which he
chooses his words obviates any possibility of his refusing to make basic
choices altogether. Perhaps the most crucial word in the conclusion to
"Adultery" is "pray," reflecting Dugan's abject uncertainty in the face of
the dilemma he has just projected. Is our "private behavior" for the most
part "insignificant," or is it true instead that the semi-conscious drift and
subtle malignity of the average man constitute a more telling indictment of
our humanity than our more overt betrayals of one another?

Dugan's concerns in "Adultery" are to be found with variation
throughout his work. In "Not To Choose," the poet acknowledges that he
"should be someplace else," that he should refuse to be the slave of habit
and deny ". . . the sweat/ of inhumane endeavor and its trash:/ goods,
deeds, credits, debts." But when he finally pays heed to those mysterious
voices that urge him to "Choose, choose," he finds it is too late, that he
is not ". . . in shape for choices,/ choices. No! Instead, I leave/ the dirty
business by the back/ window, climb down the fire escape,/ and sneak
out of town alive/ with petty cash and bad nerves . . ." Dugan feels that he
is somehow not of this world, that while situated within it and feeling
himself hedged by the most obvious and blunt realities, he is not prepared
to deal with it. He can neither accept the world nor reject it, nor conceive
a way to alter its course. What he fears most is that neutrality which predicts the death of the spirit, but more and more it appears to him that this
is indeed his most authentic reality. In "The Working World's Bloody
Flux," the speaker struggles against any inclination to commit himself to
a personal and potentially satisfying vision of things. Dugan is a skeptic
where the imagination is concerned, and he refuses to hope that his visions
or anyone else's can impose even a degree of permanence or order on a
frightfully deceptive and chaotic reality. According to Dugan, when one
feels most tempted to abandon inhibition, to submit to the imperatives
of passion, or simple fancy, one must flee, and failing successful escape,
". . . build a fort of reason in her country." In Dugan we find ourselves
desperately clinging to the quotidian, to what we defiantly know, for
only in this way can we be spared that ultimate disillusionment we want
to try to endure, and yet fear so much. Dugan's is a poetry of a man who
almost tries, and who is acutely sensitive to the magnitude of his loss.

Dugan is very much an original poet, which is to say that he never
sounds like any other poet so much as he sounds like himself. Still, there is
a kind of ennui in this verse that makes me think of Baudelaire, of his

compulsive fascination with the details of his own suffering, and of the relentless sincerity that led the great French poet to probe every aspect of what once seemed a morbid sensibility, though now strangely tame and moral. Eliot's still perfect essay on Baudelaire includes the following observation: "Indeed, in much romantic poetry the sadness is due to the exploitation of the fact that no human relations are adequate to human desires, but also to the disbelief in any further object for human desires than that which, being human, fails to satisfy them." How well this serves as a description of Dugan's poetry, as well as of Baudelaire's. And how clearly it enables us to see the nature of the tensions evoked in such poetry, though Baudelaire's is obviously the more heroic struggle, and consequently produces a wider range of tensions. With Baudelaire it is possible to speak, as Eliot does, of good and evil, of salvation and damnation. Such terms sound faintly preposterous where Dugan is concerned. His structures are too fragile, his temperament too subdued to sustain convictions of that sort. "Baudelaire was man enough for damnation," Eliot wrote, and we cannot but agree. It is difficult to imagine Dugan granting any authority that kind of ultimate dominion. Dugan's, we must remember, is a world in which judgments are relative, in which all relations are at best tentative. It is a world in which one may occasionally refer to impending catastrophe, but in which the dominant reality is "the daily accident" Dugan evoked in his first memorable volume.

And what is "the daily accident" but the inevitable skirmish that reveals our inadequacy, just at the moment when we have finally propitiated nagging doubts, or at least managed temporarily to forget them? Always there is the faceless authority, incomprehensible and unreasonable, and yet impossible to dismiss. Always the vaguely drawn circumstances assume a rigidity that is inexplicable, and yet effectively works to suppress revolt. In so many of Dugan's Kafkaesque structures, the speaker seems willing to go to his own imminent destruction, or at least to some severe punishment, in expiation of crimes he may not have committed. How often in Dugan, as in Kafka, one feels tempted to shake the speaker, to force him to acknowledge the absurdity of the largely abstract proposition to which he has assented, and according to the terms of which he no longer feels free to exercise independent, rational judgment. One thinks, for example, of one of Dugan's early poems, entitled "Tribute To Kafka For Someone Taken":

> The party is going strong.
> The doorbell rings. It's
> for someone named me.
> I'm coming. I take
> a last drink, a last
> puff on a cigarette,

a last kiss at a girl,
and step into the hall,
                                        bang,
Shutting out the laughter. "Is
your name you?" "Yes."
'Well come along then."
"See here. See here. See here."

Dugan's perception in a poem like this is neither of a sociological nor of a
political nature. It tells us not so much about the modern world as about
the effects of the modern world on a sensibility which has but barely
retained the will and energy to defend its right to exist. "Tribute" and
poems like it mark the almost total surrender of those pretensions to
innocence which according to both Dugan and Kafka are wholly incommensurate with the human being's insistence on his rights as an individual.
"See here. See here. See here." suggests the poet's persisting demand for
a measure of justice, but not for justice of an ordinary kind. As W. H.
Auden wrote of Kafka's hero in *The Trial:* "K. knows he is guilty, he does
not know of what, and his whole efforts are directed not to proving his
innocence but learning the cause of his guilt."

Like Kafka's characters, then, Dugan begins with the assumption of
guilt, largely founded upon his refusal to function comfortably as an
accomplice in the ongoing processes of his society. Even when he gives in
and follows along, as is the usual case, he dreams of a more stirring and
human denouement. Always Dugan posits an irreconcilable opposition
between the needs of the individual and the obligations of that individual
to his society. And so long as the human brain will continue to examine
the realities that threaten and finally overwhelm it, so long will the opposition be renewed. In "Two Hatreds Of Action," the Coward sees his de-
generation in the following terms:

Fifes drilled through my ears
and found my trouble: brains
coiled in the greys of self,
and reamed them with the shrieks
of civic cadence.

The troubling element is the brain, but without it there is no life worthy
of man: "My brains are drummed/ out of the corpse and wheedled away."
What seems to underlie so much of Dugan's verse is the conviction that the
world is a miserable place, but that to be aware of it is in no way protection against its insidious charms. The best one can do is now and again
to negotiate a temporary truce, often a bitter agreement in which one
vows not to think in return for promises he knows cannot be kept. In one

poem, the speaker determines to suspend disbelief, to commit himself to the world so that he may learn from it, to play on "as if all horrors are mistakes." Only, of course, Dugan must know that they are not mistakes, that brutality is more a way of life than a remediable nuisance. In one of his most ambitious and prophetic pieces, "On Zero," Dugan laments the debilitation of those imaginative resources which at one time could enable us better to control and pacify our perceptions, and which could give form and coherence to visions of violence, "and hold them helpless in the will/ and tractable to Liberal errands."

For us, Dugan claims, as we have no longer any belief in the vital capacity of the imagination fundamentally to improve the human condition, so we can no longer believe in those generous social instincts to which we have all along attributed our ability to survive. At our best, we endure by cultivating an amused detachment, an absurdist orientation, in which the worst we can possibly experience seems more than a little ridiculous alongside the more crucial perception of nullity as the predominating fact of man's existence. This is the "broad view," or so it has been called. Failing to adopt this kind of "cool," there are other alternatives. These, too, are "Qualifications Of Survivors":

> Hide in cesspools, sleep well
> on broken glass, and eat
> shit. Kiss the whips,
> hold the wife for rape,
> and have good luck:
> stumble behind a lamb
> before the bomb bursts
> and crawl out of the wreck
> to be the epitaph:
> "The good ones die first,
> but I am not so bad:
> Americans are worse."

This is the poem of a man who has spent years of his life cringing behind office desks, the poem of a man who frequently thinks of himself ". . . as an aging phoney, stale, woozy, and corrupt/ from unattempted dreams and bad health habits." And his predictable low-keyed humor, so often remarked upon by others, does little to mitigate the stinging venom of self-contempt that courses through so much of Dugan's work. His is a bitter eloquence. If the cadence is austere, it is rarely impoverished, and the muscular flow of his terse diction is rarely purchased at the expense of complexity. Dugan invites us to witness with him, without any redemptive qualification, the sordid spectacle of our common humiliation. It is a strangely unimpassioned witnessing, but then, as Dugan thoughtfully reminds us, "Americans are worse."

FOURTEEN

ON ADRIENNE RICH: INTELLIGENCE AND WILL

The title of Adrienne Rich's sixth and most recent book of poems is *The Will To Change*. As a title it declares emphatically the centrality of that will in the poet's life and work, and indeed, it has provided an unmistakable thrust in the poems she has written since 1958 or so. Now it seems to me that most of our contemporaries value this will to change all too much, not because they are politically radical or personally nimble and adventurous in any striking way, but because such a will has taken on the qualities of an ideological fashion. To be sure, fashions in the realm of intellect do necessarily bespeak particular emotional commitments and frames of mind, and may not therefore be reduced to the status of intellectual phenomena pure and simple. But we know that ideological fashions frequently detach themselves from underlying emotional factors and assume in time a life and momentum of their own. So important is the will to change in Adrienne Rich's mature work that it may well serve as primary focus in any consideration of her poetry, for it is her understanding and treatment of the ideological dynamics involved that will have much to say about the kind of intelligence we respond to as we read the successive volumes. At the same time, we must try to do justice to the wide range of insights, indeed to the variety of wills, represented in this very singular poetry.

The poet has had an abiding sense of her life and work as split in a decidedly simple and predictable way. As a young woman she had thought of herself as neat and decorous, cultivating a solid look, "Neither with rancor at the past/ Nor to upbraid the coming time," as she described it

From *Salmagundi*, Spring-Summer 1973.

wistfully in "At Majority" (1954). In those years, things had a certain weight and poems could express them in all their apparent accustomedness and density. It was not as though the young poet were entirely unaware of the abyss of uncertainty, but she had a confident way of holding it off, of handling it elegantly so that it seemed at most a mildly threatening idea. Her poetic skills, lavishly praised in the early fifties by Auden and Jarrell among others, seemed altogether a match for any difficult notions or untoward sensations that might have disturbed that wonderful poise and control, whether of self or of the aesthetic medium. All at once, though, in the poems of the late fifties, a more embattled and urgent air began to creep in, and the poet discovered that she had been covering up, not controlling merely, but wilfully evading. There is a certain tidiness in the discovery as she seeks to evoke it in the volume *Snapshots of a Daughter-in-Law* (1963), but we know in the perspective of subsequent volumes that the experience was in fact deeply important to the poet. Where in 1954 she could announce: "Now knowledge finds me out;/ in all its risible untidiness/ it traces me to each address,/ dragging in things I never thought about" ("From Mourning Glory To Petersburg"), she handles her material much more substantively, if still a bit programmatically, in "The Roofwalker" (1961):

> Was it worthwhile to lay—
> with infinite exertion—
> a roof I can't live under?
> —All those blueprints,
> closings of gaps,
> measurings, calculations?
> A life I didn't choose
> chose me: even
> my tools are the wrong ones
> for what I have to do.

The single, controlling image demanding control of all particulars in a given poem is perhaps the most consistent element in the volume *Snapshots,* and accounts for the still formal quality we sense in the various poems. They deliver up their treasures rather too explicitly, we feel, and the note of discovery becomes so pointed and anticipated that we are grateful even for outbursts of spite or anger that break the pattern. But best of all are the rare introductions of specific tensions the poet wishes to work through rather than to resolve. In the ten-part title poem (1959-1960) she asks of herself, of women generally, "Pinned down/ by love, for you the only natural action,/ are you edged more keen/ to prise the secrets of the vault? has Nature shown/ her household books to you, daughter-in-law,/ that her sons never saw?" There is no clamoring here for definitive answers, no triumphant declarations of the courage to change as though change were all one could conceivably ask of anyone truly human. The poet's self-concern here is seemly and reasonable. She wants to know about herself, her secrets, her gifts. She does not speak yet as though perpetual motion were the ideal state, the will to change the index of perfect maturity. Her business, to the degree that she can make it out, is to feel herself, to think beyond formal categories, to reject whatever is merely habitual on behalf of what she can discover as potentially to be won. Most important of all, she does not blithely reject the past as though it had nothing to tell, nor dismiss orderliness and the clean lines of a modest behavior for undifferentiated passion. The lust to be wholly contemporary has not yet become dangerously compelling.

In what is surely her best book to date, *Necessities of Life* (1966), Adrienne Rich moves steadily to inhabit the world and to make contact with that self she had thought largely repressed and almost forgotten. It is a volume not so much of youthful discovery as of sobering expansiveness, a coming out into a challenging universe armed with all the gifts of steady vision and confident warmth we associate only with a very mature person. Adrienne Rich achieves in the poems of this volume a dignity and casual elevation that are altogether rare in the poetry of any period. Imagination here is in the service of intelligence in a way that might well dampen the poetic ardor of most poets, more committed as they are to the sheer vagrancies of creative inspiration. The remarkable thing about the poems in *Necessities,* though, is that they betray no decline of invention, no thinning of poetic texture, nothing in the way of mere reasonable constraint. They are rich in a quality I can only call character. They bear, everywhere, the marks of a rare and distinguished personhood which we take as at least an implicit celebration of our being. But the poems themselves can say ever so much better what I mean to describe. Here is "After Dark" (1964), of which it would be unfair to quote less than the full text:

I

You are falling asleep and I sit looking at you
old tree of life
old man whose death I wanted
I can't stir you up now.

Faintly a phonograph needle
whirs round in the last groove
eating my heart to dust.
That terrible record! how it played

down years, wherever I was
in foreign languages even
over and over, *I know you better
than you know yourself   I know*

*you better than you know
yourself   I know
you*   until, self-maimed,
I limped off, torn at the roots,

stopped singing a whole year,
got a new body, new breath,
got children, croaked for words,
forgot to listen

or read your *mene tekel* fading on the wall,
woke up one morning
and knew myself your daughter.
Blood is a sacred poison.

Now, unasked, you give ground.
We only want to stifle
what's stifling us already.
Alive now, root to crown, I'd give

—oh,—something—not to know
our struggles now are ended.
I seem to hold you, cupped
in my hands, and disappearing.

When your memory fails—
no more to scourge my inconsistencies—
the sashcords of the world fly loose.
A window crashes

suddenly down. I go to the woodbox
and take a stick of kindling
to prop the sash again.
I grow protective toward the world.

II

Now let's away from prison—
Underground seizures!
I used to huddle in the grave
I'd dug for you and bite

my tongue for fear it would babble
—Darling—
I thought they'd find me there
someday, sitting upright, shrunken,

my hair like roots and in my lap
a mess of broken pottery—

wasted libation—
and you embalmed beside me.

No, let's away. Even now
there's a walk between doomed elms
(whose like we shall not see much longer)
and something—grass and water—

and old dream-photograph.
I'll sit with you there and tease you
for wisdom, if you like,
waiting till the blunt barge

bumps along the shore.
Poppies burn in the twilight
like smudge pots.
I think you hardly see me

but—this is the dream now—
your fears blow out,
off, over the water.
At the last, your hand feels steady.

The echoes in such a poem serve only to enhance one's sense of its largeness, its breadth of vision and informed intelligence. Nothing in the way of irrelevant local texture removes our concern from the very grave and beautiful relation that is evoked, a relation that is as much a communing of a soul with itself as it is the working out of affections between the generations. The tension here is not between idea and image, between abstraction and concretion, but between what we know and what we feel. It is the business of the poem to do justice to both, to see to it that the one is at least to some degree informed by the other. There is no pristine self here, no absolutely authentic being the discovery of which is exclusively potentiated by a cutting loose from all that is customary and embedded. How gratifying that the father's actual or imagined *"I know you better/ than you know yourself"* should be dealt with not by way of severe rejection or denial, but in the context of the words, "woke up one morning/ and knew myself your daughter./ Blood is a sacred poison." Relation is something we make, to be sure, but it may be conferred as well, and this the poet gracefully acknowledges in the poem as a way of coming to terms with her own inclinations. As she ponders the relationship, projects for herself a consoling vision of it that is at once conclusive and fragrantly evocative, her associations become progressively literary, but there is no ounce in them of the inauthentic. The poetic echoes refresh the context by reminding us of comparably moving treatments of similar themes. At one point she exclaims, "no more to scourge my inconsistencies—" and we think of Lowell's farewell to his grandfather in *Life Studies.* Or, as we read the first three stanzas of part two, we think of Sylvia Plath's ritualistic efforts to make contact with her father. Or we call to mind Lear's farewell to Cordelia as we ponder such lines as "I'll sit with you there and tease you/ for wisdom, if you like," and so on. This is a poetry that can afford such echoes, for as it is generous with its emotions without railing or ranting, so can it securely draw upon an entire tradition to substantiate its sincerity. In a work less open, less generous, the associations might seem insufficiently modulated or assimilated, perhaps even calculated. Here they strike us as fine.

I have chosen to look at "After Dark" because it is a wonderful poem and because it illuminates by contrast what has lately happened in Adrienne Rich's work. We notice in this poem that the speaker is not pleased that "the sashcords of the world fly loose." Though she struggles to win her own sense of self, she yet feels the need to be known, to be seen if not quite seen through. How beautifully she puts her impulse in the line "I grow protective toward the world," for we understand that the impulse of which she speaks is nothing less than the mature desire to resume coherence in the face of progressive assaults on those stable props that constitute our necessity and at least part of our definition. That "blunt barge" is more than the vehicle of death here. It is, in fact, an emblem of that coming home to which each of us must incline, not in the sense that we simply resign ourselves to things as they are or to our eventual demise, but in the sense that we acknowledge what belongs, inescapably, to each of us. As the poet recalls the murderous fantasies of childhood she senses — as she sensed when still a child — the degree of her participation in her father's death, and we are impressed with the profound ambivalence of most such relationships. The poem's conclusion in no sense banishes this ambivalence, or resolves it, but it allows for a final expression of affection that further validates the sincerity of that ambivalence.

Not all of the poems in *Necessities,* superb as most of them are, have quite that air of intense sentiment, so bittersweet in "After Dark." In "Side By Side" (1965), for example, the poet gives us something considerably more fragile, more suffused with that silken ethereality we conventionally associate with woman's poetry. No doubt about it, it is a woman's poem, but to say so in this case is not so much to describe its limitations as to do homage to its fragrance:

> Ho! in the dawn
> how light we lie
>
> stirring faintly as laundry
> left all night on the lines.

You, a lemon-gold pyjama,
I, a trousseau-sheet, fine

linen worn paper-thin in places,
worked with the maiden monogram.

Lassitude drapes our folds.
We're slowly bleaching

with the days, the hours, and the years.
We are getting finer than ever,

time is wearing us to silk,
to sheer spiderweb.

The eye of the sun, rising, looks in
to ascertain how we are coming on.

We may think, upon first encountering such a poem, that it demonstrates the gift of a certain style without any corresponding gift of thought. And surely, "Side By Side" is not a poem rich in ideas. What it has is a flexible central image the exploration of whose nuances constitutes the heart of the matter. We feel about the poem that it has, if not strength, then a kind of tenacity, a tenacity that is a function of persisting focus. "The eye of the sun," explicitly evoked in the final stanza, is the dominant presence throughout, we feel, and we are not a little struck by the seeming benevolence of its steady illumination. "We are getting finer than ever," the poet announces, "time is wearing us to silk,/ to sheer spider web." How fortunate, we are tempted to exclaim, how lovely that we should be "getting finer than ever" with the passage of time, that our lot should be refinement rather than impairment. The element of passivity, though frequently unwholesome elsewhere, is in this poem so lightly evoked that it comes to seem a positive strength. No doubt, the mildly ironic domestic image of laundry hanging out to dry in the opening stanzas at once establishes the basically congenial nature of the vision, so that we are prepared to accept what we read as at least partially fanciful. This initial sense is surely confirmed at the poem's conclusion in the image, simultaneously wry and hoary, of the sun as proprietary eye looking in at his tender morsels, the suggestion of delicious consumption surely playing in the margins. I do not want to make more of the poem than it deserves, but surely it records with a fidelity both grave and delighting the trancelike sense of life's passage, the experience of confronting less, where once there lay ahead only more. What we miss in the poem is that exquisite particularity Adrienne Rich is so skilled in embodying in her major work, but we are pleased all the same with what we have, in all its quiet ambivalence.

If we ask what are the sources of such ambivalence, what allows the poet to be so unflinching while yet so pleasant, so generous, we should have to speak again of character, but also and more precisely of the poet's sense of the rhythms of experience, the necessary alternations of dream and reality in the life of the spirit, the cultivated tension between knowing and feeling. In the poem "Not Like That" (1965) the speaker woos a picturesque extinction, a deliberate forgetfulness that prepares one for nullity of a most encompassing sort. She envisions herself in a domesticated cemetery — "The turf is a bedroom carpet" — and muses: "To come and sit here forever,/ a cup of tea on one's lap/ and one's eyes closed lightly, lightly/ perfectly still/ in a nineteenth century sleep!/ it seems so normal to die." As she works the shadows of the portrait, probing its secrets, she concludes that it is not extinction she wants, but some soothing vision of ultimacy such as we find perpetually available to us as children. Perhaps it is the very availability of childish consolation that announces to the older poet the insufficiency of those earlier visions. This has nothing to do with simply growing up and accepting the fact that we can no longer delude ourselves with childish fancies. What the mature poet determines to banish is the tendency to drift. She refuses to allow imagination to go its own way, to seek its objects in any guise. Not just the fantasies, the easy consolations, but the very time of childhood "was a dream too, even the oatmeal/ under its silver lid, dream-cereal/ spooned out in forests of spruce." In the remarkable image of dream-cereal the poet tells us she refuses to be nourished by anything patently insubstantial, rejects easy regressions as the means to any satisfying identity. Such symbolic returns have about them a death-like air when too regularly or lavishly indulged, and the static portraiture of the seated figure, "eyes closed lightly, lightly," surely stands in this regard as starkly emblematic warning. Things are not still, not permanent, not easy, though we are sometimes tempted by "the warm trickle of dream/ staining the thick quiet" — a dazzling image bespeaking at once the coziness and puerility of the all too available. The final lines are bracing: "The drawers of this trunk are empty./ They are all out of sleep up here."

The rejection of the dream-life, the emergence into clarified perception and knowing interaction with the things of this world, is central to the poems of *Necessities*. The will to change is considered within a relatively stable context, for the poet here presupposes a way of life. It is nothing so exalted and distinctive as the old high way Yeats wistfully remembers in the poems of Coole Park or in the "Prayer" for his daughter, but it has its decided features. Chiefly these features have to do with a decision to work through one's problems, to be attentive to one's needs and to the shifting demands of one's environment and companions, to work always at breeding flowers from the refuse heap of the contemporary situation. Involved as well is a growing commitment to what might be called social reality, as though one could not legitimately expect to know oneself or to deal with one's personal limitations without considering the degree to which they are conditioned by external actualities. What we have quite frequently in these poems, and to a much greater extent in the later work, is the spectacle of a vivid intelligence working to avoid being overwhelmed by brute matter. In "Open-Air Museum" (1964) the poet wonders at frail flowers sprouting in the town dump, and feels she has been brought "face to face with the flag of our true country:/ violetyellow, black-violet,/ its heart sucked by slow fire." Fragments of shattered dreams lie about, "the rose-rust carcass of a slaughtered Chevrolet," scraps of a photo-album, a three-wheeled baby carriage. But it is not the poet's function simply to mourn what is past, or to shake her fist at a civilization that betrays its best hopes. The emphasis of her poem lies in the lines "those trucked-off bad dreams/ outside the city limits/ crawl back in search of you." Her heart counsels that she listen carefully for the intermittent "Cry of truth among so many lies." There is no stratification of meaning here, no loose weaving together of various levels of intention that yet remain distinct, but a total human situation truly observed. The poem creates an enduring illusion of virtual experience, in Susanne Langer's terms. Our sense of the poem is of having entered a world that is whole and clearly related to the world we customarily inhabit, though not literally coextensive with it. What we recognize, are never permitted to forget in Adrienne Rich's poems, is that the materials we are shown constitute events in the poet's mental and emotional life. We do not expect, and never feel that we get, transcriptions of reality such as a theory of verisimilitude might enjoin upon the artist. Nor do we get, or expect, discursive argument of a philosophical nature. All we are shown carries with it that peculiar baggage of associations and tensions that the poet customarily lugs around, as though it were strapped forever to her back. She may shift the weight from time to time, may dance about to lighten the load, may even, temporarily, forget her burden, but it is there, and she will acknowledge it in time.

In "Like This Together" (1963), the poet's understanding of her work as in some basic way a clarification of life, her own and others', is verified in a whole range of particulars. She informs us in a recent interview (*The Ohio Review*, 1972) that "what it means to be a man, what it means to be a woman. . . . is perhaps the major subject of poetry from here on." But such an approach seems almost parochial set against the more embracing drive of "Like This Together" and comparable pieces. Not "what it means to be a woman" but how to preserve one's essential humanity is the underlying thrust of her poem. What threatens is the disintegration of the immediate physical landscape, an erosion of stable landmarks that leaves us without concrete roots, "sitting like drugged birds/ in a glass case," unable to break out for want of identifiable objects towards which we may press ourselves to struggle. So the civic disaster, the blight of perpetual and empty urban renewals is a reminder of the hollowness of most other renewals undertaken in the spirit of escape. "They're tearing down the houses/ we met and lived in," she cries. ".... soon our two bodies will be all/ left standing from that era." And on. It is a miserable scene, dank and impoverished, and it leaves the lonely soul with no recourse but to "old detailed griefs/ [that] twitch at my dreams," an aftermath of "miscarried knowledge." But it is not victimization that Adrienne Rich courts, despite her obvious affinities with the victims of recent confessional verse. She takes what we may call a more active approach to the body of her fate most of the time. The marvelous final stanza, part five of her poem, puts the case as follows:

> Dead winter doesn't die,
> it wears away, a piece of carrion
> picked clean at last,
> rained away or burnt dry.
> Our desiring does this,
> make no mistake, I'm speaking
> of fact: through mere indifference
> we could prevent it.
> Only our fierce attention
> gets hyacinths out of those
> hard cerebral lumps,
> unwraps the wet buds down
> the whole length of a stem.

To read such a stanza is to have rather a sharp sense of how the world appears to a woman of intelligence and purpose, who is yet capable of considerable pain. It is a sequence of lines that impresses much more than affirmation, more than the blithe overcoming to which so many of our poets since Emerson have directed their energies. And, as an important aspect of its message is the exalting of "fierce attention," just so does the poem ask us for careful scrutiny if we would glean its fullness. In particular we shall need to address cautiously the lines: "Our desiring does this,/ make no mistake, I'm speaking/ of fact: through mere indifference/ we could prevent it." Prevent what? we may at first wonder. Prevent "dead winter"? "Our desiring"? Actually, of course, the poet refers to something we may call the impaling past, the past imperfectly apprehended that locks us into sterile patterns, rehearsed postures, that blocks our way when we would step out and experience ourselves as creatures of quite remarkable extension. Shall we be anything but creatures of "fierce attention," the poet wants to know, and she is well advised to ask, for indifference, a function of cultural disorder and the breakdown of established authority, is surely among the central blights of our period.

The 1969 volume *Leaflets* seems to me to mark a decline in the poet's career. There are some brilliant things in the volume, patches of exquisite writing, several perfectly achieved poems, but the sense one takes from the volume is of things coming apart, not the texture of the universe merely, but the fiber of the poet's attention. She seems, if I may say so, less careful about what she says. She says, in fact, silly things, of a sort we cannot easily ignore or attribute to passing inattention, while moving on to the nearest reassuring sentiment. When a mature and accomplished poet writes ("In The Evening," 1966): "The old masters, the old sources, haven't a clue what we're about,/ shivering here in the half-dark 'sixties," we are forced to stop and vent serious doubts about the entire enterprise. What is the poet after? She seems too shrewd for us to say it is simply rage or utter desperation that prompts her to declare the perfect uniqueness of her own burdened moment. Is human experience in general so radically disparate that even the old masters could fail to intimate our problems, provide us with a clue? Apparently the poet believes in the specialness of her experience, though frankly nothing she tells us seems to me in the least astonishing. But that is not really so important. What matters is why she feels compelled to make us feel we have no clues. She apparently does not wish to play the role of victim to the hilt, so that vulnerability is but one of the notes she regularly sounds. And even when indulging such a posture, she resists the temptation to wring it for all it's worth, so that she appears at once vulnerable and wryly ironic. In "Flesh And Blood" (1965) she begins with "A cracked walk in the garden,/ white violets choking in the ivy," and we anticipate a slightly offbeat but gruesome cataloguing of small disasters. We get instead some mild reminiscence and a line like "Nobody's seen the trouble I've seen/ but you." The play on the song title is casual and flat and encourages a kind of pleasurable if silently knowing wink between poet and reader. The tone is similarly right and more or less satisfying in "Holding Out" (1965) with its flavor of Frost or David Wagoner, the word "maybe" hovering over every insight: "Maybe the stovepipe is sound,/ maybe the smoke will do us in/ at first — no matter." Why, then, the insistence upon the radical unfamiliarity of our vulnerability in poems like "In The Evening," a poem, by the way, that bears more than slight resemblance to "Dover Beach," both in the dire situation it posits and in the persistent clinging together of the two central figures.

In *Leaflets* and in *The Will To Change*, Adrienne Rich labors, it would seem, under the notion that we are inevitably period-creatures, that to deny the fact is to deny our very being. She tells us in "The Demon Lover" (1966) that "A new/ era is coming in./ Gauche as we are, it seems/ we have to play our part." Taken by themselves, such lines surely point in but one direction. The fact is, though, that they may not be taken in isolation from a great many other lines which not only qualify but openly contradict them. What I conclude is that Adrienne Rich wishes with all her strength to be other than a period-creature. She wishes, that is, to retain that sense of self displayed so handsomely in *Necessities of Life.* The problem is that progressively she falls prey to ideological fashions like the will to change, so that, though she is too intelligent ever to mouth petty slogans, she allows herself to be violated by them. They touch her verse with an almost programmatic wand. The underlying energy and tension remain, but they grow less and less visible as the set assertions come staggering forward:

> The friend I can trust is the one who will let me have my death.
> The rest are actors who want me to stay and further the plot.
> - - - - - - - - - -
> If the mind of the teacher is not in love with the mind of the student,
> he is simply practising rape, and deserves at best our pity.
> - - - - - - - - - -
> Leroi! Eldridge! Listen to us, we are ghosts
> condemned to haunt the cities where you want
> to be at home.
> - - - - - - - - - -
> I have learned to smell a *conservateur* a mile away:
> they carry illustrated catalogues of all that there is to lose.
>   (quotations from "Ghazals," 1968)

To think that the poet who could write so persuasively of her father's loss, of her own hard-earned, satisfying growth, should be so snide about having something to lose. What can she be thinking when she writes of smelling "a *conservateur*"? Does the poet imagine that men who have something to lose are necessarily blind reactionaries? Does she hold at no value the fruits of a man's labors when he is able to taste and savor those fruits? I ask such questions not to suggest that the poet has lost her senses — far from that — but to suggest how charged she has become with the nauseous propaganda of the advance-guard cultural radicals. Such sentiments as I've quoted from Adrienne Rich's poems are not, I insist, serious expressions of her intelligence but reflections of a will to be contemporary, to please those who are nothing but contemporary, and who therefore can have little sense of the proper gravity of the poetic act. Sincere they may well be, some of them, but the density of language, the gravity of the word well chosen and scrupulously employed are surely considerations beyond their characteristic sense of things. That Adrienne Rich should have "fallen in" with such models is greatly to be lamented, for her development as a poet cannot be a happy one under such an influence.

I say this recognizing full well that one is not supposed to confuse the content of poems with their specific value as poems. The idea does seem to me a little ridiculous, taken generally, but I can see the point of such an objection where the works of certain other poets are at issue. If a poet is a radical innovator who brings experimental resources to his craft that may alter the direction of poetry in his time, he is surely entitled to be examined in a special way. Or if the poet is possessed of a voice so grandly authoritative that it strikes us as in some sense the expression of an entire age, so again will we need to deal with it in a special way. Adrienne Rich is neither a radical innovator nor the voice of an age. We think of intelligence when we read her best work, and we miss that intelligence when we examine much of her recent verse. It is no use pretending that what she says does not matter, or oughtn't to, or is marginal, by comparison with the brightness and energy of her line or the sharpness of her diction. It matters to us as readers that she should speak of practising rape when "the mind of the teacher is not in love with the mind of the student." How many students have minds, we should wonder when confronted with such a line, that any sensitive and intelligent person could love? How many of us can love what we at best but barely know? When I repeat such questions to myself, particularly in connection with the work of someone I admire as much as Adrienne Rich, I try to recall other lines, better urgings from the same body of verse. I remember, for example, "How did we get caught up fighting the forest fire,/ we, who were only looking for a still place in the woods?" The quality of such a line is more than plaintive. It is touched, perhaps, by a certain pride, but it is not altogether misplaced, at least. The suggestion is that we could not but take our place fighting the blaze, and this is no doubt what many serious people feel. Such sentiments, as the heart of a poet's work, are surely acceptable provided that they are meaningfully hedged, provided that they are accompanied by other sentiments that sufficiently undercut or challenge them, so that readers are called upon for participation rather than unambiguous assent. Only in scattered poems do we feel the presence of this fruitful tension as we go through the last two volumes. One slight poem in *Leaflets* called "The Observer" (1968) quietly establishes the tension of which we speak, a tension that abides as much in the poet as in the poem. What impresses me about this poem as well is the measured coherence of the vision, a coherence no doubt impossible for the poet trying to capture the unstable rhythms of the contemporary western scene. Where most often in *Leaflets* we have fragmentary observations, notations jotted in the tumult of manning the front lines, here we have a sense of something approaching duration, the picture to be pondered in place of the frantic words trailing beyond our grasp:

> Completely protected on all sides
> by volcanoes
> a woman, darkhaired, in stained jeans
> sleeps in central Africa.
> In her dreams, her notebooks, still
> private as maiden diaries,
> the mountain gorillas move through their life term;
> their gentleness survives
> observation. Six bands of them
> inhabit, with her, the wooded highland.
> When I lay me down to sleep
> unsheltered by any natural guardians
> from the panicky life-cycle of my tribe
> I wake in the old cellblock
> observing the daily executions,
> rehearsing the laws
> I cannot subscribe to,
> envying the pale gorilla-scented dawn
> she wakes into, the stream where she washes her hair,
> the camera-flash of her quiet
> eye.

Other poems in *Leaflets* one ought to read, for pleasure and provocation, include "5:30 A. M.," "The Key," "Abnegation," and "Nightbreak."

We began by speaking of the centrality of the will to change in Adrienne Rich's mature verse, and surely it is time we turned to that subject as a central focus in what remains to be said here. It is difficult to avoid such a turning in looking at the volume *The Will To Change*, of course, but few are the readers who seem ready to front the subject directly. A reviewer for the New York Times Book Review spoke of the volume's ". . . tough distrust of completion," and declared that "The poems are about departures, about the pain of breaking away from lovers and from an old sense of self." The observations seem accurate enough, but they do not tell us much. The poems in this recent volume are about more than departures. They are about the will to be both self and other, to embody at once both presence and possibility. They are, in fact, about the will not to be left behind, not to be deluded, not to rest with one's achievements or comforts. "A man isn't what he seems but what he desires:/ gaieties of anarchy drumming at the base of the skull," she tells us in one of *The Blue Ghazals* (1968). A familiar enough idea, looked at casually, but why the insistence upon anarchy, we should like to know. Why such further lines as "Disorder is natural, these leaves absently blowing." Absence, disorder as natural: and only a few years earlier she had spoken so fiercely of the blight that is rampant disorder, of the indifference and inattention that permit the wasting of our endowments. In another of *The Blue Ghazals* the poet writes: "Everything is yielding toward a foregone conclusion,/ only we are rash enough to go on changing our lives./ An Ashanti woman tilts the flattened basin on her head/ to let the water slide downward: I am that woman and that/ water." The terrible downward glide is evoked in these poems as an inevitability to which we lend ourselves as a mark of honor, of lucidity. But to describe our drift as in some sense honorable is not to see how terrible it is, I'm afraid, and I doubt the poet has lately stepped out of the current long enough to attend to this problem. In "I Dream I'm The Death Of Orpheus" (1968) she presents "A woman feeling the fullness of her powers/ at the precise moment when she must not use them/ a woman sworn to lucidity." What is this terrible lucidity, we wonder, that it should prevent us from using our powers: some such thing occurs to us to ask as we move through any number of poems here.

As earlier intimated, the will to change is at the heart of Adrienne Rich's thought and work, and it has much to do with this terrible lucidity. For what the poet insists upon is nothing less than full revelation of every motive, every shabby instinct and cheap thrill that drives her on. Now it is customary today to applaud a whole host of writers, prophets and other culture-heroes for their frankness, and surely we do not need to be reminded of the degree to which frankness has become a salable commodity. There is nothing offensive or commercial in Adrienne Rich's poetry, but it shares with other contemporary work a quality of impatience and of rashness that is a little disappointing. She is too ready in her poems to see the "Meanings burnt-off like paint/ under the blow-torch" ("Our Whole Life," 1969). Oh, she knows the toll the blow-torch will take, writhes a good deal under its too steady heat and glare. What disturbs us is that she should have so little faith in the usefulness of resistance. For the *conservateurs* she had ready contempt, but for the anxious wielders of the blow-torch, for the more openly murderous of her own intellectual instincts, she has no strength to resist. She laments that we are "Always falling and ending/ because this world gives no room/ to be what we dreamt of being," but she mistrusts the very idea of being anything solid and loyal. How often does she tell us that change and the will to change are all. More and more I think of Adrienne Rich's recent project as a kind of perpetual hungering relieved by nothing at all, for nothing we take in can satisfy this hunger to know, to devour, to transform, to move on. In

"Images for Godard" (1970) we read: "the notes for the poem are the only poem/ the mind collecting, devouring/ all these destructibles," and later, "free in the dusty beam of the projector/ the mind of the poet is changing/ the moment of change is the only poem." And is the only reality worth knowing about, apparently.

The effect of all this on Adrienne Rich's writing has not been good, for though the poet need not manifest the organic wholeness of the traditional novelistic vision, obviously, she is responsible for more than a series of intensely noted fragments. There is some pleasure in watching her manage her combination of intimate detail and abstract rumination, in pondering her attempt to forge an authentic language deserving of the name dialogue, but we are impressed by the absence of that steady largeness of vision, those marked traits of character formed and expanding, that we marveled at in her earlier writing. The will to change has turned the poet from wholeness to analytic lucidity. Or perhaps it would be more appropriate to say that, unable to live according to those calmly alternating rhythms we think of as the emblem of a poised maturity, the poet has had to turn to the will to change to validate her hungers, to provide the stamp of authenticity she sought. I don't know for certain. What seems to me clear is that a point has been passed beyond which the poet has ceased to be herself, that blend of instinct and learned wisdom, innocent eye and educated adult, who knew there was a limit to will, and worth in steadfastness. Now that she has begun to speak of nature, of doing her thing, giving herself to the performance of "something very common, in my own way," I don't know that we may hope for very much from her verse beyond striking fragments. I shall have to hope for a resumption of that other toughness so well expressed in "Snapshots Of A Daughter-in-Law." It may be fitting to conclude with a few lines from that poem, to remind ourselves of the course we have traveled:

> mere talent was enough for us—
> glitter in fragments and rough drafts . . .
> - - - - - - - - -
> our mediocrities over-praised,
> indolence read as abnegation,
> slattern thought styled intuition,
> every lapse forgiven . . .

Those of us who believe in the altogether special and distinguished qualities of Adrienne Rich's best work will not, I hope, forgive lightly her recent lapses, nor praise overmuch her more indulgent intuitions.

FIFTEEN

HOWARD NEMEROV'S TRUE VOICE OF FEELING

In Yeats's "Adam's Curse," a poem Howard Nemerov has no doubt read
and pondered like the rest of us, the speaker remembers how the long
labor of love "had all seemed happy, and yet we'd grown/ As weary-
hearted as that hollow moon." Yeats, of course, knew what had to be
done to deal with the weary heart; in fact, he built out of it that quality
of hard detachment and bracing emptiness of solitary experience which
identify his work. Nemerov has had a harder time, it would seem, so that
in his most recent work the temptation to succumb to weariness, to cut
off the real and imagined entanglements that wound the self immoderately
and seduce it from its lonely rigors, has grown ever more persistent. The
very title of his latest book, *gnomes and occasions,* suggests how grave the
situation has become: the gnome, conventionally a wise or pithy saying
early associated with puckish creatures, in Nemerov's hands becomes
largely a weapon, a way to cut off discourse, a denial of communion and
that generous elaboration of insight which is the mark both of freshness
and human appeal; occasions, conventionally suggesting the poet's resort
to low-intensity stimulation and a propensity to write from the top of
the head, in Nemerov gives us more than we'd expected, if not quite
enough. Happily, the occasions to which Nemerov has responded in the
past have frequently been sufficiently broad and various as to liberate
the full range of his talents and insights, so that he's moved briskly from
commemoration through eulogy and celebration to lucid meditation. The
weary heart has come increasingly to bewilder and torment Howard Nemerov, but he has, in a sense like his master Yeats, learned well the gift of
hard detachment. In his best moments, early and late, this gift is a func-

From *American Poetry Review,* May-June 1975.

tion not of coldness, nor of deliberate estrangement from the world, but of the strength to consider the world in its fullness and elusiveness, to transform it in the medium of his poetry into a rhythm of sad though still encouraging observances.

In reading some of Nemerov's recent verses, we are sometimes put in mind not merely of Yeats, but of others who have more directly addressed the issue of the true or authentic self. One thinks, for example, of Hawthorne's injunction, "Be true! Be true! Be true! Show freely to the world, if not your worst, yet some trait by which the worst may be inferred." This in the interest of sincerity, Lionel Trilling has recently encouraged us to presume. Is Nemerov's "Thirtieth Anniversary Report of the Class of '41" (*gnomes and occasions*) primarily guided by an impulse to sincerity? It is an issue much worth considering.

> We who survived the war and took to wife
> And sired the kids and made the decent living,
> And piecemeal furnished forth the finished life
> Not by grand theft so much as petty thieving—
>
> Who had the routine middle-aged affair
> And made our beds and had to lie in them
> This way or that because the beds were there,
> And turned our bile and choler in for phlegm—
>
> Who saw grandparents, parents, to the vault
> And wives and selves grow wrinkled, grey and fat
> And children through their acne and revolt
> And told the analyst about all that—
>
> Are done with it. What is there to discuss?
> There's nothing left for us to say of us.

I suspect something other than the will to sincerity in Hawthorne's sense is at work in this poem of Nemerov's, as in many like it that he has lately written. While it is true that he here gives us what we need to infer, not perhaps the worst but at least the indelicate, we are more impressed by what would seem to be the contrivance of a mask. This mask has as much to do with the striking of various cool postures as with the modest extravagances of wit. Always a poet capable of wearing emotion on his sleeve, and of subverting that emotion in accessions of almost wasteful frivolity, Nemerov has learned too well how best to disarm critics of those earlier subversions. The fellow who delivers his thirtieth anniversary report is a poised, and in some respects an invulnerable fellow. He has suffered, but he is tight-lipped and relatively withdrawn — he doesn't want to talk about it. The ceremonial occasion of his address is seized upon not as an opportunity to renew human contacts or to open up a range of enquiry, but to consolidate and confirm a decision already made, and according to which we know what we know, and what we know is what had to be. Wit in this context is not an aspect of play, but of archness and resistance to play. The curve of the feeling expressed is drawn by constraint rather than by lightness. The cool, unimpassioned observer of experience falsifies that experience by exaggerating the objectivity and stark clarity with which he approaches it. What we object to in such a performance is the unchallenged submission to necessity, in Wordsworth's words, to "things as they are in themselves . . . unmodified by any passion of feeling existing in the mind of the describer."

I stress this aspect of Nemerov's work so early in my remarks because in so many poems he faces up to this submission, often struggles successfully to overcome it. Nemerov has had to work hard to achieve a voice all his own, and in so doing he has discovered for himself what others before him found: that the studied restraint of the stoic's mask conceals all manner of internal chaos and ambivalence, and that in an age like ours the affectless level stare into the blank eyes of the grey inane may well be taken for courage and honesty. In fact, the mask answers not at all to problems of voice and vision this particular poet has had to confront. Contrary to what so many have said of Nemerov, his characteristic idiom is not the language of unruffled calm or serenity. Always he has written with a sharp sense of troubled waters threatening beneath placid surfaces. When he has let himself go, setting imagination free to locate the source of disturbances pulsing around and within, he has come to visions more deeply compelled than the somber riddles of a less venturesome imagination. Here and there he affects an almost Audenesque detachment, it is true, as in these lines from "Sunday At The End of Summer" (*Selected Poems, 1950-1958*) in which the speaker stands by, watching others struggle against the ravages of a late-night storm:

> Ours was the Sunday's perfect idleness
> To watch those others working; who fought, swore,
> Being threshed at hip and thigh, against that trash
> Of pale wild flowers and their drifting legs.

More often, though, as in the poem "Brainstorm" from the same volume, what is torn and shown "Naked to nature" is what the poet willingly engages:

> He came to feel the crows walk on his head
> As if he were the house, their crooked feet
> Scratched, through the hair, his scalp. He might be dead,
> It seemed, and all the noises underneath

> Be but the cooling of the sinews, veins,
> Juices, and sodden sacks suddenly let go;
> While in his ruins of wiring, his burst mains,
> The rainy wind had been set free to blow
> Until the green uprising and mob rule
> That ran the world had taken over him,
> Split him like seed, and set him in the school
> Where any crutch can learn to be a limb.
>
> Inside his head he heard the stormy crows.

Of such writing one may speak in terms of elegance and simplicity, but not of cold restraint or serenity. Nor do we adduce weariness of heart to account for so firm and measured an utterance. While the diction of such a stanza is perhaps more conventional, and the rhythms more tightly reined, than one would like, it surely indicates the prospect of mysteries to come, of linguistic forces soon to be set loose. This is not a poet who will be content with elegant surfaces and exquisite poses.

The weariness that has always threatened Nemerov, and that would seem to account for his recent gnomes, has never been a function of linguistic exhaustion. Verbal facility has in fact always been one of his great strengths, and though Allen Tate has lately spoken of Nemerov's "great 'plain style,' in which there is nothing 'poetical' about the language," I should think that readers brought up in the Williams-projective verse tradition would find his writing very "poetical" indeed. Not long strings of adjectives, but a subtly heightened diction and rhetorical inflection color the verse, make it "poetical" in a sense not really described by Tate's remarks. Consider the opening lines of a slight piece titled "Above" (*gnomes and occasions*):

> Orange translucent butterflies cruising
> Over a smoke of gnats above the trees
> And over them the stiff-winged chimney swifts
> Scythe at the air in alternating arcs
> Among the roofs where flights of pigeons go
> (Slate as the roofs above and white below)

Or this brief poem called "The Rent In The Screen" (*gnomes and . . . . .*):

> Sweet mildness of the late December day
> Deceives into the world a couple of hundred
> Cinnamon moths, whose cryptic arrow-shapes
> Cling sleeping to a southward-facing wall
> All through the golden afternoon, till dusk
> And coming cold arouse them to their flight
> Across the gulf of night and nothingness,
> The falling snow, the fall, the fallen snow,
> World whitened to dark ends, how brief a dream.

Surely we know what Tate means when he speaks of the "great 'plain style,'" but it is useful to stress that in Nemerov's hands it is not so plain as the epithet suggests. Even when Nemerov is most conversational one sees more than the plain style at work in his impeccable precisions, a ripeness in the language that has little in common with the plain style sometimes beautifully managed by a Frost or a Jarrell. "Beyond the Pleasure Principle" (*The Blue Swallows*) opens with the following conversational accents, but we cannot mistake the crafting that controls the language for mere simplicity:

> It comes up out of the darkness, and it returns
> Into a further darkness. After the monster,
> There is the monster's mother to be dealt with,
> Dimly perceived at first, or only speculated on
> Between the shadows and reflexions of the tidal cave,
> Among the bones and armored emptiness
> Of the princes of a former time, who failed.

What, then, has made the poet weary where he has been weary? Since Nemerov's sheer linguistic inventiveness seems inexhaustible, and he has not given evidence of any grave incapacity in the conceptualization of poetic situations or broad forms, we ought perhaps to look elsewhere for suitable explanations. The content of Nemerov's work has always been quite various, so that in a typical volume, and without the poet's explicitly informing us as to what we might anticipate, a variety of independent sections will isolate from one another particular kinds of Nemerov poems.* Among these are political poems, satires, dramatic or dialogue poems, riddle or proverb poems, and so on. Obviously there is considerable overlap from one category to another, and I think it is clear that Nemerov's best work is as various as the kinds of poems he writes. No doubt the poem of the mind, of consciousness pondering itself and its relation to its materials, is the poem that better than any poet of our time Nemerov has mastered and experimented with, but neither are there many poems of our century that can match Nemerov's lyric evocations of beekeepers or Negro street-cleaners or scholars in the stacks or sightseers. The powers of sustained reflection and of celebratory invocation are so highly developed in Nemerov that one can consider only with some annoyance the weariness that afflicts a volume like *gnomes and occasions,* despite the lovely poems it nonetheless contains. I should have to say that the weariness seems mostly a matter of the poet's too consistently entertaining

* For detailed examination of these various kinds of poems, see "The Poems of Howard Nemerov" by James M. Kiehl (*Salmagundi,* No. 22-23, spring-summer 1973); also in *Contemporary Poetry in America* (Schocken Books, December 1974).

strenuous doubts about the possibility of achieving a durable innocence or freshness and of renovating a moral vocabulary, which is the language of the soul in action. At his best, and that is after all how he truly deserves to be considered, Nemerov's freshness and lyricism are indisputable, and though it is not easy to think of innocence in connection with one so worldly-wise, he so frequently moves us to wonder over the glory of beautiful things that we might almost concede to him that capacity for radical self-renewal that more readily characterized a Yeats, or a Blake.

What I am suggesting is that Nemerov is a poet of bad conscience, a poet trained in irony and *double entendre* whose instinct is to banish them and attain to transparence, to a vision clear and unmistakably right, though tainted still by memory and artifice. It is a project that comes bursting forth here and there in Nemerov's volumes, tumbling with delight into the domain of nature's careless embrace, the compulsive irony and slightly malevolent twinkle of the inveterate poseur suspended if not entirely banished. The weariness of heart we find in all those other poems, in which the essential project is not realized or attempted, is the result of the poet's falling once again into what he at some level of consciousness considers the inevitable, if not the true or essential pattern. While he aims at "a moment's inviolable presence," something "Perfected and casual as to a child's eye/ Soap bubbles are, and skipping stones," he finds himself with the perfected and casual as it appeals to the eye of the mordant ironist and tired dandy. What after all can be more perfected than the closed aphorism or gnome that beckons to no beyond, smugly pronouncing judgment upon this or that with no hint of a desire to say more or betrayal of anxious insufficiency? Nemerov's ironic wit is his gift and his burden, and it is his awareness of just this fact that has prompted his elaboration of a mask to certify as inevitable and authentic a dark insouciance that has always been more problematic and dramatic than it has been real. The weariness, one supposes, will only be confronted for what it is, if ever, when the project of the essential self has been unambiguously embraced. Then alone will the poet come to cease the exhausting posturing that goes against the grain of his most valuable gifts, which entirely transcend irony and the metaphors of wit.

Listen to Nemerov in his criticism: "Sometimes it appears to candid reflexion that great works of art give no meaning, but give instead, like the world of nature and history itself, materials whose arrangement suggests a tropism toward meaning, order and form, give, often in a tantalizing way, the prospect of meaning somewhere beyond, beyond. What, finally, does Hamlet mean?" Now this is no ideal reflection the likes of which would have little bearing upon Nemerov's art, but a profound expression of those essential impulses it is Nemerov's passionate project to entertain. It has nothing whatever to do with the little gnomic riddles the poet is wont to tell, but it tells us a great deal about a necessary, which is to say appropriate and sympathetic, approach to Nemerov's "The Beekeeper Speaks . . . And Is Silent" (*The Blue Swallows*). In some ways Nemerov's greatest and most satisfying poem, it begins not altogether promisingly, in a tone that combines downright foolery with archness and that contains more than a trace of self-congratulation. What we cannot be sure about, though, as we read the opening lines for the first time, is the degree to which they serve to characterize the speaker, rather than to aggrandize the poet. Going back over the poem, with the affection it is bound to inspire, we are astonished that the "prospect of meaning somewhere beyond, beyond," as Nemerov says, should emerge from so impatient and headstrong a beginning.

> Bees aren't humble, they don't notably bumble,
> They tend to run a touch Stakhanovite,
> If you'll allow the lofty title to
> A hedonist who works himself to death
> Flying at every blossom in the orchard
> In a madness of efficiency at pleasure,
> Like a totalitarian Don Juan
> In serious pursuit. . . .

But the tone eases considerably, as the persona of the crusty old beekeeper emerges, in a line like "There's that much nonsense to a hive of bees," or in these from stanza two:

> . . . ; it brings in dough
> All right, and it's a way to make a living
> Still has a shade of mystery about it;
> People who need you come round all respectful,
> But not quite friendly, maybe a little scared:
> They damn well should be, it's a mystery.

Slowly Nemerov introduces the element of mystery, softening his insistence by the use of everyday old-fashioned colloquialisms like "it brings in dough" and "they damn well should be." Nemerov doesn't much like to yield to the mysteries without a struggle, and the resistance here comes in the form of those marvelously colorful locutions that everywhere punctuate the beekeeper's address: "The damn fool growers," "five bucks a hive," "I got in this game young," "It's in the cards that some of them will sting," and so on. By the time he reaches stanzas four and five, though, the ground has been set. The beekeeper's dedication to his calling has been routinely established, and we feel we've known for a long time what that calling entails, its promise of danger and the extraordinary proximity it offers to the fluid energies of all life. We are ready for a heightening of the rhetoric and a more resolute elaboration of the mysteries previously intimated. The elaboration represents, as Nemerov has himself written, "a tropism toward meaning, order and form," rather than a definitive elucidation that might settle the doubts and anxieties generated by the poem:

> The bloodstream is a venom in itself,
> Sometimes I think to hear it hum in me.

What Nemerov has elsewhere called "The Protean Encounter" is unmistakably announced in these final lines of stanza four. Here is the encounter itself:

> And sometimes, too, not only in the night,
> Lying awake, hearing life hum away,
> But at the first of summer in the field
> Releasing life and death in black and gold
> Bullets that shake the petals back and forth,
> And not the petals only, but the boughs,
> With many-winged furies bearing futures,
> I have felt myself become at first a bee,
> And then the single-minded hive itself,
> And after that the blossoming apple-tree
> Inside the violation of the swarm—
> Until I am the brute and fruitful earth,
> Furred with the fury of the golden horde,
> And hear from far upon the field of time
> The wild relentless singing of the stars.

What do these concluding lines of the poem mean? It is difficult to say without crudely oversimplifying Nemerov's insights. At one level the lines say no more than that in dream, as sometimes in wakeful reverie, the beekeeper imagines himself transformed into a bee, then into the hive, and finally into the essence of nature itself. He does not think, in the frame of the poem, as he tells his story, that he has in fact achieved that transformation, but something in his telling of the imagined experience seems more real, more certain, than any denial rational intelligence can make. Why should this be so? Because Nemerov's language here is a good deal ahead of his thought, because the will to imagine is greater here than the will to contain. Meaning emerges in the pregnant spaces between intention and word, in Nemerov's formulation, "beyond, beyond." And if we ask, with Nemerov, what finally does the beekeeper's transformation mean, we can answer only that it expresses a wish, not so much to transcend the limitations of one's condition, as to embrace those limitations creatively. The tropism of which Nemerov speaks is a tropism towards coherence, an impulse to gather in one's arms that fluid force which moves briskly through every dynamic thing. The object is not to stop its course or to identify perfectly with it, but to love and treasure the protean encounter with it as the very test of all that is quick with life. To be "inside the violation of the swarm" is to be not merely "carpeted," as Nemerov suggests in an earlier figure, but to be lifted out of one's limited and subordinate truths of identity and confronted with the enigmatic at the heart of all experience. This is, after all, what Nemerov has called upon in his various celebrations of the protean encounter. "The poet asks a simple question," he has written, "to which moreover he already knows the unsatisfying answer. Question and answer.... they assert the limits of a journey to be taken. They are the necessary but not sufficient conditions of what really seems to matter here, the protean encounter itself, the grasping and hanging on to the powerful and refractory spirit in its slippery transformations of a single force flowing through clock, day, violet, greying hair," etc.

The unsatisfying answer, which is a condition of the journey upon which we are conducted in "The Beekeeper Speaks . . . And Is Silent," is that the bloodsteam is not a venom in itself, and that the beekeeper's flight may not finally be taken for more than it is: it is a flight of *imaginary* release, and what relation it bears to actual flight or the prospect of ultimate release is a speculative rather than fully achieved relation. But, as Nemerov tells us, these do not serve as "sufficient conditions of what really seems to matter here." We are concerned more with the inviolable presence of a better answer than with the reasonable assurance that we know what we know and higher truths be damned. For the duration of Nemerov's poem, at least, we are permitted a glimpse of what a higher truth might be, in this case the conviction that in fact a simple force flows "through clock, day, violet, greying hair," and so on. It matters to us because it helps to heal the gap between mind and world that imprisons and diminishes the individual experience. By individual experience I mean that experience of the fundamentally creative imagination in which the individual dreams in harmony with the archetypes rooted in the human unconscious. This is not a matter of simple perception, according to which the poet sees better than the rest of us what is present to all, and through the process of imagination deftly combines fragments of perceived reality. The "question and answer" proposed by Nemerov as the limiting condition of the poetic journey taken leave us only with what we knew we had all along. To act upon us with the force of something at once fresh and lovely, the poetic images embodied in the protean encounter must release us from the familiar necessity wherein poets and sages "get busy/ Revising their visions conformably with fact." ("A Relation of Art and Life," *The Blue Swallows*) No such revision takes place to chasten the beekeeper of Nemerov's poem, who makes his way under the auspices of "the wild relentless singing of the stars."

What we have seen, then, as a kind of provisional entry into Nemerov's art, is that he is least afflicted by weariness when he is least submissive to things as they are in themselves, when the creative faculty is least subject to the imperatives of rational intellection. Ought we to demand of a learned, sophisticated, and highly secular poet that he suppress what he knows in the interests of vision? Even were we inclined to do so, we'd be certain nothing could come of such a demand. In fact, it is Nemerov's conviction that there is a "mindfulness" in things, and that it is possible for the poetic imagination to make contact with this mindfulness. To revise one's vision "conformably with fact" is a very different matter, for fact has to do with an objective approach to things, an attempt to get at what is already present to sight. For Nemerov it is the object of imagination to make visible what is not altogether clear, to conceive the relations among things, so that we have a process of embodiment in abstract forms, wherein here and there the visible world appears — as Nemerov says in "The Painter Dreaming in the Scholar's House" (*gnomes and occasions*), from "the abstract elements of language" we get, miraculously, more than "the point, the line, the plane, the colors and/ The geometric shape." And when we get more than we could deliberately have bargained for, "It happens as by accident, although/ The accident is of design." The poet does not, then, willingly suppress his powers of rational intellection, by which he would decline to look at the evidence for this and that and refuse to accept the modest injunctions of common sense as they might refer to one or another aspect of his visionary enterprise. He is instructed in the art of operating on many levels at once, inviting reverie and the critical faculty to work freely in the smithy of his imagination. The generous and attentive eye of the poet, like the painter's eye, will see "How things must be continuous with themselves/ As with whole worlds that they themselves are not." In Nemerov's view, this must be so, because though violet and greying hair are not perfectly similar, and though spirit and sense seem often irreconcilably opposed, there is an impulse in imagination to come at things and qualities as they might be, rather than as they appear to be: "and in his hours of art," says Nemerov, "there shines a happiness through darkest themes,/ As though spirit and sense were not at odds."

The work of art, in this instance the poem, is conceived as a temporary structure, housing as a vital principle the energy that informs every object and living thing and that drives all things in the direction of the broadest continuities. In this sense, what is and is not are, fleetingly, one, and the hardest objects may be said to have the texture of wind. Nemerov's beekeeper likens the bloodstream to a venom, imagines his body "Furred with the fury of the golden horde" — deeply committed to his work, moved as he has been by the passionate recurrences of nature's cycle, he has come to that greatest of integrations, between dream and meaning. Preoccupied with the actual, with bees and hives and sales, he arrives "as by accident" at a place more in-between than here or there, a place unknown to common sense though not inimical. The achievement, for Nemerov, is more a matter of will and creative energy than it is a reflection of personal integration, for Nemerov is a deeply divided spirit: "As though spirit and sense were not at odds" describes very well the nature of his successes. What Nemerov cannot do is take his heritage for granted, to count upon an ordered sense of values both received and acceptable to his reason. Though moved by impulses we do not customarily identify as contemporary, Nemerov is very much of his time, and in his memorable poems we discover not the trained and polished ambiguities of metaphysical wit so much as simple and profound uncertainty. That he manages to express this uncertainty in a context of lucid meditation and frequently ecstatic illumination is something we can only marvel at. In a recent poem from *gnomes* . . . entitled "Lines and Circularities," Nemerov remarks, "How many silly miracles there are/ That will not save us." The only thing that can save us, apparently, is a kind of modest though not yet passive vision, the vision so grandly possessed by Nemerov's beekeeper, for one.

The quality of vision to which Nemerov is attracted is no familiar quality to which American poets in general are drawn. It is quite a complicated matter, in fact, and readers anxious to understand precisely Nemerov's relation of art and life may find themselves a little puzzled by it all, somewhat like the speaker in "Questions" (*gnomes* . . .) who asks: "And does the temptress of the To Be Known/Summon across a sea that has no shore?" Nemerov does not set us permanently adrift, but he has a way of speculating on epistemological and visionary issues that suggests we look for comfortable analogies where no analogy will really help. All sorts of poets have recently expressed a desire to take us to the things of this world, to fill us with love and admiration for the universe as it is, without distortion by the creative faculty, no matter how inspired and intelligent. Frequently Nemerov seems to offer some such thing, and because we know an impulse to that sort of clarity cannot really account for the poems of his we like best, we are suspicious of him when he does stake a claim to such a project. We think of a gorgeous poem like "The Mud Turtle" (*The Blue Swallows*), for instance, a poem worthy of comparison with Elizabeth Bishop's animal poems, in which the personality of the poet is almost entirely suppressed and the dignity of creatureliness is modestly but unmistakably asserted. Nemerov's poem is submissive to the objective presence in the world of the turtle, but even in such a poem, where Nemerov virtually refuses to impose his fancies upon the object he examines, there is a riddling interposition of consciousness which is the mark both of personality and of the will to alter and shape. Much of the poem is in the nature of quiet, straightforward observation:

> Then when they turn him on his back
> To see the belly heroically yellow,
> He throws himself fiercely to his feet,
> Brings down the whole weight of his shell,
> Spreads out his claws and digs himself in
> Immovably, invulnerably,
> But for the front foot on the left,
> Red-budded, with the toes torn off.
> So over he goes again, and shows
> Us where a swollen leech is fastened
> Softly between plastron and shell.

But there are also lines like the following:

> His lordly darkness decked in filth
> Bearded with weed like a lady's favor,
> He is a black planet, another world
> Never till now appearing, even now
> Not quite believably old and big,
> Set in the summer morning's midst
> A gloomy gemstone to the sun opposed.
> Our measures of him do not matter,
> He would be huge at any size;
> And neither does the number of his years,
> The time he comes from doesn't count.

In such lines there is a good deal more of the poet's voice than we find, say, in a Bishop poem, or in a poem by Richard Wilbur, for that matter. If there is not quite the desire to abandon what is seen for what is imagined, there is a mobility here that impresses, an aspiration towards freshness of imagery and possibilities of insight not immediately conveyed by the turtle itself.

But "The Mud Turtle" is an unusual poem in Nemerov's canon, and I have chosen to look at it only because it is a fine poem and because it least readily serves to demonstrate the point I wish to make. For Nemerov, the object of poetry has to do with the cultivation of a protean encounter by means of which we apprehend the world and in some sense come to see, in his words, "what and in what way we are." I do not know that

"The Mud Turtle" contains intimations of what we are, although the dignity with which Nemerov's creature bears his hurt and learns to take "A secret wound out of the world" may serve as a vivid lesson to us of proper and graceful behavior. What we can surely say, though, is that the turtle serves, if only by contrast, to point up the pettiness of most human pursuits, and as such intimates to us, if not what we are, what we might be. In Nemerov's terms, speaking of metaphor in general, "what is known is proposed as a presumptive demonstration of what is not known, what can be seen as a reflexion of what cannot be seen." Thus the sensible properties of the turtle intimate to us possibilities of being in the world that we had not, perhaps, imagined so vividly before.

But the question of art and world remains a knotty one, and may be best addressed by examining the title poem of Nemerov's finest book to date, *The Blue Swallows*. It is a gorgeous piece, standing somewhere between Nemerov's many abstractly ruminative poems and his more concretely observant works, generally less explicitly thematic than "The Blue Swallows." It will be well for the reader to keep in mind, as he reads the poem, how elusive is the program Nemerov charts, for though he tells us here that "poems are not the point" and that "Finding again the world" is, the poem's burden is in no sense as easy as the message wants us to think it is.

> Across the millstream below the bridge
> Seven blue swallows divide the air
> In shapes invisible and evanescent,
> Kaleidoscopic beyond the mind's
> Or memory's power to keep them there.
>
> "History is where tensions were,"
> "Form is the diagram of forces,"
> Thus, helplessly, there on the bridge,
> While gazing down upon those birds—
> How strange, to be above the birds!—
> Thus helplessly the mind in its brain
> Weaves up relation's spindrift web,
> Seeing the swallows' tails as nibs
> Dipped in invisible ink, writing . . .
>
> Poor mind, what would you have them write?
> Some cabalistic history
> Whose authorship you might ascribe
> To God? to Nature? Ah, poor ghost,
> You've capitalized your Self enough.
> That villainous William of Occam
> Cut out the feet from under that dream
> Some seven centuries ago.
> It's taken that long for the mind

To waken, yawn, and stretch, to see
With opened eyes emptied of speech
The real world where the spelling mind
Imposes with its grammar book
Unreal relations on the blue
Swallows. Perhaps when you will have
Fully awakened, I shall show you

A new thing: even the water
Flowing away beneath those birds
Will fail to reflect their flying forms,
And the eyes that see become as stones
Whence never tears shall fall again.

O swallows, swallows, poems are not
The point. Finding again the world,
That is the point, where loveliness
Adorns intelligible things
Because the mind's eye lit the sun.

A beautiful poem, to be sure, but how lacerating the perspective Nemerov takes through most of it, how ungrateful he seems for his own power to conceive relation and make it seem both persuasive and inevitable. I have always felt this way about some of Stevens's more somber reflections, though Nemerov's temperament is generally more sanguine, the spirit of his poems consequently more impish. It is really quite curious, all this business in Nemerov about the mind's helplessness, its addiction to unreal relations and absurd ascriptions. Nemerov has rarely seemed to anyone an enemy of mind, and after Stevens it is hard to imagine what difference it can make to worry over the fact that neither mind nor memory can perfectly retain the shape and impression of blue swallows. That is not what poetry, as a medium of mind and memory, can do: so much has been conceded, by Nemerov as by other poets of intelligence and modesty. The poet who wrote "The Blue Swallows" has also written that "So far as poetry is *for* anything beyond contemplation, we may say that it exists for the purpose of producing more poetry." Such a statement is consistent with the aesthetic Nemerov has developed in many essays during the past dozen years or so, and is further refined in his contention, from another essay, that "a fine poem is not so much a thought as it is a mind." Which is to say, not the thought of the way blue swallows divide the air, but the processes of the mind as it "weaves up relation's spindrift web" is what will matter to us. Will the processes of mind matter more even than the blue swallows? Insofar as we are engaged in reading a poem, the answer is, certainly, for blue swallows are, can be, but an aspect of mind when they are reflected through the prism of the poet's language. What we have in Nemerov's poem is truly the language of imagination. In

Hazlitt's predication, and a reasonably catholic notion it is, such language "conveys the impression which the object under the influence of passion makes on the mind."

How, then, do the swallows act upon Nemerov's mind? They make him uneasy, press him to find a way to imitate and thereby to capture what is ineffable. That he cannot do so is a matter of considerable disappointment to the poet, and he is driven therefore to denigrate not merely his unique powers but his calling as well. Since poems cannot give us the world as the world deserves to be represented, we had best turn from poems altogether, or so the poet suggests in a manner at once almost plaintive and angry. Throughout, of course, we are treated to a demonstration of poetic mastery that leaves us grateful and amused, amused that one who has taken such pains to fashion an exquisite lyric should simultaneously mock his preoccupations as of little worth. Thus, even as he insists upon our helplessness, he moves us to admire the way he leaves the word "helplessly" dangling there on the third line of the second stanza, until finally it is rescued three lines further down the page. Such is the "feebleness" of Nemerov's verse.

But there is more to the general uncertainty we, at least, must feel as we read the poem, for though mind is mocked as simple, anxious, and literal, the product of "grammar-book" cultivation, the meditation concludes by reflecting that in the world, "loveliness/Adorns intelligible things/Because the mind's eye lit the sun." So we have moved from a concern for reality as it might be taken in by any pair of "opened eyes emptied of speech" to a concern for "intelligible things" whose loveliness is consequent upon "the mind's eye." It is not clear just how Nemerov gets from the one to the other, for there is nothing like a transitional passage in the poem to effect a change of mind or heart. If, after all, it is the mind's eye that "lit the sun," and we've no need to posit sources in nature or in the cosmos, why bother to lament intellectual pretension and foolishness and tease us with specters of ineffability? All that seems certain here is that the poet does not feel satisfied with our customary approaches to the world poets conventionally probe and celebrate, and that his allegiance finally is to the intelligible and to the powers of imagination. The dialectical turn of Nemerov's mind is unmistakable here, though its expression is perhaps less ordered than in other poems. What is so striking about "The Blue Swallows," of course, is the rich simplicity of the phrasing, the elegant compression of the line. Is there any other poet of our time who can manage the lofty casualness of Nemerov's opening stanza? I think not.

The dialectical tension so teasingly displayed in "The Blue Swallows" is a regular feature of so many Nemerov poems that one has little trouble fitting together a pattern that may explain our uncertainties. In "One Way," for instance, from *The Blue Swallows*, Nemerov hopefully conjures "a world/Whose being is both thought/And thing, where neither thing/Nor thought will do alone/Till either answers other;/ Two lovers in the night/ Each sighing other's name/Whose alien syllables/Become synonymous/For all their mortal night/And their embodied day." Here, though, the embodying imagery is not sufficiently visual or particular, so that the ideas are not so much deepened as simply told. "In The Black Museum" (*The Blue Swallows*) is similarly directed, though it proceeds somewhat more obliquely, announcing its contention with "When all analogies are broken/ The scene grows strange again. At last/There is only one of everything" and following with "one mask/To every skull, that is the end of art." Strangeness, in this view, is a function of a fantasied return to things as they are, to a universe in which not imagination but naked perception reigns. It is an impoverishing prospect, but Nemerov's evocation is itself so dryly abstracted that by poem's end he seems almost embarrassed, and takes cover in a concluding analogy seemingly contrived to subvert the seriousness of his observations:

> Or as two mirrors vacuum-locked together
> Exclude, along with all the world,
> A light to see it by. Reflect on that.

An earlier poem, entitled simply "Writing" (*New and Selected Poems*), represents a more conventional treatment of the theme, but is not on that account less effective. The characteristic inflection of Nemerov's voice is less developed here than in his recent poems, but there is a quality of casual elegance in some of the lines that we recognize and respond to. The poem opens with the pleasant suggestion that at any number of points in experience, "world/ and spirit wed" — we know this from the way we respond to skaters as they "curve/all day across the lake, scoring their white records in ice." The record they leave behind of their journey, according to Nemerov, delights us, "even without a meaning," for somehow the sense of their lives, a generalized meaning, is communicated, as "the blind bat surveys his way/by echo alone." Further, the record left behind in some sense reflects not only the recorder but the circumstances in which he has come to be what he is: "A nervous man/ writes nervously of a nervous world, and so on." Surely we know what Nemerov is getting at, or almost. But the poem takes a substantial turn in its second and final stanza, a turn to which we've already grown accustomed in considering the dialectical tension of Nemerov's vision:

Miraculous. It is as though the world
were a great writing. Having said so much,
let us allow there is more to the world
than writing; continental faults are not
bare convoluted fissures in the brain.
Not only must the skaters soon go home;
also the hard inscription of their skates
is scored across the open water, which long
remembers nothing, neither wind nor wake.

If it is the burden of "Writing" to celebrate the evanescent identity of world and spirit and to help us resign ourselves to the ultimate elusiveness of the world, there are any number of Nemerov poems that survey the same questions with a good deal less equanimity. In "Hide and Seek" (*gnomes* . . .) he concludes on this difficult note: "An explorer said the stars were moved by love—/Then what great light's black space the shadow of?" Or consider this brilliant poem from *The Blue Swallows*, called "The Breaking Of Rainbows," surely one of the finest short lyrics Nemerov has written, a poem in which the poet's usual measured reserve is not accompanied by even a trace of studied or ironic dryness:

Oil is spilling down the little stream
Below the bridge. Heavy and slow as blood,
Or with an idiot's driveling contempt:
The spectral film unfolding, spreading forth
Prismatically in a breaking of rainbows,
Reflective radiance, marble evanescence,
It shadows the secret moves the water makes,
Creeping upstream again, then prowling down,
Sometimes asleep in the dull corners, combed
As the deep grass is combed in the stream's abandon,
And sometimes tearing open silently
Its seamless fabric in momentary shapes
Unlikened and nameless as the shapes of sky
That open with the drift of cloud, and close,
High in the lonely mountains, silently.
The curve and glitter of it as it goes
The maze of its pursuit, reflect the water
In agony under the alien, brilliant skin
It struggles to throw off and finally does
Throw off, on its frivolous purgatorial fall
Down to the sea and away, dancing and singing
Perpetual intercession for this filth—
Leaping and dancing and singing, forgiving everything.

In "The Breaking of Rainbows" the words accumulate by the simplest means an almost intolerable excitement, resonant as they are without demanding of us that we locate authoritatively the source of their excitement. A prophetic ardor works in this poem to cast a grim eye upon all human efforts to reflect and hold the world in its course, for such efforts are necessarily assaultive in this view — no matter how brilliantly conceived the projects of spirit, of creative mind, Nemerov suggests, it is finally an "alien" and heavy yoke we impose upon the living stream, as the oil in Nemerov's poetic figure is "heavy and slow as blood." Stevens's "The Idea Of Order At Key West" comes to mind here, though Nemerov makes fewer concessions than Stevens, and works out his insights in a less elaborate and leisurely way. We must also remark, of course, how in Nemerov's poem the water, as the embodiment of original energy and spontaneous force, almost wildly conceived as it is in such expressions as "frivolous purgatorial fall" and "abandon," is also conceived as pursuing its way not indifferently, but "dancing and singing/Perpetual intercession for this filth" — despite the brute smugness of our customary assaults and vaunted appropriations, expressed as an "idiot's driveling contempt," we are somehow to be forgiven in a vision that had not seemed at first charitably disposed to our depredations. It is, to be sure, the abandoned confidence of the stream that so enables it to forgive everything, even the "agony" to which it is needlessly subjected.

We have seen that Nemerov's vision is tense with ambivalence, and that his expression of that vision is extremely various, even considering the relatively small range of his poems that overtly trade in epistemological questions and the general theme of artistic vision. One in particular, that comes at these matters tangentially, is worth noting, again for its apparent shifting of direction, and for its generous projection of law as a function of man's estate. "September, the First Day of School" (*gnomes* . . .) treats the father's pain of separation from his young son, passed now into the hands of those who will insist he submit to arbitrary rules and learn what he is told he must. No sooner is the situation established, though, the inevitable betrayals of the rich dream-life underscored, than the poet bows nobly to it all, as we enter part two of the six-stanza poem. Note that it is not mere resignation the poet expresses here, but an active hope for and sympathy with what must happen; he is not here on the side of nature in any "frivolous purgatorial" guise, though of course his feelings remain quite generous.

> A school is where they grind the grain of thought,
> And grind the children who must mind the thought.
> It may be those two grindings are but one,
> As from the alphabet come Shakespeare's Plays,
> As from the integers comes Euler's Law,
> As from the whole, inseparably, the lives,

The shrunken lives that have not been set free
By law or by poetic phantasy.
But may they be. My child has disappeared
Behind the schoolroom door. And should I live
To see his coming forth, a life away,
I know my hope, but do not know its form

Nor hope to know it. May the fathers he finds
Among his teachers have a care of him
More than his father could. How that will look
I do not know, I do not need to know.
Even our tears belong to ritual.
But may great kindness come of it in the end.

What interests me most about this, more even than the ease with which Nemerov manages to make ominous grindings seem not merely necessary but grandly promising, is the implied equivalence between law and poetic phantasy, and their shared capacity to redeem otherwise "shrunken lives." Nemerov's readiness, finally, to entrust the child to those who trade in "a stuff/So arbitrary, so peremptory,/That worlds invisible and visible/Bow down before it," as he put it in part one of his poem, is explained, then, though confusion remains. What works in these poems of Nemerov is a profound conviction in the mysterious efficacy of language, in the power for good of sheer articulacy, provided the speaking instrument be finely trained. The biological father, in Nemerov's poem the poet himself, may have more than he can manage in what he calls "My selfish tears" to deal successfully with the necessary instruction and nurturing to independence of the child. A sentiment, an urging of the heart, must become formal if it is to hold fast before the rush of experience that would otherwise daunt and frustrate it, confusing one object with others, paltry pleasures with enduring joys. Nemerov doesn't allow himself to speculate too closely on the outcome of ambitious designs, but he knows that design is deeply woven into the fabric of things. We may not, individually, make the laws to which we submit or defiantly react, but it is a human business to know which they are and to will consent or defiance. In this sense, for Nemerov to wish for his child instruction in law or poetic phantasy is to wish for the child that kindliness of spirit which comes often to those who dream reasonable dreams. Earlier in his poem Nemerov had spoken of the biblical Joseph whose "dream got him such hatred of his brothers/As cost the greater part of life to mend,/ And yet great kindness came of it in the end." Clearly Nemerov's hope is that his young son may achieve such consummation at a less dire cost, as who would not wish for his child?

"September, The First Day of School" is one of those poems whose voice is so immaculately singular that it constitutes a true signature. Only a handful of poets ever come to such a signature, and it is important that we have in mind what Nemerov's is peculiarly good for. It involves a curious mixture of intellectual candor, a really impressive probity of mind, and a species of tenderness touched by sorrow. In an earlier poem like "Shells" (*The Salt Garden*) in which each of these qualities is amply present, we see as well Nemerov's curious inclination to undercut his own resonant solemnities, as if a little embarrassed by his involvement in his vision, his attentive obedience to the rhetorical pulse he has set throbbing in the poem. Remarking on the abandoned seashells he finds scattered on the shore, picking one up, he is moved even to announce the obvious, that "The life that made it is gone out," and bestirs himself to make something of it, to discover in place of life, a meaning.

> Its form is only cryptically
> Instructive, if at all: it winds
> Like generality, from nothing to nothing
>
> By means of nothing but itself.
> It is a stairway going nowhere,
> Our precious emblem of the steep ascent,
>
> Perhaps, beginning at a point
> And opening to infinity,
> Or the other way, if you want it the other way.

How disarmingly Nemerov draws attention to the made-up quality of his metaphorical elaborations. One doesn't know precisely what response is called for by "if you want it the other way" — does it express, one wonders, a kind of impatience with the inevitable equivocations to which all metaphor and analogue give rise, or is it nothing more than a generous invitation to each of us to extend and elaborate the figure of the shell in our own way? Insofar as the image of the stairway speaks directly to the issue of Nemerov's signature, it may at least be said to indicate Nemerov's tutelary impulse, as well as his ability to introduce unexpected locutions and tonalities even into pieces as closely integrated and clearly focused as "Shells." That these impulses and capacities do not always serve the poet well is an obvious fact, and could hardly be otherwise given the range and various ambition of Nemerov's canon.

Consider the tutelary dimension, for example, how remarkably well Nemerov at his best makes it a function of a more general intellectual candor, so that the desire to take us gently by the hand, almost as an older child will address a younger, strikes us with a freshness that is less a mark of simplicity than of sheer enthusiasm. In "Deep Woods" (*Mirrors and*

Windows) we read of a place "too still for history," a place that invites the heart to take "a kind of rest," to yield to a darkness "which does not flatter with profundity." And yet it is not rest the poem goes on intricately to impress, but instruction of a very special sort. The burden of it all is that we may not gain genuine entry into Nemerov's unstoried woods unless we are equipped to understand with him what they are not, but might be. It is a variant of "The Blue Swallows" Nemerov plays for us here, but with a tutelary gusto that makes the later and more famous poem seem tame by comparison. "This unlegended land," he would have us understand,

> Is no Black Forest where the wizard lived
> Under a bent chimney and a thatch of straw;
> Nor the hot swamp theatrical with snakes
> And tigers; nor the Chinese forest on
> The mountainside, with bridge, pagoda, fog,
> Three poets in the foreground, drinking tea
> (there is tea, and not so many as three)—
> But this land, this, unmitigated by myth
> And whose common splendors are comparable only to
> Themselves; this leaf, line, light, are scrawled alone
> In solar definitions on a lump
> Of hill like nothing known since Nature was
> Invented by Watteau or Fragonard
> In the Old Kingdom or the time of Set
> Or before the Flood of Yao (or someone else
> Of the same name) in the Fourth, or Disney, Dimension.

Such writing strikes us as sincere in the most extraordinary sense of that term. In the words of Hulme, a master theorist surely, we recognize a special degree of sincerity "when the whole of the analogy is necessary to get out the curve of the feeling or thing you want to express." Nemerov wishes, that is, to teach us, whether in "Shells" or "Deep Woods" or "September, The First Day of School," and he does so in a manner at once bracing and delightful. But what does he wish to teach? I should have to say that at his best, Nemerov aims to teach us how to be sincere, to be what we are, and to express what we feel in a way that will make those feelings available to others like us. Nemerov's object, then, is nothing less than the grand object assigned poets long ago by Coleridge: "to cultivate and predispose the heart of the reader."

To what, we may well ask, does "Deep Woods," particularly the fragment quoted earlier, predispose the reader, and which faculties can it be said to cultivate as an aspect of Nemerov's tutelary project? Is the reader's heart predisposed to celebrate a land "unmitigated by myth/ And whose common splendors are comparable only to/ Themselves"?

Surely, though the idea of a condition unmitigated by myth has always appealed to Nemerov, as we have observed, his poetry celebrates a transparence that is more the product of artifice than of unself-conscious innocence. He may deliberately direct us to the plain ripple and occasional flash of an ordinary world, but the vision is inevitably instructed in ways that bear little affinity to anybody's notion of an unlegended land. An imagination like Nemerov's compulsively multiplies resemblances — it can do no other — and though he does not complain about the malady of the quotidian, he is as little content with it as others who have labored in its measured embrace. Like Stevens, Nemerov is committed to an ethic and aesthetic of metamorphosis, according to which "Three poets in the foreground" become an acceptable element in the representation of deep woods, whether or not they constitute an essential feature of the phenomenon as it is available to ordinary intelligence. The reader, then, is predisposed to an acceptance of the contingent as a function, at least in part, of the poet's involvement in his medium. The poet cultivates the reader's sympathy for devices many of which would seem to go against the grain of his overt intentions. Without resorting to mannerism, Nemerov instructs his reader in a vision of possibility which is responsive to a whole range of restraints shaped by the character and intellect of the poet.

The will has very little to say about the role such restraints will play in the formulation of the poet's vision. Nemerov has always been uncomfortable with over-insistence in poetry, and his best work has characteristically avoided just those wilfully decisive elaborations of a position that compel agreement and dissolve the mysteries associated with reverie and psychic resistance to one's own formal certainties. Always the texture of the verse allows for qualification of the position overtly taken, not in the interests of some queasy relativism, but as a celebration of metamorphic faculties given consistent rein by the poet's sense of his own needs and special gifts. What we get, then, is tension, rather than a species of neurotic anxiety, the latter consequent upon futile attempts to insist upon conclusions that will not occur. If the tensions in a poem like "Deep Woods" do not come from juxtaposition of elements in antithetic blocks, they may at least be said to emerge from a continuous alternation of sentiments. Nemerov knows and does not know what are the hard facts and less stable realities with which we must all learn to deal. To be properly instructed, the reader must come to accept that what can be known or proved, including the commonplace realities poets pride themselves on apprehending, is always a limited and subordinate truth. Nemerov's truth is not the unstoried truth of deep woods, but the degree to which intelligence and wit are liberated in the encounter with an object universe that might otherwise have stood mute, disheartening in its awesome self-possession and impenetrability. We learn, that is, to respect our own best faculties, as we understand how Nemerov's characteristic probity of mind is finally indistinguishable from self-respect.

The generosity to oneself and to one's largest ambitions is not always easy to sustain, most of us have discovered for ourselves, but much of Nemerov's recent verse reminds us, with its gnome-like provocation, that the case is frequently even more serious than we'd imagined. The poet is too often tempted to that vexatious questioning that can issue in nothing even moderately satisfying, either to himself or to his reader. Subjected to such questioning, the poet falls prey to what Keats, in a letter to Shelley, called "'self-concentration' — selfishness, perhaps," ending in that "irritable reaching after fact and reason" Keats impugned as unworthy of true poets. Too compulsively to ask the question, "Am I getting it right," or "Have I given the not-me its essential due" is to urge upon ourselves the bad conscience we earlier described as the source of weariness and futility. The weariness issues ultimately in "self-concentration," a morbid sensitivity to the seductive challenge of things in the world, a challenge, moreover, which we know at once we shall not successfully master. The ironist in Nemerov is a dangerously passive figure, for whom the necessity to transcribe accurately and the resultant guilt upon his failure to do so cause great anxiety, and stir hopeless evasions. The poet of *gnomes* ... , unlike the great master whose work all must celebrate, becomes too much the "collector," in the words of his beloved theorist Owen Barfield, "the man who cannot grasp the reality of anything but *percepts.*" Such a collector, Barfield goes on to suggest, "will become the connoisseur, that is, he will collect either *objets d'art* or elegant sensations and memories." There are nothing but limited truths and glib sensations, though touched with a kind of elegance, in "Myth and Ritual" (*gnomes* ...):

> You come down to a time
> In every poker game
> Where the losers allow
> They've lost, the winners begin
> Sneaking into their shoes
> Under the covered table;
> You come down to that time,
>
> They all go home. And hard
> As it is to imagine
> A fat and rowdy ghost
> Pee in his empty glass
> So as not to miss a hand,
> That's how it happens; Paul
> is gone, and Stanley is gone,

The winners have risen with cash
And checks and promising papers
And drifted through the cold door
Forever, while the host,
Like some somnambulist
Or sleepy priest, empties
Their ashes into the dawn.

Randall Jarrell once wrote: "As one reads Stevens' later poetry one keeps thinking that he needs to be possessed by subjects." He goes on to argue that in Stevens's later work he "has had only faintly and intermittently the dramatic insight, the capacity to be obsessed by lives, actions, subject-matter, the chameleon's shameless interest in everything not itself, that could have broken up the habit and order and general sobering matter-of-factness of age." That last critical expression of Jarrell's describes with considerable appropriateness Nemerov's "Myth and Ritual," and most of the gnomic utterances in his latest volume. It's not the case that such poems of Nemerov's fail entirely to repay careful reading, only that the "capacity to be obsessed by lives, actions, subject-matter" we found in "The Beekeeper Speaks . . . And Is Silent" and other masterworks encourage us to hope for more. The reader of *gnomes* . . . will not be entirely disappointed, of course, even in his most extravagant anticipations, for here and there the distinctive voice of the poet resonates, its palette of light and dark colorings wondrous to behold, the wit warm, the sentiments unashamedly earnest. The last poem in the book, a substantial piece, is a consummately beautiful thing, a poem no reader would for a moment mistake for anyone else's. "Beginner's Guide" is its title, and when I read it I like to think it deliberately instructs us in the proper anticipation of volumes yet to come, even as it serves to remind Nemerov himself of that radical innocence he will need to recover and nurture if he is to be what, for himself, he most needs to be. The poem is too long to quote in its entirety, so I shall quote only the concluding stanzas. Earlier in the text the poet had spoken of collecting Field Books, Guides to flowers, birds, and stars, and of his desire to learn names, press samples, collect knowledge of all there is to know. To be such a collector, the poem suggests in its mildly importunate way, has nothing in common with murdering to dissect or blazoning trophies, or aiming to accumulate mere percepts or the data of sensible experience. To collect in the spirit of Nemerov's "Beginner's Guide" is to assimilate what is in the world to form a rich interplay between object and self, heightening our faculties in ways at once unmistakable and modest.

Was it a waste, the time and the expense,
Buying the books, going into the field
To make some mind of what was only sense,
And show a profit on the year's rich yield?

Though no authority on this theme either,
He would depose upon the whole that it
Was not. The world was always being wider
And deeper and wiser than his little wit,

But it felt good to know the hundred names
And say them, in the warm room, in the winter,
Drowsing and dozing over his trying times,
Still to this world its wondering beginner.

We believe Nemerov when he says these things, believe in the embodied vision of a good soul, because the object universe, the common world to which it responds, is hard and real enough to resist the realization of that vision. The redemption to which Nemerov's vision gives utterance is a human redemption, consistent with powers of human imagination and critical intelligence. The spiritual restlessness that underlies all of his work, as "Beginner's Guide" clearly indicates, has in it no necessary discouragement to hope or generosity or expansiveness of feeling. These are qualities which, along with others we have cited as characteristic of the poet, best describe his true signature and are the source of the consolation we take in his achievement.

INDEX

PS
221
B58

Boyers, Robert.
    Excursions: selected literary
essays.

PS221 B58
+Excursions : sel+Boyers, Robert.

0 00 02 0197739 4
MIDDLEBURY COLLEGE